A SHEARWATER BOOK

Leadville

Lead ville

The Struggle to
Revive an
American Town

Gillian Klucas

Island Press / SHEARWATER BOOKS

Washington . Covelo . London

A SHEARWATER BOOK
Published by Island Press

Copyright © 2004 Gillian Klucas

SHEARWATER BOOKS is a trademark of
The Center for Resource Economics.

Library of Congress Cataloging-in-Publication data.
Klucas, Gillian.
Leadville : the struggle to revive an American town / Gillian Klucas.
p. cm.
Includes bibliographical references and index.
ISBN 1-55963-385-9 (cloth : alk. paper)
1. Abandoned mined lands reclamation—Colorado—Leadville. 2. Mineral
industries—Environmental aspects—Colorado—Leadville. 3. Water—Pollution—
Arkansas River. 4. Hazardous waste site remediation—Colorado—Leadville—
Citizen participation. I. Title
TD195.M5K58 2004
363.738′4′0978846—dc22

British Cataloguing-in-Publication data available.

Printed on recycled, acid-free paper ♲
Design by Teresa Bonner
Manufactured in the United States of America

10 9 8 7 6 5 4 3 2 1

For my parents, Robert and Carol

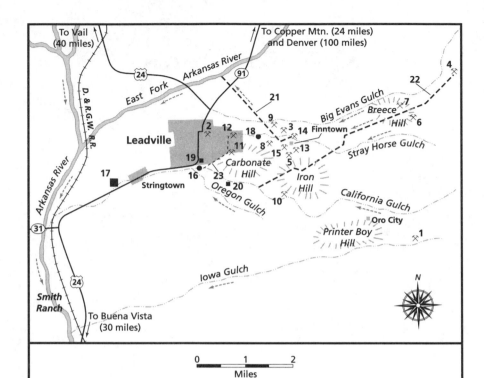

0   1   2

Miles

Mines

1. Black Cloud
2. Coronado
3. Denver City
4. Diamond
5. Greenback
6. Ibex
7. Little Jonny
8. Maid of Erin
9. Matchless/Baby Doe's Cabin
10. Minnie
11. Penrose
12. Ponsardine
13. R.A.M.
14. Robert Emmet
15. Wolftone

Mining Structures

16. Apache Tailing Piles
17. Arkansas Valley Smelter
18. Hamm's Tailing Pile
19. Harrison Slag Pile
20. Yak Treatment Plant

Tunnels

21. Leadville Mine Drainage Tunnel
22. Yak Tunnel

Other Features

23. Starr Ditch

Contents

Leadville

Prologue

Leadville, Colorado, sits on the Continental Divide above a beautiful high valley in the Rocky Mountains, at 10,200 feet the highest incorporated town in North America. Just over the passes to the north lie the ski resorts of Copper Mountain, Vail, and Breckenridge; to the west over Independence Pass, drivable only in the summer, is Aspen. Picturesque Leadville averages two hundred inches of snow a year, and snow flurries have even graced the Fourth of July parade. The temperature can dip to thirty degrees below zero, but rarely reaches eighty in the summer. At that altitude, it's hard to keep coffee warm, baking is a challenge, and a flight of stairs leaves most visitors gasping for breath.

In 1998, living in Denver, I had never heard of Leadville until I learned that the residents were battling the Environmental Protection Agency (EPA) to preserve their mine waste dumps. At the time, I knew little about historic mining, and I couldn't imagine the desire to save a "waste dump" or who would be interested in doing so. I moved away before I could find out, but my curiosity simmered, and several years later I had an opportunity to spend a few days in the town.

Leadville is a friendly place, and that August I was soon exploring the hills in old pickup trucks and learning about much more than the waste rock piles that have dotted Leadville's hillside for more than a century. The story, I learned, reached far beyond historic preservation or even environmental protection to a town struggling for nearly twenty years to retain a way of life—a mining identity—in the face of economic hardship and governmental intervention. But something had happened in the three years since I had first heard about Leadville's bitter fight. Resentment against the federal government was still there, but I sensed a new spirit of cooperation between the EPA and the townspeople that I hadn't anticipated.

Just before leaving town, I was standing beside the Arkansas River talking with a rancher when dark clouds suddenly blew over the mountains. As a few flakes began to fall, I watched the Arkansas winding its way down the valley. It had been explained to me that, despite the breathtaking scene, for miles the river and meadows were poisonous to fish, wildlife, and livestock that relied upon them. I realized I was more intrigued and perplexed by the complex problems facing restoration of abandoned mining sites than I had been before I arrived. As I turned away from the river, churning now by wind from the advancing storm, I was anxious to get off the mountain, but I knew I would be back. I wanted to know if this new cooperative spirit I had witnessed in town could possibly lead to the river's revival.

A year later I moved to Leadville to get to know the town better and to try to understand its past, including its fascinating journey over the past twenty years, and its prospects for the future. Subsequently, I spent hundreds of hours talking with the people who appear in this book and many more who do not; I became a regular at city, county, and federal government meetings; and I spent hours in the library scouring through more than twenty years of local newspapers.

In Leadville, I found many of the complex challenges facing the nation as we attempt to restore the environment after more than a hundred years of extracting minerals from the earth, and other disruptive practices. The scope of the waste left behind in Leadville and elsewhere is astonishing. This subject is larger than Leadville, and larger even than the dozens of other western mining towns grappling with similar issues. But Leadville is illustrative of the challenges we, as a nation, must face in deciding what to clean up, who pays for it, and how much risk to our health we are willing to accept.

The story that follows is about a mountainside covered with mining ruins, a blue-collar town, and a powerful federal agency, but it begins and ends with the river.

1

Living Downstream

Doc Smith didn't get the message until late afternoon, after he had finished his chores and made his way across the snowy pasture toward home, his heifers watching his progress from behind a gnarled wood fence. It had been a good day for working outside; only thirty-five degrees but sunny, and the air at two miles above sea level warmed to a degree that surprised visiting flatlanders. Doc crossed the wide dirt driveway and climbed the wooden steps to his house one at a time, leading with his right leg, his left leg followed stiffly behind. At the top, he stomped the snow from his boots and entered the cluttered hominess of the combined dining room and kitchen, the center of activity at the Smith Ranch.

The message Doc found waiting for him was from Dr. Dennis Linemeyer, the young man who had replaced him at the veterinary clinic. Doc was only fifty-two years old, but times were tough and the town could no longer support two vets. Besides, Doc had a ranch to tend. He picked up the phone and sat down at the dining table beside the antique woodstove that warmed the room.

Dr. Linemeyer told Doc he had received a call earlier in the day. The man wouldn't leave his name, but he had a warning: "Tell Doc Smith his river is going to run red." That was all the anonymous caller would say, but it was enough. Doc knew what that meant because something similar had been happening to the river for years, though usually on a Friday night before a long holiday weekend and this was Wednesday. Doc had never been alerted before, and he wondered what that could mean. He went back outside and trudged three hundred yards down the driveway to have a look.

The Arkansas River, one of the longest in the United States, begins modestly on the side of a craggy mountain high up in Colorado's Rocky Mountains just ten miles north of Doc's ranch. It quickly makes its way to the valley floor and snakes southward, losing altitude but gaining momentum as it travels 120 miles through the wide Arkansas River Valley before turning southeast across the Kansas Plains to Arkansas and entering the Mississippi River. When Doc stepped onto his old railroad tie bridge that afternoon and peered over the side, he could see the river's rocky bottom through the clean, icy-cold water.

Doc straightened up and looked east toward town and the hills rising behind it and wondered what was coming. Then he turned west and headed back home—a compound consisting of his log-and-wood-panel house; a vacant 1870s farmhouse; several large barns, deep brown from a century of harsh winters; and a number of sagging old structures long since abandoned. Colorado's two highest peaks, Mount Massive and Mount Elbert, towered over his rustic homestead and the snowy surroundings.

Throughout the evening, Doc worried about the anonymous warning and continued to check the river, but found nothing unusual. After the ten o'clock news, he grabbed a flashlight and his coat and tramped through the snow to the river's edge for one last look before bed. Shining the light into the water, Doc couldn't see that the river was already changing, and in a strange way, he was disappointed. He had expected something to happen and began to think the caller had been wrong.

Doc went back to his house, climbed the stairs to the bedroom, and packed a few clothes for a meeting in Gunnison the next day before getting into bed. Lying in the darkened room next to his wife, he remembered all of the other times he had worried about the river and wondered what he would find in the morning.

Earlier that day, five miles east of Doc's ranch, rusty-hued sludge had poured out of an old tunnel cut into the hillside, a "Danger! Do Not Enter" sign affixed to one of the decaying wooden beams holding up the tunnel's entrance. The sludge entered California Gulch, one of many crevices dug into the mountains by glaciers that drain snow and rain into the valleys below. But this sunny winter afternoon, the gulch carried a vast toxic hemorrhage that cut a swath through fresh snow as it plunged down the hillside past dormant aspens and pine trees. It edged by the hard-knocks town of Leadville, picking up toxic strength as it flowed past the enormous mound of mining spoils that loomed at the end of Leadville's main street. The sludge continued flowing west, over silvery green sage; past Stringtown, a collection of trailer homes and run-down wooden structures; and through the shadows of undulating gritty black hills before entering Doc's beautiful valley. There it poured into the Arkansas River.

For days previously, the sludge had been backing up into the Irene mine shaft. The Yak Tunnel that normally drained groundwater from the Irene, among numerous other mines, must have been blocked by the rotting timbers and rock walls that periodically toppled over and prevented the contaminated water from draining into California Gulch. The manager of ASARCO Inc., the mining company responsible for the tunnel, decided it was time to go in and have a look around.

Nine ASARCO employees had ducked past the "Danger!" sign and entered the tunnel. With the light affixed to their hard hats leading the way, the men walked along the sludge-covered floor of the tunnel, their passage clearing a channel. Along the way, they encountered several areas of fallen timber and rock that dammed the flow of water and "slime," as the manager would later note in a handwritten report. In some areas, the stagnant water reached chest height. Working in the dim light with little fresh air, the men removed much of the timber and rock obstructions so that "a considerable flow was running" by the time they left the tunnel.

"None of the newer people enjoyed this trip very much," the manager wrote in his report. "We all got very wet, very orange and very cold. I, nor did any one who made the trip before, quite expect the gravity of the problems we saw." The old timbers were in terrible shape, and the group agreed that more blockages within the year were inevitable.

It would be hours before the consequences of ASARCO's trip into the tunnel would be known, but they were devastating. The toxic torrent let loose consisted mainly of "yellow boy," a miners' term for the iron hydroxide that gave the river its rusty color, plus an assortment of other heavy metals, all dangerous in high quantities: zinc, copper, cadmium, manganese, lead, and arsenic. In recent years, the Yak had been draining 210 tons of these metals into the Arkansas River each year. California Gulch had long since been stained a permanent rusty orange.

Mining's toxic by-product came from the hills, but for over one hundred years it had been flushed downstream, unchecked and unregulated and out of sight to those working in the mines. And it had had a disastrous effect on the valley below. For three miles south of the confluence of California Gulch and the Arkansas River, through the Smith Ranch, the Arkansas River had long been considered a dead zone. No wildlife, most notably fish, could survive the metallic-tainted water. For another sixty miles beyond the dead zone, few trout survived more than a couple of years.

Ranchers had been using the Arkansas River to irrigate their land and water their livestock for generations. The accumulation of metals from 130 years of mining the hills had taken its toll; acres of barren ground pocked the meadows, and the grass that did grow there was so mineral-rich that the foals and calves that grazed on it were poisoned to death.

The Smith family had taken the brunt of the contamination, living in the midst of the dead zone since 1879, when Doc's grandfather, Henry, first homesteaded 160 acres of verdant meadows below two vast mountain peaks and the sparkling Arkansas River meandering right through the middle of it. Back then, timothy grass grew "as high as a horse's back," and Henry and his new neighbor, Huey Young, built an irrigation ditch, still known as the Smith-Young Ditch, to spread the clean, cold river water over the meadows. Doc's grandfather was in business, making hay for the area's milk cows and the mules that lived underground in the mines. But over the last twenty years of the eighteen hundreds, more and more waste from the mining operations was dumped into the Arkansas River, which soon became "rolling mud," as Henry described it. Timothy grass turned to stubble, and Henry's once-successful hay business floundered. Even then, Doc's grandfather knew the source of his problems. To prove it, he gathered up soil from his meadow and sent it over the mountains to the Agricultural College of Colorado in Fort Collins. The reply—the Environmental Protection Agency (EPA) would excitedly refer to it as "The Letter" seventy-five years later—dated July 30, 1906—confirmed Henry Smith's fears.

> Dear Sir:
> The sample of soil and letter pertaining thereto were duly received. The letter has been misplaced so I cannot answer your questions except as I remember them. You apparently know exactly the cause of your trouble i.e. mine water and mill tailings. The sample sent is so rich in the latter that we would think that you must have gathered the sample from the bottom of a ditch or stream. There is a large amount of soluble iron and zinc salts present either of which are injurious in such quantities.
> *Yrs, W. P. Headde*

Mining, bringing fame and fortune to those just a few miles away, was killing Henry's meadows and his livelihood. All he could do was build another irrigation ditch, the Smith Ditch, to carry water from a creek farther west in the mountains. It was a long haul, but the water was cleaner, diluting the effects of the Arkansas River, and grass grew again, though not as it had thirty years earlier. Henry's son, Jim—Doc's father—decided livestock would be more profitable, and the ranch began raising cattle. But by 1940, as Leadville's mines increased production of lead and zinc in anticipation of World War II, the calves and foals began to come up lame and many died. And the cows were too skinny, unable to bulk up like cattle at the southern end of the valley. Jim Smith couldn't give his problems a name, but he knew they stemmed from the same place his father's had—mining waste draining out of the hills, and he would tell his son that many times over the years.

His son, Bernard—to become "Doc"—had grown up on the ranch watching the livestock suffer and he decided to become a veterinarian. He returned from school in the mid-1950s to be Lake County's only vet, starting his practice in the basement of a new house, built just a few yards from the 1870s farmhouse he and his father had grown up in. Doc was small in stature with a fine-boned handsomeness and well-groomed like his father and grandfather. In another era he would have been considered a "gentleman farmer," as his grandfather had once been. Doc had what his wife would later describe as the Irish Catholic belief that the longer and harder one suffers the more points earned with God, something her German Protestant background didn't share. Doc earned a lot of points his first year back on the ranch.

The winter of 1957 had been cold—more snow and ice than normal, and the ground was frozen into slick concrete. By spring, the ranch was behind schedule; nearly May and the yearlings had not yet been dehorned or vaccinated. One day, Doc and a ranch hand were rushing to round up some unruly calves. "I was the guy who was always in too big of a hurry," Doc would recall. He turned his horse quickly on the frozen ground and all four legs went airborne. As the horse crashed on its side, Doc heard his left leg snap like a willow stick. It didn't seem too bad at first. The hardened mountain men made a splint and eventually got Doc to the Leadville hospital, ten miles away, a few hours later. But Doc had fractured his lower leg in four places and crushed the blood vessels. Rushed to Denver—four hours over Loveland Pass in those days—the doctors amputated his leg just below the knee. Only in his mid-twenties at the time, Doc would never fully recover, fighting feelings of inadequacy and gritting through the pain of working the ranch on an amputated leg the rest of his life, though he rarely let on and most people in town never knew despite his stiff gait.

Over the years, Doc earned a reputation for his patience, teaching young ranch hands to "cut nuts," the western tradition that gives restaurants the prized Rocky Mountain oysters, and for his acrimonious sense of humor, softened by an impish smile and a sense of tease in his gravelly smoker's voice. He brought to the ranch a redhead named Carol he had met on a blind date in college. Her lovely smile belied an even wickeder sense of humor than Doc's. Though she'd grown up on the outskirts of Denver, still a cow town then, Carol loved the ranch, and Doc admired her toughness. Their good-natured humor helped them raise eleven children. Carol survived the neonatal onslaught by becoming a laid-back mother and housekeeper. If future surgeon George ended up wearing dirty, mismatched socks to school because he hadn't bothered to pick up his clothes, that was fine with Carol. And she rarely wore her glasses in the house so she wouldn't see the dust bunnies gaining mass in the corners.

But the contaminated ranch left them so poor the children were sometimes allowed just half an egg at breakfast. A high-altitude meadow should produce about two tons of hay per acre. "The best I ever got, when my wife wasn't pregnant and was working her buns off out there, was up to 0.88 tons per acre. You can't make a gosh darn living."

Their troubles intensified in 1971 when ASARCO opened another lead, zinc, and silver mining operation up on the hill, sending yet more waste through the Yak Tunnel and into the Arkansas River. Doc complained about the contamination in public meetings, which didn't make him popular with the mining companies, especially ASARCO. "I'm not sure when I began to have intimate relations with the bosses at ASARCO, but we swore at each other. I didn't take them kindly, and they thought I was a pain in the ass." Doc may have been a pain in the ass, but that was about it. With no clear regulations in place to stop the mining companies from dumping waste, Doc had no leverage.

But by 1970 a nationwide environmental movement was underway, with the first Earth Day held in April of that year. Companies in all industries were being pressured to clean up their acts. Pushed by the public, Congress began to address some of the more egregious environmental problems, creating the Environmental Protection Agency in 1970 and two years later passing the Clean Water Act, with its mandates to clean up contaminated rivers. Doc thought finally something would get done. His persistence led to a meeting on September 20, 1972, in Leadville's plain brick county courthouse. There, twenty-five men—mining company officials, local politicians, and state and federal representatives of the mining associations, health departments, forest services, the young EPA, and Doc—discussed, for the first time, the possibility of cleaning up California Gulch.

Orin Diedrich, a well-liked and practical county commissioner, complained that "those who have taken money out of the mines in the past have left us with a mess." ASARCO officials, however, claimed that its mining operations discharged little or no contamination, and state officials, at that time, agreed. Denying responsibility would characterize the mining companies' tactic over the coming decades-long battle once government officials finally resolved to address the hazardous waste that extracting the Earth's resources left behind. The county would do nothing to hinder mining operations, Commissioner Diedrich assured the group. Leadville's economy was thriving that year but, as it had for a century, it relied solely on one industry, mining, and no one, particularly the local politicians, wanted to contemplate its end in Leadville. They could envision the economic and social turmoil that would follow. At this initial meeting, Doc and the county commissioners were the only ones advocating cleaning up the gulch. An official with Colorado's health department suggested that "maybe the best solution is to leave it lie where it is right now. With the proper amount of funds, the water could be cleaned up, but it may not be worth it."

Not worth it? Doc realized that no one, not even the state's health department federally mandated to clean up contaminated water, was going to do anything. Doc spoke up. He wanted to see something concrete happening, he said, not watch the issue die of indecisiveness amidst the mumbled "looking into it" assurances coming from the agency minions.

After the meeting, Doc stood up and stepped stiffly into the aisle. Three scowling ASARCO employees, as big as NFL linebackers, were moving toward him. He thought they weren't going to stop. "They're going to run right over little Bernie." Doc was frightened, but he refused to budge. He put his hands on his hips and said, with as much nonchalant friendliness as he could muster, "Hi. Can I talk to you?" Doc explained to the men that he didn't want to shut down the mines, just clean up the gulch. They glared down at him and brushed past, leaving him standing in the aisle. It was an unnerving encounter, one that he would remember vividly thirty years later as the moment he first understood the danger of antagonizing such a powerful interest.

The morning after Doc received the anonymous tip about the river, he dressed in a suit and tie for his meeting in Gunnison, said good-bye to his wife and kids, and went out to his car. He drove slowly down the driveway and rounded the bend to the river.

Doc braked hard. Though the river had periodically been discolored in the past, the scale of what he saw now was unprecedented. Doc made a U-turn and hurried back to the house. He didn't want to be late for his meeting, but he wanted to make sure that this time the discharge didn't go ignored. He quickly wrote out a list of places for his wife to call: the local sanitation department, the Colorado Department of Wildlife, and especially the Denver TV stations and newspapers.

He got back into his car and, as he bounced over the railroad tie bridge, he looked at the colorful river winding its way down the valley. He knew the toxic concoction was headed straight for the pump station that carries Arkansas River water out of the valley and over the mountains to supply the populous Colorado Front Range with drinking water.

Doc smiled. "We got 'em," he said aloud. "We finally got 'em."

2

Boom Years

Doc Smith could not have known that cold morning he woke to a red Arkansas River that the event would mark the beginning of a long, fierce battle over cleaning up what mining had left behind for more than a hundred years. For the next twenty years, he and many of his Leadville neighbors would find themselves caught in the middle of what would become the latest chapter in Leadville's colorful mining history, a chapter that would also redefine the association that the multinational corporation ASARCO had long had with the town.

The Guggenheim family didn't create American Smelting and Refining Company (ASARCO)—J. P. Morgan, the Rockefellers, and other industrialists of the late nineteenth century did that—but within two years of the company's formation in 1899, the Guggenheims controlled it. Meyer Guggenheim and his seven sons had set out to dominate hardrock mining and smelting in North America, and by the turn of the century they had succeeded. The mining industry created most of the Guggenheim fortune so well known for its philanthropy today, and it started in two unlikely Leadville mines named the A.Y. and the Minnie. Forty years later, the family cut its ties to ASARCO, Leadville, the mining and smelting industry, and the environmental mess they had helped create around the globe in pursuit of a family dynasty. How fortuitous their choices were would only become clear many years later, when, in the 1980s, the U.S. government began to clean up that mess—suing mining companies to pay for it—with the powerful new law that came to be known as Superfund.

Meyer Guggenheim already owned interests in the A.Y. and Minnie, two mines sitting side by side in California Gulch, when he came for a short visit to inspect his new investments in 1881. Miners panning for gold had first arrived nearly a quarter century earlier but it wasn't until later, when the miners dug into the earth and discovered rich veins of silver, that the mining boom that created Leadville began. The town was only four years old when Meyer arrived, but it was already the mining capital of the United States. Nearly $15 million in gold, silver, and lead had been mined and processed in the hills east of Leadville the previous year alone, and 1881 promised to top that. Meyer was late jumping into the prospecting game, but he hoped the A.Y. and Minnie would still land him among the silver barons.

It didn't look promising. Both mines were flooded and couldn't be worked. A discouraged owner had sold his shares to Meyer for $5,000, and Meyer knew he would have to invest thousands more for pumps and other equipment if he wanted to see if the mines contained silver. It had taken fifty-three years, but he finally had the money he needed to take that risk.

Meyer had been born in 1828 in a Switzerland ghetto suffering under harsh, restrictive laws. He took up tailoring and peddled his skills and wares in Europe before emigrating to Philadelphia at the age of nineteen. The short, thin young man was reserved socially, but he charmed the Pennsylvania housewives he met on his door-to-door sales. Quick to recognize business opportunities, he soon expanded his tailor business to selling household necessities. Meyer married his stepsister, Barbara, and the family grew to include eight sons (one died as a child in a horse riding accident) and three daughters. As his sons matured, he groomed them in the family business. By the time Meyer, now sporting white, bushy muttonchops, visited Leadville in

1881, he had amassed a small fortune, primarily from importing lace and embroidery from Europe. But he dreamed of more. He wanted to be on par with the Astors, the Rockefellers, and the Rothschilds. And he wanted a dynasty for his sons.

Looking down the dark shafts of the flooded A.Y. and Minnie could not have seemed the beginning of a dynasty. But all around, fortunes were being made. Up and down California Gulch was an industrial complex operating at full steam. Wood-planked buildings of the shaft houses, ore houses, mills and offices, long wooden ore chutes, and mounds of crushed rock blanketed the treeless hillsides. Logs to construct more buildings and to shore up the underground tunnels were piled about. Streams of railroad cars crisscrossed the gulch, hauling ore. The sky was thick with smoke that billowed from tall, narrow chimneys. Below ground, miners were carving a honeycomb of tunnels as they blasted rock to release the silver-bearing ore that would make the mine owners richer. Day and night, horses, mules, and men scurried about moving rock. The same scene was playing out nearby, in Stray Horse, Evans, and Oregon gulches and on the surrounding hills, areas that would become well-known battlegrounds a hundred years later.

Just west of the mining district, Meyer witnessed the chaos of a town growing by a hundred people a day. Leadville's population had exploded to fifteen thousand in just a few years. A mass of humanity, horses, and wagons crowded the dusty streets at all hours. Newcomers remarked on the constant din of men talking in the streets, railroad trains, and wagons coming and going, saloon music, and around-the-clock construction trying to keep pace with the expanding town. Some services couldn't keep up; the odor of trash and refuse from outhouses wafted across town along with industrial smoke. But by the time Meyer visited, Leadville's wealth was beginning to transform it from a mining camp into a real city. Railroads had pushed over the passes the previous year, halving the length of the trip from Denver to ten hours and lowering the cost of goods. Walking along the boardwalk of Harrison Avenue or Chestnut Street, Meyer would have seen gas streetlamps and telephone poles with tenpin cross arms. An assortment of two- and three-story brick buildings with tall, ornamental windows and cornices were replacing the original, hastily built wood-frame structures. Most of the buildings now had plumbing. Storefronts advertised banks, lawyers, books, mercantiles, laundries, saloons, and furniture stores. An imposing county courthouse with decorative, arched windows had recently been built, its cupola topped with a statue of Lady Justice standing above all else in town.

Leadville now had churches, schools, and a hospital. Women served afternoon teas, men joined social clubs, and both could attend performances at the Tabor Opera House, an opulent theater with a wooden walkway three stories above ground connecting it to the luxurious Clarendon Hotel next door. Although a lynching across the street had prevented a large turnout on opening night in November 1879, the opera house gave Leadville a boost of sophistication, particularly when Oscar Wilde, Sarah Bernhardt, or Harry Houdini came to town. The opera house's owner was a source of envy and hope to the thousands of bedraggled newcomers pouring into Leadville. He had struck it rich just three years earlier.

Horace Tabor, his wife Augusta, and their young son had arrived at the base of the Rocky Mountains in 1859 after they'd heard gold had been discovered near a new mining camp known as Denver City. Sixty million years earlier, the land lay flat under a vast, shallow sea, bearing the scars of its previous existence as the Ancestral Rockies, which had already lived for millennia and eroded away, swallowed once again by an ancient sea. But thousands of miles to the east, a fissure running down the middle of the Atlantic Ocean was widening. As the ocean floor parted, the North American plate slid over the top of its neighbor, the Pacific plate. As the tectonic plates ground together, North America crumpled, bulged, and folded in on itself where it was weakest, sending the Earth's crust soaring. The violent upheaval and glaciers that followed fractured the mountains into millions of faults, cracks, and fissures.

The Pacific plate submerged below the North American plate melting as it descended into the Earth's fiery interior and propelling molten blobs of liquid, crystals, and gases toward the continent's surface. The magma carried with it water, oxygen, and minerals with the power to create civilizations—iron, copper, lead, zinc, silver, gold, arsenic, sulfur. Magma that reached the surface burst forth in dazzling volcanic eruptions. More rarely, it stalled in the hard rock of the Earth's crust and oozed into the mountains' cracks and faults. As it cooled, the magma crystallized into rich veins of mineral deposits. By 1859, mountain erosion over millions of years had left some of those veins a mere day's shoveling from the surface or had worn them away, sending minerals washing down mountain streams. Providence provided Colorado with a swath of riches spanning 350 miles diagonally across the state from north of Denver to the San Juan Mountains in the southwest.

When news was heard that a few miners had tapped into this rich mineral belt, an estimated one hundred thousand miners—the 59ers—poured into the Rocky Mountains. Soon, mining camps located at the edge of the mountains along what would become Colorado's Front Range teemed with prospectors. It wasn't long before a few of them left the crowded camps, such as Black Hawk, Cripple Creek, and Georgetown, and traveled up the Arkansas River in search of gold deeper in the mountains. As prospectors neared the Arkansas headwaters, they passed through a narrow gorge and into a wide, verdant valley still carpeted with snow. Dense thickets of willow bushes, their delicate silvery maroon stems reaching over the men's heads, fanned out from the riverbanks. The men fished for cutthroat trout and hunted the antelope, elk, mule deer, and bison that grazed freely on the valley floor. To the west soared the Sawatch Range and the highest mountains in what would become Colorado. To the east, the smaller, smoother Mosquito Range beckoned some of those early prospectors. A dense forest of lodgepole pine, Engelmann spruce, and groves of aspen covered the hillsides and nurtured the woodland creatures that lived there. The men panned for gold in a narrow gulch that carried clean, snow runoff during the spring down a gentle slope to the Arkansas River. Gnarled bushes of big-tooth sage, clumps of hardy grass, and lupine grew alongside the intermittent stream. After those early prospectors struck gold in that remote, scenic spot in the Rocky Mountains, the landscape would never be the same. They named the ravine California Gulch, in the belief—or hope—that it would prove as wealthy as the land far to the west had a decade earlier.

For the next few years, ten thousand miners journeyed over the treacherous mountain passes to stake their claims in California Gulch, Horace and Augusta Tabor among them. The couple helped establish Oro City, a one-street village of tents, log cabins, saloons, and the Tabor's general store that stretched along the upper gulch. The placer miners turned over the earth looking for gold that had washed down the streams. They used sluice boxes, long wooden troughs with riffles across the bottom, and a stream of water to break up what the miners shoveled into the sluice. Flakes of gold would catch on the riffles as the gravel washed downstream. It was an inefficient method that required a tremendous amount of water. The snowmelt or rain trickling down the gulch could not accommodate all of the sluices and by the time what little water was available reached the lower claims, it was an unusable thick mud. So the miners built a series of dams and ditches to divert other mountain streams to their claims. One became known as the Starr Ditch, named for Thomas Starr, an Irish immigrant who arrived in California Gulch in the 1860s and who later became an early Leadville resident (and Doc Smith's great-uncle). He undertook the extensive project of digging a three-mile ditch to bring water to his placer claim.

At nearly two miles above sea level, California Gulch was a difficult place to live and work. Digging and shoveling in the dry, thin air quickly left miners gasping for breath. Respiratory diseases were common. Snow could fall in any month, even during the short summer season, and the permafrost was just a few feet down. In addition to the lack of water, miners complained about the thick, black sand that constantly clogged their sluice boxes. With all of the activity, the gold available to placer miners didn't last long. Most miners earned what they could quickly and left. By 1865, only a few hundred hardy hopefuls, including Horace and Augusta, remained. Oro City was nearly deserted. In just those few years, spanning the period of the Civil

War, California Gulch had changed dramatically. The population had swelled and receded. Trees had been chopped down to build cabins, sluices, and ditches, leaving a barren landscape stubbled with stumps. Erosion and placer mining had washed much of the topsoil and surface rock down the gulch and into the Arkansas River. But as altered as California Gulch had been by the placer miners of the 1860s, the impact on the land would not compare to the underground mining that followed.

In 1874, a pair of veteran miners returned to California Gulch to work Thomas Starr's old placer claim armed with a new, more efficient hydraulic technique. The two men quickly realized that the "black cement" miners had been scraping out of their sluices for more than a decade was lead carbonate, an ore containing silver. They secretly began buying up claims in California Gulch. Like those who had recognized the gulch's lead carbonate before them, the men knew that transporting the ore out of this remote land for smelting, the process that extracts metals from the rock, would be difficult, costly, and time consuming. Would there be enough wealth in these hills to warrant the expense and aggravation of mining and living under such difficult conditions? They were counting on it.

The two miners convinced a representative from a smelting company in St. Louis to examine the lead carbonate they had been collecting. August Meyer, who went on to become a leading Leadville citizen, recognized the potential in the men's ore and agreed to haul three hundred tons of it by oxen 130 slow miles to the railroad in Colorado Springs for shipment to St. Louis. Though the freight costs negated any profit, the ore was rich in silver. The smelter's owner, Edwin Harrison, decided that California Gulch was indeed promising enough to have its own smelter, and in 1877, he built the Harrison Reduction Works down the gulch from Oro City. With the placers worked out, miners now had to go underground for gold and silver, but having a smelter next door made mining for silver in the remote region feasible. The silver boom was on.

Thousands of people again swarmed into the high mountain valley, the trip still a bumpy, dusty twenty hours by stagecoach from Denver over dangerous mountain passes. Horace and Augusta, sensing a renewal for Oro City, had returned several years earlier. The couple, however, soon moved their general store down the gulch from Oro City to a new town residents were calling Slabtown, named after the pinewood slab boards used to construct the shanty homes and businesses that were popping up near the Harrison smelter. As the town rapidly expanded, residents began building attractive brick commercial buildings amongst the early rough-sawn businesses, and elaborate Victorian-style homes soon resided next to one-room log cabins. Slabtown's hardworking miners, hoping for the lucky strike, mixed with the wealthy beneficiaries of mining, some of whom had been digging holes themselves not long before. The area's leaders decided that "Slabtown" was not refined enough for a Silver Queen, and so they renamed their new town Leadville. They hired a marshal to tame the disorderly town, pulled out tree stumps left behind in the haste to build, and laid out streets. The wide street running north of the Harrison Reduction Works was named Harrison Avenue after the smelter's owner who had made the "Magic City" possible.

Other smelters soon joined Harrison's and within a few years as many as eighteen operated at any one time. The smelters' furnaces ringed Leadville, melting the ore the miners dug up to separate out the silver and gold, which were then shipped to refineries for further processing. The thick, red-hot smelter waste resembling molten lava was poured outside and left to cool into a hardened, black "slag" rich in arsenic and lead. Acres of slag accumulated around the smelters, and Leadville discovered that it made a nice blacktop that could be used to tame the muddy avenues, and they spread it liberally and often throughout town for the next hundred years.

In the early days, when most of the ore consisted of low-burning carbonates, smelters used charcoal to raise the temperatures in the furnace. Trees were chopped down, thrown into cone-shaped kilns and reduced to ashes. The kilns competed for trees with the valley's thirty sawmills. Throughout Colorado, forests were decimated to build the mining towns and feed the early smelter furnaces belching a thick, yellow smoke of arsenic, lead, and other metal particles into the air. Later, as the miners dug deeper, they pulled up ore rich in sulfides, mostly pyrite, or fool's gold. Sulfides burn hotter, lessening the need for charcoal in smelters, but the chimneys now emitted a sulfuric acid mist.

Milling, another method of separating ore from metals, left behind its own distinctive waste. After grinding the rock into fine granules the size of talcum powder, the ore was put into vats of water and given a "bubble bath." Chemicals added to the water caused the silver to become water-repellent and cling to air bubbles floating to the surface where the metal mixture could be skimmed off the top. The process was less efficient than smelting, leaving about 40 percent of the silver behind as waste along with lead, arsenic, and pyrite. But milling, which became more common in later decades, served to concentrate minerals found in lower-quality ore before it was sent to the smelter or refineries. In the early days of milling, the leftover sludge and water were dumped straight into the rivers and streams. The finely ground slurry—fluvial tailings—soon clogged up the streams. Later, the tailings were dumped into piles, which would become well known to the generations that followed for their toxic effect on the Arkansas River.

As the prospecting season got underway in 1878, Horace Tabor had not yet hit the bonanza, but he did not have long to wait. With the success of his general store, he could afford to grubstake prospectors, supplying them with picks, shovels, and food in exchange for a split in whatever they might find. That spring, two prospectors from Germany he had grubstaked struck silver on Fryer Hill and just like that, Horace Tabor was a rich man. The Little Pittsburg Mine made Horace and Augusta $2 million over the next two years. Two more lucky strikes that became the Chrysolite and Matchless mines earned Horace another $10 million. He was an extravagant spender, financing a number of luxurious buildings in Leadville to boost the town's respectability among the wealthy elite, including the Tabor Grand Hotel on Harrison Avenue, a posh, four-story hotel featuring Leadville's first elevator. Despite his wealth, Horace remained popular with working-class miners because he had retained his rough western edge. He never adopted the airs of the mine owners from the East who got rich off of Leadville and left town without looking back. In 1878, Horace became Leadville's first mayor and would later become Lieutenant Governor of Colorado and then a U.S. Senator. But it was Horace's scandalous personal life, not his generosity and political prominence, that made him a Leadville legend. In the early 1880s, Horace divorced the prim, well-liked Augusta only after he had already married a glamorous, voluptuous, and divorced young woman named Elizabeth Bonduel McCourt Doe—Baby Doe.

Other stories of fortunes quickly made continued to bring the ambitious to Leadville in the hopes of striking it rich. Marshall Field of Chicago, for example, invested wisely in Leadville mines. David May, a Bavarian Jew who immigrated to America at age fifteen, landed in Leadville and opened his first clothing store on Harrison Avenue. It was the humble beginning of the May Department Stores Company and eleven nationwide chains, including Lord & Taylor, Filenes, and Foley's, now worth $14 billion. One of May's Leadville clerks was a spirited young woman named Maggie Tobin, who went on to marry James Brown. The Little Jonny mine made the Browns multimillionaires, and Maggie later became famously portrayed in books, movies, and a Broadway play as the Unsinkable Molly Brown for her survival and heroism during the sinking of the *Titanic* in 1912.

By the time Meyer Guggenheim visited Leadville in 1881, newcomers hoping to strike it rich for the first time were already too late. The underground mines were now so large and complex that it required a substantial investment such as Meyer was willing to risk to get a mine operating. The most a poor prospector could hope for was to find a job in an established mine, work a small claim farther away, and, if he got lucky, sell the claim to someone who could afford to take a risk and invest in mining it.

Back in Philadelphia after his Leadville visit, Meyer did not have to wait long for his own gamble to pay off. Two months after dewatering the A.Y. and Minnie, his miners struck silver, and he was suddenly a much wealthier man. While six of his sons continued in the lace industry, he sent twenty-three-year-old Ben to live in Leadville and learn the mining business. Ben was handsome, charismatic, and adventurous. He had chafed working in the family's New York offices and was happy to find himself in a rowdy mining camp out West. The Guggenheims bought a house in Leadville a block west of Harrison Avenue. Ben lived in the richly furnished, six-bedroom Italianate-style house, but after a day at the mines, he preferred consorting with the rougher parts of town his father most likely avoided. Leadville may have had all the finery for the upscale crowd, but it also had all the depravity of a storied mining camp.

More than a hundred saloons accommodated gambling, drinking, and dancing. Hundreds of prostitutes worked the streets and brothels, most of them west of Harrison Avenue along State Street (now 2nd Avenue), Tiger Alley, and the even more depraved Stillborn Alley. Outlaws Jesse and Frank James kept a low profile while they lived in Leadville, but infamous gambler Doc Holliday—pale, emaciated, and dying of tuberculosis—called attention to himself during his years in Leadville by shooting two people, one a constable. Claiming self-defense, Holliday was acquitted on both charges. Gunfights and murders were commonplace, and nearly every man, including Ben Guggenheim, carried a gun to protect against claim jumpers and robbers.

Throughout the 1880s, the A.Y. and Minnie produced vast amounts of silver for the Guggenheims. Meyer returned in 1884 to dedicate a new plant, which, the *Evening Chronicle* wrote, "looks like a miniature mosque of Constantinople, and Papa Guggenheim is the sultan." Before the mines were done, they'd produced $15 million in silver and lead, and the Minnie had become one of the most productive silver mines in America. Though Leadville's silver made Meyer Guggenheim and his sons very wealthy men, hundreds of other mines such as the Little Pittsburg, the Robert E. Lee, and the Colonel Sellers were making other men wealthy as well. Two mines, even in the Magic City, could not make a dynasty.

By 1887, Meyer realized that the smelters were earning twice as much money as the mines. The real profit was in smelting. So Meyer sent Ben to Denver to learn the smelting business. By the next year, Ben had moved 120 miles south to Pueblo, a dusty, little community that was emerging as an industrial center, to help build and manage the family's first smelter. Now that the family's fortune lay solidly in the mining industry, the Guggenheims sold their lace business and began importing cheap Mexican ore to their Pueblo smelter, flooding the U.S. market with inexpensive silver. Upset by the subsequent drop in silver prices, other U.S. industrialists forced the passage of the McKinley Tariff of 1890 that essentially eliminated the importation of Mexican silver. Smelters that had relied on Mexican ore were forced to close, but the Guggenheims simply expanded their business into Mexico, building two new smelters and buying up mines there. Within five years, the Guggenheims had become an industrial power in Mexico. In the new century, however, even as the A.Y. and Minnie became less important to the family fortune, the Guggenheims ties to Leadville would remain strong for a time.

Ben wouldn't participate in this new stage in his family's saga. He had already been sent back east, married the daughter of a wealthy family, and retired—to the chagrin of his father—from the family business to travel in Europe and launch his own, unsuccessful businesses. In 1912, at age forty-seven, Ben would sink with the *Titanic* a hero, as the history books tell it, making sure the women and children were given seats on the lifeboats ahead of the men trying to push their way past.

3

The Fortunes of ASARCO

A poor peddler built the Guggenheim empire, but ASARCO was born big. By the end of the nineteenth century, the smelting and refining business was hurting. Competition was fierce, lead and silver prices had plunged, and employees were agitating for better working conditions. In that era of giant mergers and weak antitrust laws, consolidation of the smelting industry seemed the answer to improving business for everyone. In April 1899, the American Smelting and Refining Company (the name was changed to ASARCO Inc. in 1975) was born from the merger of seventeen corporations comprising sixteen smelters—including the Arkansas Valley Smelter just south of Leadville—eighteen refineries, and many more mines. Upon its formation, ASARCO dominated the smelting and refining industry but for one important holdout. The Guggenheims had refused to join unless on their terms—control of the new company. ASARCO had refused, and the two companies began to battle for dominance in the smelting market.

The struggle was brief. Soon after ASARCO was formed, Colorado passed a law mandating an eight-hour workday for all mine, mill, and smelter employees, most of whom were then working ten- or twelve-hour days. In retaliation, ASARCO, which owned several important smelters in the state, lowered wages to match the shorter workday. When employees struck, every ASARCO smelter in Colorado shut down. Just a few months later, the Colorado State Supreme Court ruled the law unconstitutional, but by then the Guggenheims had already captured the market. ASARCO's stocks dropped along with its profits. The company needed new capital and again sought to bring the Guggenheim family into the company, this time accepting that it would control ASARCO. When the negotiations were finished, the Guggenheims owned 51 percent of the company, one brother was president and chairman of the board, another brother became treasurer, and three more brothers sat on the board.

Meyer had at last secured his dynasty. He died just a few years later, in 1905, at the age of seventy-seven and worth $77 million (about $1.5 billion today). With the power of a dominant company behind them, Meyer's sons continued their father's ambitions, expanding ASARCO's operations around the globe. The Guggenheims—ASARCO—were routinely vilified for their tactics. Early conservationists called them "industrial spoilers" for buying up huge swaths of pristine land for mining exploitation, particularly in Alaska. The media called them profiteers, monopolizers, and power mongers for absorbing huge profits at the expense of poorly paid workers, for mercilessly breaking strikes and competition, and for exploiting the economies and labors of developing countries. Arguing capitalistic freedom, the Guggenheims drove up mineral prices and were devastating competition in the mining industry, some claimed, even during World War I until President Woodrow Wilson demanded they lower their prices.

For forty years, the Guggenheims controlled ASARCO; former U.S. senator from Colorado, Simon Guggenheim, remained president— the second brother to hold the office and the last Guggenheim to sit on ASARCO's board—until his death in 1941. In the 1930s the aging Guggenheim brothers, in deciding what to do with their respective fortunes, discovered philanthropy and eventually, through gifts to aeronautics, the arts, and medicine, replaced their infamous reputation as industrial spoilers with one of generous humanitarians.

Over the course of the twentieth century, ASARCO, during and after the Guggenheim years, became one of the world's biggest smelting and mining companies and a powerful global economic force. The company mined and processed gold, silver, lead, zinc, coal, and diamonds in operations that ranged from Alaska to Chile, and from Utah to Angola, but in later years it specialized in copper. Many of its U.S. sites—including Tacoma, Washington; El Paso, Texas; East Helena, Montana; and Leadville, Colorado—would be criticized for the damage they caused to the environment and the public's health, and ASARCO would again be routinely accused of putting the company's profits ahead of the public's welfare.

Leadville did not fare as well as ASARCO in the new century, though not as badly as many other mining towns. Throughout the 1880s, silver prices had been declining, in part, because of too much silver on the market. To bolster the nation's economy, President Benjamin Harrison had signed the Sherman Silver Purchase Act of 1890, authorizing the government to buy 4.5 million ounces of silver each month to exchange for paper money. But the nation was soon in the grip of a panic over depleting gold reserves in the U.S. Treasury, due in part to the fear that less-valuable silver would replace gold as the monetary standard. Many blamed the economic crisis on the Sherman Silver Purchase Act, and President Grover Cleveland urged Congress to repeal the act. The price of silver plunged.

The silver crash of 1893 forced mines and smelters to close and fortunes to crumble in silver mining towns throughout the West. In Leadville, miners fled for new opportunities and the wealthy silver barons of the 1880s disappeared. Horace Tabor, who had spent so lavishly, lost everything in 1893 and died in poverty six years later of appendicitis. After his death, Baby Doe and their two daughters, Elizabeth and Silver Dollar, moved into a squalid one-room shack to await a return of fortunes at the now-silent Matchless Mine east of Leadville.

But unlike most mining towns, which either faded into ghost towns or turned to tourism, the Magic City's luck held. Colorado's Mineral Belt is particularly rich and diverse in Leadville's section of the Mosquito Range, containing not just silver and gold, but copper, lead, manganese, and zinc. For twenty-five years, miners had been tossing these less glamorous minerals into the waste piles. After the silver crash, it would be these base metals that would for a time save Leadville and its mining industry.

In the late 1890s, another venture got underway in Leadville that would boost the mines' profitability and assist the town's economic recovery. At the time, it was considered the Leadville Mining District's "most magnificent enterprise," and it would have profound environmental consequences for the Arkansas River and for the valley where Doc Smith's grandfather was already troubled by his struggling hay business. For years, pumps had been used to dewater the mines of the shallow groundwater that flooded the mine workings. Several mine owners, including August Meyer, who had been instrumental in bringing Leadville its first smelter, decided that the mines could be dewatered and worked more profitably by allowing the groundwater to drain downhill through a large tunnel rather than by the more expensive method of pumping the water out. They started the tunnel in California Gulch near where the A.Y. and Minnie were still hauling out silver for the Guggenheims. For the next thirty years, the Yak Mining, Milling and Tunnel Company drove the tunnel northeast four miles through the mining district, ending high up in the Mosquito Range at the Diamond mine at the top of a pretty, little valley of wetlands and waste rock piles called Evans Gulch. As the Yak Tunnel progressed, mine owners built laterals to drain their mines into it. An underground rail line in the tunnel, electrically driven by 1904, also hauled ore out of the mines through this tunnel to a nearby mill.

Throughout the twentieth century, Leadville's economy cycled with the mineral market, thriving during the war years and just getting by in between. During World War II, the federal government offered price incentives to encourage the production of copper, lead, and zinc, and Leadville's mining district boomed once again. By the 1940s, milling had become more efficient, and John Hamm, an entrepreneur who had arrived in 1935, believed the mineral wealth left in the early waste piles was worth reprocessing. The self-described "dump rat" built the Hamm's Mill just a mile east of Harrison Avenue in Stray Horse Gulch and began reprocessing old, prominent waste dumps like the Maid of Erin, the Wolftone, and the R.A.M. After the war, Hamm left town in search of new opportunities. His legacy to Leadville was a gigantic tailing pile loaded with sulfur, lead, zinc, and other metals. On windy days, the pile's fine, sandy particles blew across town.

In the federal government's urgent need for metals during World War II, it began digging its own ill-fated tunnel to dewater the "downtown mines" not served by the Yak. In 1943, the Bureau of Mines planned to drive the Leadville Mine Drainage Tunnel three miles, beginning just north of Leadville and heading south through the mining district, in under two years. By the end of the war in August 1945, the tunnel had reached little more than a third of that distance. In 1950, the Korean War prompted the Bureau of Mines to resume digging, but progress stopped for good at the end of the war in 1952 at just two miles. In the end, the tunnel not only wasn't completed in time to supply the war effort with metals, but it also wasn't deep enough to drain most of the mines it originally was intended to dewater. But the government's tunnel was extensive enough to drain 2.5 million gallons of contaminated groundwater a day into the Arkansas River.

With the end of the Korean War, Leadville's boom days were gone for good. A few mining companies continued operating sporadically, depending on the mineral market. For the townsfolk it was a quiet time, but up on the hill, the buying, selling, and agreements made during this period would become significant thirty years later when the government sought out companies to sue for the contamination. ASARCO bought up and consolidated mining claims in the district and operated the Irene Mine. Resurrection Mining Company, a subsidiary of Newmont Mining Corporation, had been operating mines and a mill in Leadville since the late 1930s and had purchased the Yak Tunnel in 1942. In 1955, the two companies became partners. Under Resurrection's management, the Joint Venture operated several mines that drained through the Yak. By 1957, dismal metal prices forced the mines to shut down, and in 1961, ASARCO closed the Arkansas Valley Smelter—the last of Leadville's smelter smokestacks stilled after eighty years in operation. Then in the early 1970s, after discovering new metal reserves, the two companies spent $14.7 million to dig a new shaft and build a mill five miles up the hill. When the Black Cloud Mine and Mill began operating—with ASARCO as the controlling partner—it employed about two hundred miners and was the only major mine operating in the Leadville Mining District.

ASARCO's new lead and zinc mine was too small of an operation to sustain Leadville, but during the slow mining times of the late twentieth century, the town had been rescued once again, this time by a little-known mineral with a hard-to-pronounce name being mined twelve miles north of town since the 1920s. But by now Leadville was no longer the Silver Queen or even the Magic City. It had to look to its past, to the waste dumps, crumbling headframes, and mining buildings that remained in the hills east of town to remember the glory years.

Leadville's contribution to western mining and the East's industrial growth was staggering. Over the course of a hundred years, nearly a billion dollars worth of lead, silver, copper, zinc, and gold came out of the mountains east of town. Only a tiny fraction of it stayed in Leadville, however. With the exception of Horace Tabor's hotel and opera house, the money was sent off to Denver, Chicago, New York. Leadville was left with the environmental destruction.

In the rush to expand westward, settlers gave little thought to the environmental damage they caused. To early newcomers, the Rocky Mountains and its bounty must have appeared endless. But the land could not long support the mass of people that swarmed to the area after gold was discovered in 1859. Within just a few decades, the region's natural abundance was nearly wiped out. Forests were decimated; herds of antelope, bison, and elk were hunted to near extinction; streams were fished out. In the upper Arkansas River, the yellow-fin cutthroat, unique to the area, was fished to extinction.

Leadville

The sheer scale of mining and its disturbance of the land in heavily mined areas is hard to comprehend. In the eight-square-mile Leadville Mining District, for example, surveys over the years have identified 1,329 mine shafts, 155 tunnels, 1,628 prospect holes and 1,800 other types of man-made cavities spanning a total underground network of several hundred miles. More than two thousand waste rock piles, from house-sized bumps to soaring cones streaked with oranges, yellows, reds, and browns; tailings from numerous mills; and the slag piles of forty-four smelters continue to dot the landscape. Every square inch of dirt had been turned over at least once.

The most harmful and enduring environmental result of western mining stems from acid mine drainage. When groundwater percolates through the porous geology and the numerous cracks and faults into mine workings, it reacts with sulfides in the ore and oxygen in the air to create sulfuric acid. The acid eats at the tunnels' walls, dissolving metals—the iron, cadmium, lead, copper, zinc, arsenic, mercury, and manganese—and feeding sulfur-loving microbes that speed up the chemical reaction. The entire brew flows out to the streams or seeps into the groundwater. Above ground, the waste rock piles and tailing piles also contain the toxic combinations of sulfur and other heavy metals. Rainwater or snowmelt passing over the piles adds the final ingredient to create sulfuric acid, releasing the piles' metals to wash down the waterway. This simple chemical reaction unleashes a host of complex environmental consequences.

Iron draws the most attention to itself, marking the path of acid mine drainage a rusty orange, and it was the metal responsible for turning Doc Smith's river red. But it's the metals that can't be seen that wreak the most damage. Acidic water and some of the metals it carries kill plants, insects, fish, other aquatic life, and mammals. The effects are passed up the food chain. Cadmium, for example, concentrates in the willow bushes growing along riverbanks, causing weak bones and kidney and liver damage in the birds and other wildlife that feed on them. As the metals accumulate on the riverbanks and floodplain, they kill or stunt the vegetation and poison young animals that graze on it, not just the ranchers' cattle and horses, but the valley's elk, antelope, mule deer, and bighorn sheep. Once lodged in the soils, the cadmium, zinc, and lead persist for thousands of years before eroding away.

Tailing piles also pose unique risks. The ground-up ore generates even more acid mine drainage, and wind and water erode the piles, carrying metals into neighboring land. To migratory birds, the acidic water accumulated atop tailing piles can look like an inviting muddy pond. Hundreds of birds—entire flocks of snow geese, plovers, and ducks—have been killed after drinking the acidic water.

Acid drainage occurs in nature as well, wherever sulfides, water, and air come together. Some areas in the Rocky Mountains beckoned prospectors to try their luck because of the orange-tinted water naturally found there. But for the most part, the amounts were small, wetlands helped filter the metals, and nature had adapted. Mining radically magnified the amount of acid drainage pouring into streams simply by exposing pyrite to water and air and giving the contaminated runoff a direct route to the gulches and rivers. Nevertheless, given the existence of some natural acidic water and heavy metals, how clean is clean enough would become an important, difficult, and contentious question to answer when future generations looked to repairing the damage caused by mining.

Acid mine drainage and its environmental consequences are of course not unique to Leadville. The extent of the contamination can only be estimated, but as many as five hundred thousand abandoned mine sites dot the American landscape, roughly three hundred thousand of them in the West. Some writers put the estimates even higher. Roughly fifty billion tons of mine waste is strewn across two million acres of the United States. According to the EPA, acid mine drainage pollutes an estimated 40 percent of the West's watersheds, including those within the heavily mined Mineral Belt slicing through Colorado—despite the popular image of pristine Rocky Mountain streams winding their way down from the Continental Divide through unspoiled wilderness. Colorado's more than twenty-three thousand abandoned mines alone pollute 1,300 miles of streams. These and other Rocky Mountain rivers provide drinking water to ten million people throughout the southwest, including Los

Angeles. Restoring the environment for its own sake might not have proven a strong enough incentive for the tens of billions of dollars cleanup would require, but protecting the public's health became a powerful additional selling point.

By the 1960s, a new environmental movement was calling attention to the consequences unbridled industrial growth was having on the environment and the public's health. Politicians responded to the overwhelming popular support for environmental protection by enacting an array of environmental regulations, most notably the Clean Air Act of 1970 and Clean Water Act of 1972. Under these laws, the new Environmental Protection Agency set air and water standards, but the states were charged with ensuring those standards were met.

Regulated for the first time, industries balked. Regulations would weaken the economy, they threatened. Among the two hundred largest companies in the United States at the time, with more than $2 billion in assets, ASARCO was considered by regulators to be especially bullheaded and a barrier to environmental health for having gone to the legal mat at its mining and smelter sites throughout the West and Midwest to avoid pollution controls and violation fees.

ASARCO had faced environmental criticism elsewhere before and prevailed. It had successfully thwarted attempts to hinder mining the Alaskan wilderness, and Doc Smith wasn't the first farmer to complain that ASARCO's smelters hurt business. Farmers in California and the Salt Lake Valley in Utah had sued the company in 1912, arguing that the smelters' sulfur dioxide emissions killed their crops and ranchland. ASARCO had promised to research the problem, and the suits were dropped. At least fifteen years later—and perhaps much longer—the company decided that taller smokestacks would dissipate the acid rain over a wider area, reducing the toxic concentration in any one area below the point where crops were noticeably damaged.

But tall smokestacks didn't satisfy this new generation of regulators, who seemed to have the public on their side in the 1970s. As the pressure to put profits into environmental safeguards mounted, ASARCO considered it a legal problem, not an engineering one, and handed the problem over to its lawyers. The battle between regulators and industry played out across the nation, but ASARCO's Black Cloud Mine and Yak Tunnel in Leadville sat squarely in the midst of the conflict. It had long been known that the heavy metals found in mining waste and in the Yak's discharge harmed the Arkansas River—above the confluence with California Gulch fish could be found, directly below there were none. ASARCO was California Gulch's largest polluter and its biggest obstacle to cleanup. The company owned more than half of the hundreds of mines in California Gulch, and its active mining operation generated one-third of the Yak's discharge. ASARCO, along with its partner, Resurrection Mining Company, the Newmont subsidiary, also owned the Yak Tunnel and many of the abandoned mines that drained into it.

In the 1970s, ASARCO refused to compromise with Colorado's health department, which was trying to impose a waste discharge permit to monitor and regulate the Black Cloud Mine's hazardous releases as mandated by the Clean Water Act. The company threatened to file suit against the state and to shut down the mine, putting miners out of work, unless discharge standards were relaxed. The tactic gave the company, one of Leadville's largest taxpayers, considerable leverage against the state. Though ASARCO and Resurrection filed for a permit by a July 1, 1977, deadline, ASARCO's threats and inflexibility delayed the permit more than five years, making it the last major industrial operation in a six-state region to obtain one. In the meantime, the company was free to dump mine waste into California Gulch.

The Black Cloud is situated at the top of Iowa Gulch, the ravine just south of California Gulch. To avoid drainage into California Gulch by way of the Yak Tunnel, which was receiving so much attention, the company in the 1970s decided to dump its waste straight into Iowa Gulch, the acid and heavy metals destroying its fish and beaver populations, until the health department forced them to stop in 1978. In the end, the discharge permit was weak, addressing only waste from the active mining operation, not from the abandoned mines still draining into California Gulch and contaminating the Arkansas River. The permit required ASARCO to prevent the Black Cloud's waste from draining into the Yak and to build a treatment facility for the waste in Iowa Gulch. State officials had suggested that ASARCO build a plant that would treat all of the sludge draining out of the Yak to prevent the hazardous material from reaching the Arkansas River, but the company had refused. It was a decision that would later come to seem improvident. At the end of the decades-long permit battle, state officials admitted that, in the interest of preventing lawsuits, too many concessions had been made. "Perhaps we are now more inclined to use the regulatory power of the courts," a state official told a Denver newspaper.

In the 1970s, the states were expected to enforce the Clean Water Act. But by 1980, a new and more powerful threat was looming for ASARCO and other mining companies nationwide. The federal government's Environmental Protection Agency, a decade old now, was beginning to tackle the nation's hazardous waste. Congress had passed CERCLA, the Comprehensive Environmental Response, Compensation, and Liability Act of 1980, which President Jimmy Carter signed into law in his final hours in office.

The powerful new law was a landmark, inspired by the public's growing fears of hazardous waste, particularly acute after the Love Canal scandal near Niagara Falls, New York, made headlines in 1978. The Hoover Chemical Company had dumped toxic chemicals into the canal in the 1940s and 1950s that later leaked into hundreds of homes built on top of the area. Though the public sometimes blamed the EPA for allowing disasters like Love Canal to happen, the agency was hamstrung by long legal battles, and was forced to build a case for cleanup in court when companies sued. To remedy the situation Congress, through CERCLA, gave the EPA $1.6 billion—a Superfund—to clean up toxic waste dumps immediately and seek reimbursement from offending companies later. It was intended as a "fast track" solution to solve abandoned hazardous waste problems that too often had become mired in the courts.

Superfund was a controversial approach: clean up now and bill later. But perhaps more significantly, it gave the EPA power to track down corporate dumpers and haul them into court to recover cleanup costs in the millions of dollars. The law's intended targets were chemical dumpsites—graphic images now making the nightly news of corroded barrels leaking toxic waste dumped into a secluded, wooded gully at night. To finance the fund, CERCLA included a special tax on the chemical and oil industries. The initial program was to last five years. During the first two years, the EPA developed a proposed Superfund list of 418 of the most hazardous sites in the nation. Included were a few particularly noxious mining sites in the West, Leadville's California Gulch among them. Experts believed at least fifty thousand more sites could have made the list. But two years into the program, the "fast track" solution had started work on only five abandoned dumpsites. Decontaminating the nation's most dangerous hazardous waste sites was more complicated than originally conceived. But by 1982 another reason for the limited accomplishment emerged. Superfund had wound up at the center of a political maelstrom that eventually cost twenty-two top EPA officials their jobs, demoralized employees to the point that 40 percent of the staff quit, and left 418 communities nationwide dangling. The outcome of the political fighting about to erupt in Washington, D.C., would greatly affect Leadville for the next twenty years.

The day after Superfund became law, a new president changed the course of environmental cleanup. Ronald Reagan and his controversial interior secretary, James Watt, began deregulating environmental laws and scaling back the power of regulatory agencies created to enforce them. The EPA's budget was cut by nearly 30 percent; its research divisions, the biggest threat to justifying less-stringent regulations, took the largest hit—slashed by 42 percent. Environmental regulations passed under the Carter administration, including those seeking to prevent toxic dumping under the Clean Water Act, were suspended as soon as they took affect.

"The degree to which a 'deregulated' agency can become the handmaiden of industry became evident in a scandal that erupted last winter in which the Environmental Protection Agency was, once again, the focus," wrote Martin Tolchin and Susan J. Tolchin in the *New York Times Magazine* in 1983. At the scandal's core was Anne Gorsuch, the thirty-eight-year-old EPA administrator. She had come from Colorado's House of Representatives, one of its self-appointed "crazies," a group of ultra-conservative legislators determined to prevent government from interfering in industry. Gorsuch brought that ideology with her to the EPA. She was considered smart, extreme, defiant, uncompromising, and tough—a Denver newspaper wrote that Gorsuch could "kick a bear to death with her bare feet." The EPA's Superfund administrator, Rita Lavelle, was equally dogmatic. The thirty-five-year-old had recently been a public relations employee for a California company facing hazardous waste problems. Gorsuch had successfully fought hazardous waste legislation in Colorado, and Lavelle agreed with her boss that Superfund was a threat to industry.

The two brought Superfund to a standstill, instigating measures diametrically opposed to Superfund's fast-track intentions. Under their guidance, the EPA weakened regulations, failed to develop standards, and halted enforcement against polluters. Gorsuch and Lavelle refused to believe, at least publicly, that hazardous waste posed a serious public health risk despite the overwhelming evidence. Besides, they said, the public must get used to living with greater risk.

In refusing to spend the $1.6 billion allocated to clean up hazardous waste across the country, Gorsuch hoped to circumvent "Son of Superfund," the statute's reauthorization Congress would decide in 1985. The Reagan administration intended for Superfund to die. Part of that plan included barring mining sites like California Gulch from Superfund consideration. Pressure from the mining industry had led Congress to exclude mining's hazardous waste from the original CERCLA law unless it posed an "imminent and substantial" risk to public health. That determination was left up to the EPA.

Unlike the contained, concentrated chemical dump sites Congress initially targeted, mining sites were sprawling and complex, characterized by high volumes of low concentrations of toxic waste. By denying abandoned mining waste an explicit entitlement to CERCLA enforcement, Congress had given the EPA an excuse to exclude mining and gave the mining companies greater incentive to fight the law for years to come. Though the law would prove problematic in addressing large-scale western mining sites, without CERCLA no other legislative mechanism existed to mandate cleanup of abandoned mine sites contaminating nearly half of the West's watersheds, including Doc's Arkansas River Valley, already identified as one of the most contaminated spots in the nation. Lavelle believed that adding mining sites to Superfund's National Priority List would hurt western Republican candidates in the upcoming election. In June 1982, Gorsuch decided that mining sites would remain on the proposed list, but Superfund money would be used only to study the sites. Cleanup could only proceed after a court had ordered someone else to pay for it—returning the issue to the legal quagmire that had led to Superfund's passage in the first place.

Undermining Superfund proposals led critics to charge the new EPA administration of colluding with industry polluters, and six Congressional committees began investigating the EPA for political favoritism and mismanagement of the Superfund program. EPA employees testified to administrative cover-ups, shredded documents, and dozens of private meetings with industry representatives that resulted in Superfund listing decisions made to benefit Republican causes. President Reagan refused to hand over documents to Congress, and Gorsuch followed the President's lead and ended up becoming the highest ranking official—at that time—to be charged with contempt of Congress. The nation's editorialists considered the situation one of the most serious constitutional confrontations between the White House and Congress since the Watergate scandal, and Congressmen warned that the EPA was "out of control and falling part."

With the media scrutiny now exposing her decisions and questioning her motives, Gorsuch reversed her decision on mining and approved Superfund money for cleanup plans on January 18, 1983. The following month, as public outcry over the EPA scandal intensified, President Reagan fired Rita Lavelle, who spent six months in prison, convicted of perjury and obstruction of Congress. Her boss, EPA Administrator Anne Gorsuch, resigned in early March 1983.

A few weeks earlier, on February 23, 1983, the morning Doc Smith awoke to find a crimson Arkansas River, the phone at ASARCO's

Leadville

Leadville headquarters began to ring. An ice fisherman reported that the river was "running very red," the local game warden was spotted watching the entrance of the Yak Tunnel from the road, and people were complaining at the county courthouse. As Doc drove to his meeting, all the way down Highway 24 that follows the Arkansas River through the valley, he saw people bent over bridges, looking at the aberration—accounts of the river's color would vary from butterscotch to orange juice to blood red. The spectacle was stopping traffic as far south as Buena Vista, a little town thirty miles downstream. Chemical concentrations, particularly of zinc and cadmium, reached levels up to four times higher than standards allowed—high enough that it killed fish fifteen miles downstream. More significantly, halfway between Leadville and Buena Vista, the sludge entered the Otero Pump Station, which was hastily shut down to prevent the concoction from entering the drinking water supply to the five hundred thousand residents of Colorado Springs and the Denver suburb of Aurora.

The news was spreading. A representative from both the state's health department and the Environmental Protection Agency were on their way, and two news stations from Denver were loading up their vans for a trip into the mountains.

Twenty years later the consequences of the event were still being felt. At the time, the residents of Leadville didn't realize its significance. The river had been "running red" for more than a hundred years, a by-product of the industry that had supported their families for generations, and even the old-timers couldn't remember when fish swam in the upper Arkansas. But now it had disrupted the water supply to the populous Colorado Front Range, and various government agencies were paying attention—as far away as Washington, D.C. These proud, independent westerners didn't realize they were about to tangle with a young, cocky Environmental Protection Agency in a modern-day version of an old western standoff. In the process, both sides would be forced to address hard questions about identity and the future, with implications that would reach far beyond Leadville and the beautiful high valley that nurtured it.

4

The Shutdown

Jim Martin, a short, wiry miner, his black hair graying, didn't pay much attention when the Yak Tunnel "burped," as miners often refer to such spills (the EPA prefers the term "blowout"). As a chief engineering planner at AMAX's Climax mine twelve miles north of Leadville, Jim had spent nearly a year laying off engineers and felt lucky he still had a job himself. He had too many worries to concern himself with what was going on over in California Gulch.

Until 1982, Climax had employed half the town of Leadville and its county, supporting nearly the entire population of 8,800. Then the company had suddenly begun laying off three thousand miners, leaving just a few hundred employees. The layoffs had taken the entire town by surprise. Jim knew, because he helped the company calculate such things, that there were still five hundred million tons of molybdenite left in the mountain, more than had been mined during the company's seventy-five years in operation and enough to keep miners employed for decades.

Leadville had seen booms and busts for more than a hundred years. To many, painful as it was, this was just another bust to be waited out. Jim knew the situation in town was serious, but he wasn't too worried; he, too, thought the layoffs would be temporary. Two blocks up the street from his colorful Victorian home, past the small Heritage Museum, old mining relics displayed in its tiny yard, Jim could see the north end of Harrison Avenue. Most of the buildings along Harrison had been built during the town's boom days. Those that had survived—City Hall, where the mayor and six city council members governed Leadville; the Old Church, the turreted American National Bank housing a Goodwill Store, the Tabor Opera House now used as the Elk's Lodge—most of the half-mile long stretch of two- and three-story brick buildings with tall, arched windows wore a dark coating from a hundred years of grime and sagged from neglect. The ornate details of the buildings, built during a period of prosperity and grandeur, were now chipped, drooping, or missing, a reminder that the old Silver Queen had fallen far.

In the early 1980s, businesses still occupied the rundown buildings and people continued to navigate Leadville's crumbling sidewalks to shop in town. A noticeable exception was the Tabor Grand Hotel, Horace Tabor's monument to luxury that stretched an entire block along Harrison. For most of the twentieth century, a prominent sign had identified it as the Vendome Hotel, but by the 1980s, the only lodgers were drifters who didn't mind the grimy interior of peeling paint, boarded windows, and an upper floor that looked as if someone had tossed in a grenade—a blackened exterior with windows and frames missing, construction paper flapping in the dry mountain air. Scores of pigeons had long since made the top floor of the Tabor Grand their home. There was talk of demolishing the landmark to make a parking lot.

A few blocks south on Harrison, in the County Courthouse, three commissioners ruled most of Lake County, including the mining district. At the south end of Harrison, a huge heap of gritty black slag—smelter waste that tourists often mistook for coal—had accumulated right up to the road's edge, left there by the Harrison Reduction Works nearly a hundred years earlier. Next to it along the road and spilling into California Gulch was the World War II–era Apache Tailing Impoundment, acidic mill waste covering eighteen acres, the equivalent of about fourteen football fields. There, the road bent to the west, heading down the gulch toward Doc Smith's ranch, but first passing another slag compound—forty acres worth—left over from ASARCO's Arkansas Valley Smelter days. Mine waste was the first sight to greet visitors entering Leadville from the south.

Along the arteries running east and west of Harrison, the grand old homes of the wealthy beneficiaries of mining and the small, unadorned houses, some little more than shacks, of its workers still intermingled. Some homes, like Jim's, were maintained with fresh coats of paint, tidy yards, and beds of purple columbines. Others were surrounded by cars that hadn't moved in years and by piles of junk no longer recognizable rusting in Leadville's snowy weather. The west side of Harrison still featured Millionaire's Row, though the money was long gone—the homes much too small and Leadville much too provincial for contemporary millionaires. What was once Ben Guggenheim's home, empty and neglected for decades, had deteriorated to the point that it was lucky to be standing. The small red-light district on 2nd Avenue, still bustling and ignored by authorities in the 1960s, was now gone. But plenty of saloons still flourished to help the miners unwind, including the Silver Dollar, left over from the old boom days that had since blended an Irish motif into the Wild West theme—right down to the redheaded owner named Patty McMahon who served drinks behind the original, shamrock-decorated bar.

East of Harrison, the brown- and yellow-streaked piles of waste rock pulled from the ground nearly a century earlier still jutted into people's backyards, dwarfing the houses around them. The piles were a ready playground for the neighborhood kids. One massive pile on 5th Street, the Hamm's Tailing Pile, was a particular favorite. Kids called it "the sandbox" or "the sand dunes." Another popular playground, the Starr Ditch, originally built in the 1860s to carry water to placer miners in California Gulch, passed between the east-side houses.

Less than a mile up the east side of town, the houses stopped and waste rock piles and disintegrating wood remains of the mine buildings dominated the landscape. The piles were like the town's pets, each still known by the name of the mine that had created it: Blind Tom (named after a mule that had spent its life in the tunnels), Robert

Emmet, Pyrenees, Greenback, Maid of Erin, Fanny Rawlins, Corona-do, Clear Grit, Wolftone, R.A.M. (short for Ragged Ass Miner—the true moniker too risqué to be registered in the Victorian era books), and many more. A few, like Tabor's Matchless, still had their head-frames, the tall A-frame structure used to hang the pulleys to haul men and equipment up and down the mine shaft, and perhaps anoth-er small building or two, but little else to suggest that the entire land-scape had once been a nineteenth-century industrial mining center dominated by rough-sawn buildings, railroad trestles, and a smoke-filled sky. The Matchless Mine was now a tourist attraction. Baby Doe had frozen to death at the Matchless in March 1935 after having lived there for more than thirty years, her rags-to-riches-to-rags story now a popular Leadville legend.

In the early 1980s, only ASARCO's Black Cloud and a few other mines were still operating in the Leadville Mining District. For decades, though, the work that essentially kept Leadville a mining town long after most had disappeared was not east of town in the mining district, but at the Climax moly mine, a giant complex owned by American Metal Climax Inc., or AMAX, located twelve miles north of town. Miners like Jim had been blasting Bartlett Mountain to get at its molybdenum for generations.

Sitting atop the Continental Divide, at the headwaters of three rivers and above timberline at 11,300 feet, Climax sat between the tallest peaks in the Rocky Mountains and an eight-mile-long moun-tain valley. It was in the late 1870s, as prospectors were digging into the hills around Leadville looking for silver, that others were finding instead a bluish gray, greasy mineral they'd never seen before. Molyb-denum seemed to have little usefulness, but miners continued to bring up the unusual mineral anyway. It wasn't until World War I, when the Allies began dismantling recovered German weapons, that they realized molybdenum's potential. The Germans were using moly as a steel alloy to strengthen and increase the durability of their weapons. Demand for moly in the United States rose, and the Climax mine opened in early 1918 to meet it. But the war soon ended, and the company faced a slump in the market. It began lobbying the young automobile industry, convincing them that moly was the answer to lighten and strengthen their steel-heavy cars. The first car to use moly-reinforced steel, Wills Ste Claire's 1921 Gray Goose, cost three thousand dollars—too expensive for most early automobile buyers. But the alloy eventually caught on among auto manufacturers, ensuring Climax a stable market for its moly—and Leadville a large, solid mining employer—beyond the boom and bust cycle for minerals during the twentieth century's wars.

From its early days, Climax maintained a hectic production pace through good times and bad and was willing to take risks to stay on top. It claimed to be the world's largest underground mine and in the 1940s produced nearly all of the moly needed to strengthen the American guns and tanks used in World War II. During those years, miners passed through a chain-link fence topped with barbed wire and armed guards to work in the military's highest-priority mine. The need for minerals, especially moly, was so critical that the government allowed potential soldiers with mining experience to work at Climax instead of fighting overseas.

Climax may have been surrounded by natural beauty, but its working conditions were even worse than those in Leadville's mining district. Bitterly cold much of the year, Climax received more than three hundred inches of snow annually and a fierce wind could whip over the mountain pass. In the early years, when the railroad tracks and the road to Climax were often impassible and few comforts existed, miners were not impressed with the majestic setting, referring to their job site as "that hellhole near the sky." Even in the 1970s when mining jobs were harder to find, the company had to hire thousands of miners just to hold onto a couple of hundred.

To retain workers and compensate for the harsh conditions, the company provided Jim Martin and others who stuck it out with high wages and good benefits. Those who stayed were loyal to Climax, a company that rewarded hard work, where a man could count on working his way up the ladder no matter his level of formal education. And these workers in turn appreciated the company's generosity toward Leadville. Climax provided summer jobs and scholarships for their kids, built new schools, and donated money whenever called upon. Before Climax shut down in 1982, Leadville had the highest per capita income and the largest number of graduates continuing on to college among all towns in Colorado's rural counties. With Climax barreling along for more than seventy years, it appeared as though the good life would never end.

When Jim arrived with his family in 1962 to take a job at Climax, Leadville seemed like a fine place to settle down. It was the kind of mining town Jim liked. A tight-knit community with the friendships and camaraderie that came when men worked for the same company for essentially the same wages, their wives knew each other from community and church activities, and the kids all went to school together. Everyone was equal.

Leadville then was a bustling town of about five thousand people, mostly mining families, with just enough businesses to meet their needs. J.C. Penney had been at 7th and Harrison since 1934. There was also a men's haberdashery, three auto dealerships, a shoe store, and a theater where kids could pay with milk carton lids to watch movies. You could buy a washing machine, furniture, luggage, cameras, and jewelry and had your choice of electricians, plumbers, and auto mechanics. People from all over the area came to Leadville to do their shopping. The town still had the rough edge that had earned it a reputation as the "wickedest town in the West" a hundred years earlier. Transient miners could choose from a number of raucous bars. It was said that distributors sold more alcohol to Leadville's liquor stores and bars than to any other Colorado small town. Ma Brown owned the Pioneer Bar, where it was widely known that a miner could still drink, gamble, and buy female companionship. Upon learning of the establishment, a new district attorney began asking around about it. He soon learned that people wanted the place left alone. Ma Brown, it turned out, was a respected businesswoman.

Leadville had undergone a transformation in the years just before Jim Martin arrived. After the prosperous World War II days, the town had decided, like so many others in those early postwar years, that it could afford a badly needed face-lift—not to restore its historic buildings, but to modernize, to become a typical American city. Historic buildings were torn down to make room for the square brick-and-glass architecture that typified the 1950s. Within a decade, the town had built two new schools, a hospital, and a county courthouse to replace the 1880 building holding up Lady Justice that had been lost to fire in 1942; the 1880s sewer system was replaced and expanded; and new one-story, ranch-style houses with attached garages sprouted in the town's expanding neighborhoods. The plain functionality of contemporary 1950s now mixed with gothic Victorian complexity. By 1959, *Look Magazine* had pronounced Leadville an All American City, and the *Carbonate Chronicle* declared that its hometown had successfully transformed itself from an old mining camp to a modern American town. It wouldn't take long for the backlash.

By the 1960s, some in town were agitating for further changes. Many of them were newcomers, attracted to the area's remoteness and natural beauty. "Hippies," groused the old-timers. Leadville needed a plan for the future, the newcomers said. The town relied too heavily on one commodity—molybdenum—and needed to diversify and embrace the tourists who were beginning to discover Leadville, they argued. But the old-timers and working miners asked why. Climax was churning out molybdenum, handing out good paychecks, and helping to take care of the town's needs.

Jim didn't have time to get involved in town politics. He had a young family and a new mining job to keep him busy. Jim had never questioned that he would become a miner. The Martin family history includes the names of many of the major western mines and mining towns dating back to the 1880s, the decade in which his great-grandparents and young grandmother left New York bound for the new western mining camps. They settled first in Eureka, Nevada, and later moved to Butte, Montana. In those early days of underground mining, the job was particularly hazardous. Miners, along with their pie tins (with lunch or midnight meal), canteens, drills, dynamite, candles, and the oil lamps they needed, were lowered down a narrow vertical shaft in an iron bucket about the size of a large whisky barrel attached to a hoist cable. Depending on the size of the operation, the cable was attached to either a simple timber frame and turned on a circular whim by a horse or mule or to a headframe, sometimes enclosed in a shaft house and powered by steam. In either case, the trip up and down the shaft, controlled manually by a hoist operator of varying experience and attention span, was a dangerous ride in the dark as the bucket bounced against the shaft's rock walls. When cables broke, hoists failed, or men tipped out of buckets or lost their footing, they tumbled hundreds or thousands of feet to their death, the newspapers colorfully reporting the events, as this headline in Leadville's *Chronicle* on July 12, 1881, illustrates:

HOISTED TO HEAVEN—Terrible Accident in the Denver City Mine—John Jones Hangs on to a Bucket—And Then Drops a Sheer One Hundred Feet—The Limbs Literally Driven Into the Body

Once underground, Jim's grandfathers also faced rock and timber cave-ins, floods if accidentally hitting underground reservoirs, and fires from tipped oil lamps, sometimes suffocating far from the fire when it drew oxygen from distant tunnels. "Mucking," drilling and blasting, was also hazardous. To blast apart the ore, miners drilled six- to eight-foot holes into the rock surface, sometimes overhead, using drills powered by compressed air delivered by underground pipes from a compressor on the surface. Just before the end of their ten- or twelve-hour shift, the miners filled the holes with "giant powder" (the dynamite that was another source of deadly accidents), and lit the fuses. The air cleared somewhat before the next shift arrived to shovel the broken rock.

Miners worked in cramped tunnels in near darkness. The air was stagnant, the noise from the drilling and blasting deafening, and the odor pungent from the fumes and smoke of giant powder and from the human and mule waste left in the tunnels. Most of the mules, once lowered, never saw daylight again, spending their years strapped to a cart, hauling rock, and going blind in the dark tunnels. By the time electric-powered carts came along in the early nineteen hundreds, some of those mules had lived underground for more than twenty years.

The danger in the mines was omnipresent. In addition to accidents, the drillers and blasters also frequently developed a persistent hacking cough and shortness of breath. They called it miner's consumption; later it was diagnosed as silicosis. Drilling into the rock enveloped the muckers in a cloud of dust. The miniscule, sharp-edged particles they breathed in day after day, year after year, lodged in their lungs and often proved fatal. The drills became known as "widowmakers." By the turn of the century, "wet" drills that used water to tamp down the rock dust had been invented, but drills were expensive to replace and widowmakers remained common into the 1930s.

Like so many mining families, Jim's ancestors were plagued with mining deaths and accidents. Jim's grandmother's first husband died when a hoist cable broke. Her second husband, Jim's grandfather, died from a fall in a mine, and Jim's father suffered from silicosis. The federal government slowly began regulating working conditions after the turn of the century. But for many years, mining companies did little to ensure the safety of its miners or provide for them after an accident. In those early years the prevailing view, reinforced by the U.S. Supreme Court, was that a miner knew the risks when he accepted the job and picked up his one- to three-dollars-per-day wage. The mine owners were deemed not responsible for accidents or deaths, and injury benefits were decades away. Unable to afford medical care, miners often employed home remedies, setting bones and stitching gashes themselves. In every mining camp, men—scarred, maimed, half blind, and suppressing unrelenting coughs—lined up for work at the mines.

Because miners—and mining jobs—were easy to come by in boom times, company officials and mining employees didn't feel much loyalty toward each other. Miners quit often, rumors of better pay and better conditions prompting them to try their luck at another site. "Tramping" sent a constant migration through the mining camps, creating a transient quality to the towns that, at least in the early boom years, manifested itself in poor sewage systems, tiny, ramshackle living quarters, and few amenities beyond numerous saloons and whorehouses.

By the time Jim was born in 1930, conditions in both the tunnels and the towns had improved, but mining was still a dangerous, back-breaking profession and tramping, which would characterize Jim's childhood, was commonplace. Jim's birthplace was a temporary stop while his father worked a mine in Park City, Utah. The Depression soon drove the family to "tramp" to a number of Canadian mines until World War II brought a mining boom back to the States, enabling Jim's family to return to Butte, briefly.

Growing up, Jim attended four grade schools and six high schools. For a time he lived near James Bay, a mining camp in northern Ontario so remote the family had to fly in and so small he and his younger brother attended a one-room schoolhouse with a single teacher. For a year, they lived in Arlington, Virginia, with 3,500 class-mates, then they were off to Happy Camp in northern California and a log-cabin schoolhouse with twenty-five students. The constant moving didn't bother Jim. He was gregarious and outgoing, "a fun-loving guy, no doubt about that," who preferred playing outside with his buddies than studying in school (he was only "strapped" twice: once for playing hooky and another time for fighting).

Unlike his brother, who opted to spend his adult life in New York City, Jim preferred small towns, and he wanted to remain a part of the large, yet tight-knit western mining community. The custom of tramping extended that community of miners beyond individual towns to encompass the entire network of western mines. Wherever his next mining job might take him, a miner and his family were bound to know people they'd worked and lived with before no matter how small the town, which always amazed Jim. He also wanted to be like the miners he'd watched growing up: down to earth, hard work-ing, and skilled.

His father's near death in a mining accident when Jim was just beginning his own career didn't sway him from the mining life. Near Eureka, Nevada, in 1948, miners hit an underground reservoir, flood-ing the mine and nearly trapping Jim's father and two co-workers underground. Amidst the chaos, the three miners managed to float on the water as it carried them up the mine shaft to the surface. Mines were getting safer, but no one needed to be reminded that working underground was still dangerous. The scare prompted Jim's father to quit mining, but Jim headed for the mines of Butte, Montana.

It was there that he met Corinne, a blue-eyed, redheaded city girl who unexpectedly found herself in small-town Butte attending nursing school. Small-town living was supposed to be temporary, her roots deeply planted in Denver where her grandfather had been a prominent, long-serving politician and her father a well-liked juvenile court judge. She was one of eight children in an extended Irish Catholic family.

Corinne knew little of what a mining life entailed, but she thought Jim was fun and smart. He was an entertainer who could make everyone laugh, and he offset her quiet demeanor. The Butte months were fun times for both of them, but the Korean War interrupted their courtship. Jim shipped out to operate a rock quarry on the banks of the Hangang River near Seoul, and Corinne went back to Denver.

Jim was only in Korea four months before the war ended, but their separation lasted two years. The young couple eventually married and moved to a mining town in Wisconsin, then back to Denver and on to Leadville. Corinne was not the tramping type, especially with five young children soon in tow, and she certainly never expected to find herself living in a small town at 10,200 feet and married to a miner. But she knew it was time to end the tramping life, buy a house, and make a home. An attractive Victorian house caught her eye. It still had its old-fashioned charm: a bay window poking out onto a front porch, delicate eaves, and original woodwork. Jim didn't think much of the idea of buying it—his family had never owned a house. But Corinne was adamant, and they bought the 1899 house, its three small bedrooms barely enough room for the large family.

By the early 1980s, Jim had spent twenty years working his way up the mining hierarchy at Climax. They had been good years. Jim felt lucky he had found a place to settle down and raise a family—his wife had been right to buy the house after all. His oldest son had followed Jim into mining, carrying on the family tradition in Alaska.

Then the country fell into a recession. Iron, copper, coal, and other mining operations that supported the nation's industries were closing all over the West. ASARCO posted its worst earnings in history. People stopped buying cars, and the automobile industry began shutting down assembly lines and laying off workers. The consequences soon rippled out of Detroit, first to the steel industry, which went into a steep decline, then to the moly market. The price of moly dropped from $32.50 a pound in January 1979 to just $3.50 by December 1981.

Because steel used about 80 percent of all the moly produced—and Climax was still the biggest producer—the impact eventually reached the mining giant deep in the Rocky Mountains. Climax had weathered dips in the market before. For seventy-five years, the company's philosophy had been to charge through the down times. As it had done in the past, Climax continued to mine moly, stockpiling it to sell when the market improved, and Leadville's miners kept on mining.

The shutdown blindsided everyone. The company began laying off miners in early 1982 and continued through the fall. Officials hoped the closure would be temporary, but this time, the recession wasn't the only problem. Competition in the moly market was growing, nationally and abroad. Low-grade moly, sufficient to use as a steel alloy, is a by-product of copper mining. As the demand for molybdenum dropped, the additional competition was cutting into AMAX's market. Jim and three hundred other employees stayed on to manage the shutdown, maintain the equipment, and someday plan the mine's reopening. The *Herald Democrat* still referred to when, not if, Climax reopened.

As Jim drove up the valley to Climax each morning, the impact of a century of mining was obvious. Miners had extracted millions of tons of Bartlett Mountain's innards through a 150-mile network of tunnels, causing the mountain to collapse in on itself. The result was a half-mile-wide crater where the mountain used to be—the "Glory Hole" that greeted Jim on his commute. In the early 1970s, after equipment that could tolerate the freezing temperatures had finally been developed, the company began open pit mining. Instead of hauling rock out from the inside, moly was mined from the surface, a faster method that stripped the mountain in layers. Over the next decade, Bartlett Mountain took on the characteristic stair-step pattern of open pit mining. The 470 million tons of rock hauled out or stripped from the mountain for decades had to go somewhere. After the Climax mill ground the ore and extracted the moly, the waste was dumped into the neighboring valley, which became a 1,600-acre bowl of tailings. A well-used highway cut between the mining operation and its waste, giving drivers an up-close view of the mountain looking like a Roman amphitheater for giants above and below that, the orange swirl of acid and tailings.

In its lifetime, Climax had mined two million tons of moly worth $4 billion. The money had supported Leadville for decades. After the town's mining district had withered in the 1950s to just a few mines, the residents had relaxed into the comforting knowledge that Climax would take care of them. Leadville had managed to stave off the loss of mining far longer than its Rocky Mountain neighbors, but now that Climax was gone, the town had nothing to fall back on. Without the company, the company town went into a steep decline. Climax accounted for 86 percent of Lake County's tax base. Without it, the county's revenue plummeted from $250 million in 1981 to just $74 million three years later and continued spiraling downward over the years to a $44 million low by the mid-1990s.

As the shutdown dragged on with no encouraging news from the company, the exodus began. Half of Leadville's residents tramped, many heading for the mines in Nevada and Arizona. Houses sold for half their previous value, and foreclosures were rampant. Schools closed as more than a quarter of the children left the region. The Trailways bus service diverted its route around Leadville. J.C. Penney, Skaggs, Ben Franklin, the car dealerships, shoe stores, furniture and appliance stores, and most of the grocery stores all left Leadville. Compared to the town that needed two stoplights to manage traffic along Harrison just a few years earlier, Leadville appeared deserted.

The action had decamped north over the mountain, past the silent Climax industrial site, to places like Dillon and Silverthorne along the recently completed Interstate 70 corridor, which were now enjoying a construction boom.

Jim and his family stayed on. He was in his early fifties and still had a job, though he didn't know for how long. The value of his house had plunged, and he had children in college and one still in high school. "Where the hell was I going to go?" The family still felt relatively secure, but around him, a way of life was coming to an end, and the mental strain was increasing as the social dynamics changed. Previously good wage earners were getting by on garage sales, food banks, and fishing. Those with more resources took advantage of the low real estate prices and went into the rental business. High school students who had assumed they would work at Climax after graduation—or marry someone who did—didn't know what to do. The tight-knit camaraderie that Jim enjoyed was unraveling. The town was no longer united in that singular purpose of mining moly, and the inequities of people's lives began to surface. As frustration mounted, so did the crime rate.

Climax had provided not just new schools and roads; it had given Leadville an identity and pride in its long-standing mining-town status. Economic stability had shielded the town from having to try anything new. Alone and vulnerable, Leadville's citizens didn't know how to do anything other than mining. Residents knew they needed to find something to save the town and, at least for some, tourism seemed the logical choice. A number of former Rocky Mountain mining towns, such as Georgetown and Silverton, had successfully made the transition, but they had nearly a century's head start. Leadville's leaders were miners and lacked the knowledge and experience to fill the void. Without leadership to guide the town into a new era, outsiders in the form of consultants and real estate developers stepped in. A debate dormant since the 1960s was revived.

The trip from Denver was now a mere hour-and-a-half drive. Interstate 70 was bringing more skiers, hikers, mountain bikers, and fishermen farther into the mountains. By the 1980s, more than a million vehicles passed through Leadville and Lake County each year, but the town had never encouraged them to stay. Now they desperately needed them to. Citizens formed the Leadville Improvement Group, and with $50,000 from the state, undertook Operation Bootstrap. An effort was made to scrub clean what the *Herald Democrat* termed Leadville's "dirty face." Merchants approved a $900,000 bond and Harrison Avenue soon sported new streetlamps that mimicked the old gaslights and a new sidewalk with interlocking red bricks. (The bricks abruptly stopped at the point where town officials knew they'd receive too many "no" votes from merchants to pass the bond.) A development company promised to buy six weathered buildings along Harrison, including the former Tabor Grand Hotel, and to spend $10 million restoring them for condominiums, boutiques, and restaurants. The town produced a $40,000 promotional video, staged the Oro City Festival that included kids pretending to pan for gold in California Gulch, and launched an annual hundred-mile ultra-marathon along the Continental Divide.

While some applauded the changes, others worried that Leadville would become "touristy." Town officials wanted the business, but they didn't want to turn into an Aspen or Breckenridge. An ex-Climax miner turned writer noted in the *Christian Science Monitor* in 1983 that he feared Leadville was "being homogenized and made into a replica" of a real frontier mining town, smoothing out its rough edges to attract visitors. The ultimate irony, Stephen Voynick wrote, is that Leadville didn't need to be packaged and polished. It had been the real thing all along.

5

Overrun by Outsiders

While the town's residents debated which way to turn after the Climax shutdown, Leadville was being overrun—or so it felt—not by tourists, but by government officials—summoned by the red river, dying fish, and a jeopardized drinking water supply. "It was like a freakin' army around here," Jim recalled. EPA officials and representatives from the state's health department began making regular trips to the town. Newmont's Resurrection Mining operated out of its storefront along Harrison, and ASARCO still had its mining operation up the hill. Amidst rumors that Superfund would eventually exclude mining sites, scores of workers began roaming up and down California Gulch and the Arkansas River taking water samples, digging monitoring wells, and watching the Yak Tunnel, sometimes while standing right next to each other. To the hard-up residents, the whole affair seemed a gigantic waste of money.

The EPA official in charge in those early years was a tall, affable young man named Bill Rothenmeyer. He had first arrived in Leadville in 1980, soon after Superfund had come on line. It had been Bill's job to find Colorado's most hazardous spots for possible inclusion on the Superfund list. To rank sites, the EPA used a numerical scoring system that considered a variety of characteristics to assess risk. Mining areas in general scored highly, and Bill had found California Gulch to be one of the worst offenders because of what he termed the "extreme effect" that high volumes of acid mine drainage and toxic concentrations of iron, lead, zinc, and cadmium had on the river and its fish. EPA officials also worried about the possible metal contamination to the local drinking water supply. On September 8, 1983—with former EPA administrator Anne Gorsuch gone—Leadville was added to the National Priority List and became an official Superfund site, one of fewer than ten mining sites. Of the 418 sites added to the list its first year, Leadville's high score ranked it as one of the most polluted spots in the nation. So now, with waste rock piles and the weathered remains of mining ruins for a backdrop, Bill had technicians in space-age suits worn to protect against hazardous materials taking soil and well-water samples from the homes of families who had lived along California Gulch for generations. He suggested they drink bottled water.

Bill also worried about the area's tailing piles, particularly the monstrous, eighteen-acre Apache. Because mills required large amounts of water, their waste, the engineered tailing piles made of ground-up rock, often sit in the path of a water drainage, stream, or reservoir and for that reason are often called "dams." Unlike the mounds of hardrock waste, tailing piles, a damp slurry, are often unstable. If they become saturated in a heavy rain or flood, the piles can disintegrate— like a sand castle in the incoming tide—and wash downstream. Just a decade earlier, a tailing dam had given way in Buffalo Creek, West Virginia, and sent 132 million gallons of muddy water and coal mine waste rushing downstream, destroying the towns below and killing 125 people. In California Gulch, wooden ditches called flumes had once carried at least some of the Yak Tunnel drainage around Apache and down the gulch to the Arkansas River. But now those flumes were part of the quaint remnants of the past—broken-down piles of wood merely hinting at their intended purpose. The EPA considered Leadville's tailing piles "high hazard dams." The gulch's water runoff and the Yak's effluent now passed through Apache, soaking the pile, picking up metals, and threatening Stringtown homes that lay in the path downstream.

Compared to other towns the EPA had been to, Leadville residents took a surprising amount of interest in its work. Doc Smith and eleven others immediately formed an environmental task force to scrutinize EPA reports and offer advice. Bill held well-attended town meetings where residents voiced their opinions and frustrations about EPA and the Superfund process. They resented the use of outside consultants when so many people in Leadville needed jobs. ("It is a slap in the face reaching out to California to solve our problems. We can get the expertise of the people right in this room," said one, referring to the EPA's California-based contractors.) They offered their own solutions—mining the piles for the minerals left in them was a popular suggestion. Residents also worried that the EPA would force ASARCO and the Black Cloud out of business. The mine employed only 130 people, but it was enough to maintain Leadville's status as a mining town. "You don't want to rock the boat on ASARCO," one resident warned Bill at a meeting. That sentiment, vocalized often, kept many in town firmly on ASARCO's side and resentful of the EPA. Miners getting off work at the Black Cloud would shake their fists out the truck windows at Bill when he was out taking samples along the gulch.

Doc Smith, though, made it clear he was not on ASARCO's side. The mining companies were also collecting samples, gathering evidence in anticipation of a legal battle with the government. When an ASARCO employee showed up with Bill on Doc's ranch to ask permission to take samples on his land, Doc—with his gruff exterior and gentleman's spirit—said, "If Bill wants me to, I will." Bill shrugged. "I don't care," he said. "That's up to you." Doc turned to the ASARCO man, "Well then, get out of here." Over the next few years, Doc would grow frustrated that the EPA focused its attention on California Gulch and was doing little about the contamination already existing along the Arkansas River. By then, Doc knew that too much zinc in the soil and in the grass created a copper deficiency that caused lameness and death in his foals and calves, a condition called "osteochondrosis dis-secans." Although the soil contamination didn't have the dramatic appearance of red-streaked acid mine drainage, detoxifying the valley would prove to be equally challenging. Officials were sympathetic but, they said, until the contamination stopped flowing out of the hills, Doc's meadows would have to wait.

It was not supposed to take long. The EPA announced it anticipat-ed two to three years to study and fix California Gulch. Given the events that followed, the timeline was either wildly underestimated or an attempt to appease the townsfolk—in either case, a move that would lose its effectiveness with time. "I never dreamed Superfund would become the program it did," Bill Rothenmeyer recalled twenty years later. "I thought it would only go five years. We'd clean up the worst of it and be done."

As Bill studied the gulch and documented the damage, ASARCO managers grudgingly complied with his requests. They made it clear they expected Bill and his crew to be gone before long—just as soon as the mining industry was able to lobby the EPA successfully to drop mining sites from its Superfund hit list.

While ASARCO fought Superfund nationally, in Leadville the com-pany sought to keep the citizens firmly on its side. In 1983, after the Yak blowout, ASARCO purchased a full-page ad in the *Herald Democ-rat* to dispel "incomplete and misleading information" reported in the newspapers. ASARCO assured the community that no toxic or haz-ardous wastes had been released, merely iron hydroxide and a "very small quantity of additional heavy metals" that did not have haz-ardous characteristics; that no aquatic life had been harmed; and that nothing happened on February 23 that had not been occurring "natu-rally" for more than a hundred years. "It is important to realize that the drainage out of the Yak Tunnel is mostly from inactive and aban-doned mine claims, and as such is not regulated by any permit. This water is essentially state water. . . ." As the state's water, it was not the company's problem.

Federal and state officials disagreed, not surprisingly. The state cited ASARCO and its partner, Newmont's Resurrection Mining, for violating the Clean Water Act. The companies received no fine but were ordered to stay out of the tunnel, presumably to try to prevent further blowouts. In its rebuttal, ASARCO, as it had done in the community newspaper, insisted that "removal of naturally occurring cave-ins and material in the Yak Tunnel to permit the tunnel to continue its regular flow of the water and sediment normally occurring in the state waters in the Yak Tunnel does not constitute a 'discharge of pollutants.'" The tunnel's natural cave-ins and the resulting release of normal sediments, ASARCO repeated several times, were legally defensible "Acts of God."

God did it again two-and-a-half years later. In late October 1985, Doc awoke to find the Arkansas River again "running red." This time the color was even more dazzling than the blowout of 1983. The beautiful, muted mountain valley preparing for winter was adorned with a ribbon of errant scarlet down the middle. As Doc had done nearly three years earlier, he went back to his house to make a few phone calls. Somebody was going to pay attention to the valley.

When Lake County's sanitation director arrived at his office at eight thirty that morning, Doc's message was waiting for him. He went to have a look at the Yak and saw muddy, red water flowing out of the portal and down the gulch. The sanitation director called the state authorities to report the blowout, and for the rest of the day, he fielded phone calls from reporters as far away as Los Angeles.

The flow out of the Yak had slowed by the next morning, but at least one million gallons of sludge rolled downstream for two more days. The state once again ordered the Otero Pump Station and all water intake valves downstream closed—this time all the way to the bustling city of Pueblo 150 miles away. The blowout apparently had been caused by the sudden release of water trapped behind rock and timber that had collapsed in the tunnel. The water had finally built up enough force to dislodge the obstruction and race through the tunnel, picking up minerals and debris before pouring into the gulch. Because this blowout had occurred in the fall when the river was low, the sludge remained concentrated, amplifying the color and traveling farther downstream than the previous time. Denver's news reporters spent several days transmitting live broadcasts as they followed the red sludge on its journey southward.

Throughout his long career, Jim Martin had never concerned himself with the environmental consequences of mining. He knew the EPA was camped in his town—they were hard to miss—but he wasn't about to waste his time going to town meetings to discuss it. "Oh, I'd heard Doc Smith bitchin' about things for years, but I didn't realize the stuff that happened seventy-five or a hundred years ago screwed up his pastures. In those days, I didn't care. I had nothing to do with it." But Jim, still working for the struggling Climax, happened to be driving back from Cañon City one hundred miles downstream when the colorful plume passed by on its way to Pueblo that October day in 1985. On the long drive home up Highway 24 that follows the Arkansas River, Jim had plenty of time to watch the Technicolor river contrasted against the rocky, earth-tone bluffs. He watched the river slide through wide, flat ranchland, past towns with riverside parks and businesses catering to river kayakers. He considered the problems Doc and his family had had all of these years living in the dead zone. Leadville's mining affected the entire valley and its communities, he realized. And it bothered him. "It's wrong for us to pollute," he would say years later. "It's wrong for us to dump our contaminated water into the Arkansas and screw it up from here to Pueblo."

6

The Brown Envelope

Carol Russell sat in a heavy wooden pew, waiting as the clock on the oak-paneled wall ticked past ten-thirty on a September day in 1985. In front of her, she marveled at what looked like two hundred of Denver's most powerful and expensive attorneys crammed into tables in the cavernous federal courtroom in downtown Denver. At the front of the room, before an imposing wall of dark, cold marble, the judge was ready to begin. But one attorney—for the Leadville case—was still missing. The assembled lawyers shifted in their seats, looked at their watches, and waited.

Ten minutes later, the lawyer rushed in, apologetic. Carol remembered an irate Judge Carrigan saying: "Estimate how much each one of these people was paid to wait and double that amount. I want to see a donation to your law school." To Carol, what unfolded next was "the most amazing thing I've ever seen."

Leading up to the hearing, Carol Russell had had a rough couple of years. She had been working as a mining inspector for Colorado's Division of Minerals and Geology until 1983, when she was asked to join the Office of Health and Environmental Protection (the name would later change to the Department of Public Health and the Environment). The young, blond woman accepted what would become "the worst job of my life," after she found herself caught between three government agencies, each vying for control of California Gulch.

The EPA had just named California Gulch a Superfund site and after rifling through old county land records, officials had identified seven "potentially responsible parties" or PRPs, who had owned or operated mining claims in the area. After decades of mining in Leadville, ASARCO and Newmont's Resurrection were obvious defendants. The records also identified Hecla Mining, an international company based in Idaho that had operated a mine and mill in the area; three small companies whose names were still on the books; and Robert Elder. The EPA had sent each a letter inviting them to voluntarily clean up their share of the mess, but each one had declined the offer. Given the political foot-dragging in Washington in the early 1980s over the "fast track" Superfund program, the agency was several years away from filing a lawsuit to compel them.

The State of Colorado, however, needed to act quickly or lose its own opportunity to sue. The Comprehensive Environmental Response, Compensation, and Liability Act (CERCLA), the Superfund law, not only allowed the EPA to sue companies for the cost of cleaning up hazardous waste, but it also gave both the feds and states the right to sue in federal court for damages to the natural resources—a provision that could potentially cost the companies even more than the cleanup. The statute of limitation for filing such claims was to expire on December 10, 1983. Colorado's director of environmental programs, Tom Looby, had learned of the deadline with just a few months to spare. He quickly selected the most severely damaged sites, and a day before the statute of limitations expired, Colorado became one of only a few states to make the deadline, filing seven separate Natural Resource Damage claims under the CERCLA statute—six of them in mining areas. ASARCO learned it would be defending itself at two sites, the Globe Smelter in Denver and California Gulch. Newmont's Resurrection and the Res-ASARCO Joint Venture were also named as defendants.

The state's lawsuits had never been attempted before and became political pawns in Denver, bringing another government agency into the fray. The state's attorney general's office under Republican Duane Woodard and its health department under Democrat Governor Richard Lamm were duking it out for control of the lawsuits—apparently, literally. Carol had heard that two lawyers, one from each state office, had gotten into a fistfight at the downtown YMCA. For Carol, hired as the liaison between the two agencies, it was a tough time to be in the middle. The attorney general's office eventually gained control, hiring extra lawyers to handle the cases. As the dust settled, the uncharted task of putting a dollar value on the damage to the state's natural resources—its air, water, wildlife, and fisheries—fell to Carol and her "Nerds for Natural Resource Damage," as the experts she hired called themselves.

As the team began compiling the scientific evidence needed to prove the state's cases in court, Carol dug into the mining companies' business records. Newmont readily turned over its documents. ASARCO, however, wasn't going to make it easy. After flying to the company's headquarters in New York City for a prearranged appointment to review its files, Carol was told an insurance company had them. In another instance, when she flew to ASARCO's Coeur d'Alene mine in northern Idaho to look through additional files, officials put her in the cafeteria, forcing her to wait outside in Idaho's winter whenever the cafeteria was needed. Driving that night, after her first day in Idaho, Carol realized she was being followed. As if she were in a movie, Carol turned off roads and doubled back, but her stalker stayed with her. Scared, she returned to her hotel room. She picked up the phone, only to hear the telltale clicking of a phone tap, a sound she'd learned to recognize from a friend, a Los Angeles lawyer who worked on high-profile cases. Carol was certain ASARCO was trying to intimidate her. Determined to finish the job, she remained in Idaho for a week looking through ASARCO's files and staying in her hotel room after dark. When Carol returned home, she decided that ASARCO could deliver any additional files she needed to her Denver office.

While Carol and her team gathered evidence, Judge Carrigan's courtroom was busy with motions and hearings as the companies attempted to rid themselves of the state's lawsuits. But the cases marched steadily toward the first important step: determining liability. Were the companies legally responsible for damages to the natural resources under the CERCLA statute? Judge Carrigan was going to answer that question in all seven cases before any of them went to trial. The summary judgment hearing was set for September 20, 1985. Millions of dollars were at stake.

ASARCO remained defiant, writing in a court document: "Defendants strongly dispute that any compensable harm has occurred in the area, and would be unlikely to agree to pay damages even if a 'liability' trial found that releases had occurred."

Judge James R. Carrigan was known as a cutup in the courtroom. His clerks adored him. He waved a referee flag to call illegal motions and kept a stack of cartoons at his side. When the proceedings became tense, he would call the attorneys up to the bench and whip out an appropriate joke. His favorite was a drawing of an attorney banging a witness over the head with a badger. "You can't do your best work when you're angry. You have to take your work seriously, but not take yourself seriously," Judge Carrigan would say. Once, to loosen up a couple of "stuffed shirts from Washington, D.C., who thought they were big shots," Carrigan called them into his chambers. After they were seated, he spun around in his chair to face them in a pair of Groucho Marx glasses. "What the hell is going on here?" he asked in his best Groucho voice. Judge Carrigan was disappointed that the D.C. attorneys seemed more horrified than amused at this westerner's behavior.

But among his colleagues, the judge was known for his patience, diplomacy, intelligence, penchant for green pens, the occasional green robe, and of course his sense of humor. He sported a small mustache on his long, handsome Irish face and suffered only a mild case of that judicial malady of self-importance known as "black robe fever." Perhaps his modest upbringing kept him grounded. He had been raised the son of a baker in Hallock, Minnesota, a cold, flat speck near the borders of North Dakota and Canada, and had put himself through college and law school, finishing both degrees with honors in just five years at the University of North Dakota. In 1956, at the age of twenty-six, he married a Californian he'd met while they were both studying in New York City. Soon after, the couple moved to Colorado, honeymooning in Leadville, a thriving mining town then, and staying at the grungy Vendome Hotel (the renamed Tabor Grand) where the ceiling dripped from the plumbing above them and the floor slanted disconcertingly, but the price was right. Across Harrison Avenue from the hotel, the newlyweds ate at the Golden Burro, a popular restaurant affectionately known as the "Brass Ass" that had been serving miners since 1925.

Twenty-four years after his honeymoon in Leadville, Jim Carrigan, now a father of six and for the past four years a U.S. District Court judge, had been handed some of the nation's first Superfund cases dealing with mining sites—the state's natural resource claims. Over the last decade of his career, Judge Carrigan would help define how the nation's law covering abandoned hazardous waste could be used to clean up the western legacy of hardrock mining. He would need a new set of cartoons.

On that September day in 1985, Carol Russell settled back into the hard pew for what would surely be a lengthy liability hearing. With something approaching two hundred lawyers present, how could it not be? After chastising the tardy lawyer, Judge Carrigan dove in, addressing one of ASARCO's attorneys representing its Globe Plant. Did ASARCO own the waste material full of lead, cadmium, and zinc that state officials had seen blowing off the waste piles during their visit? Yes or no. The ASARCO attorney attempted to elaborate, but the judge allowed no sidestepping, no waffling. He wanted a yes or a no, and he rebuked ASARCO for not cooperating with Carol's team of investigators. Down the line the judge went, astonishing Carol by establishing liability for each company in all seven lawsuits in under half an hour. In his written orders, Judge Carrigan noted that there was no need for an expensive and time-consuming liability trial when the "ultimate conclusion seems obvious."

Judge Carrigan's unequivocal determination of liability that morning belied the mixed feelings he had toward the case. A law to clean up abandoned polluted sites like California Gulch was long overdue, but he felt Superfund's liability provisions were harsh and unjust. "There really aren't any defenses in this act," he would say nearly twenty years later. "If you owned it, occupied it, or polluted it, you're liable. You've got to clean it up. But I was very reluctant to impose liability retroactively." Superfund's strict, joint, and several liability were controversial. It meant that the government didn't have to prove the company was negligent. If it owned the land but never mined it, it was liable. If its actions were legal at the time, it was still liable. If the company owned only part of the land or was responsible for only part of the damage, it could be held liable for all of it; and the government need go after only the companies that could afford to pay for the cleanup. If those defendants then wanted to sue others and bring these "third party defendants" into the suit to help pay the damages, they could—and they often did.

A statute to clean up hazardous sites nationwide was overdue, but the bill would be in the billions. Who should—or could—foot that bill? The mining companies that had built fortunes on a dearth of environmental regulations and that had not had to pay any royalties to mine on public lands, thanks to the antiquated General Mining Law of 1872 or, as the companies argued, society at large? For more than a century, Americans had benefited from lower product prices that resulted from dumping waste rather than dealing with it at the time. Therefore, the companies argued, all Americans should pay to clean it up through taxes. Superfund would in that case be a huge public works project, much like the dam-building era of the previous fifty years. But that was politically unpalatable, even to those sympathetic to industry. Without CERCLA's "polluters pay" provisions, neither the federal government nor the states could afford the billions of dollars it would take—even with the tax on chemical companies—to clean up the nation's millions of acres of contaminated land and water.

In enacting such unique, tough liability standards, Congress had hoped those companies still around would be willing to settle quickly without a trial. It rarely worked out that way, however. At California Gulch, ASARCO co-owned and was the managing partner of the Yak Tunnel. The company also owned many, though not all, of the claims draining into California Gulch but had mined relatively few of them. Despite Judge Carrigan's ruling, ASARCO didn't believe it should pay millions to clean up water that drained from workings they never mined. Hundreds of people owned mining claims in the Leadville Mining District. Many of them were small, little more than family novelties divided up among grandchildren as the claims passed down through the generations. Instead of accepting Carrigan's liability judgment and settling with the government, ASARCO threatened to sue hundreds of third parties. The company could tie the courts up in knots for years and keep communities like Leadville in limbo.

At the same time Judge Carrigan was ruling ASARCO liable in California Gulch, in Washington, Son of Superfund was under negotiation. The Congressional fight over Superfund's reauthorization was long and bitter. Everyone wanted to see the program expanded, even President Reagan, now backpeddling on his deregulation stance since the fiasco that had ended with Gorsuch's resignation two years earlier in 1983. But by how much, who should pay, and should mining be included? On October 17, 1986, Congress finally passed the Superfund Amendments and Reauthorization Act (SARA) that extended CERCLA with an $8.5 billion budget. SARA embraced tougher standards than the original CERCLA and included timetables and deadlines intended to accelerate cleanups. The expanded Superfund would be paid for by additional taxes and an increase in general funds. Mining sites were still on the list.

As SARA was nearing the final hurdles, in Leadville the EPA was ready to jump in with its own lawsuit to force the mining companies to clean up hazardous waste contamination in California Gulch, and it sued thirteen PRPs. In addition to the seven the agency had identified earlier, newcomers included Newmont Mining, (Resurrection's parent company), the Res-ASARCO Joint Venture, and the Denver and Rio Grande Western Railroad, which had purchased slag piles in the 1960s and early 1980s to use the smelter waste as railroad ballast. Three other small companies with recent or historic ties were also sued.

California Gulch now had two lawsuits winding their way through Judge Carrigan's courtroom—the state's claim for Natural Resource Damages and the fed's lawsuit to compel hazardous waste cleanup. ASARCO and Newmont were defending themselves in both. With the state and feds working independently to clean up the mining district and the companies involved fighting both governments, it seemed to Leadville's citizens that no one was in charge and nothing was getting done. While Carol Russell explained the lawsuits at one town meeting, a man suggested the commissioners should "get out there and start shooting at the guys" to spur some action.

Carl Miller, chairman of the Lake County Commissioners, had no intention of shooting anyone, but he wrote letters to the EPA and the state complaining that the turf battles wasted time and money on lawyers, threatened the continued operation of ASARCO's Black Cloud Mine, and left Leadville dangling with a Superfund label over its head. "The State of Colorado and EPA have embarked on a witch hunt to destroy the prime industry of Lake County," he wrote.

By the mid-1980s, Leadville citizens were proving a vocal hindrance, and animosity between the locals and government officials was mounting. Three ex-miners had even debated the fate—hanged or merely tarred and feathered—of one young EPA employee on an errand to hook up a Stringtown residence to the municipal water supply because the family's well had tested high in metals. The townsfolk had strong opinions, disagreed with EPA plans, and offered their own solutions. They could yell and they could be cordial. Many didn't think there was a problem at all; the EPA should just get the hell out of town, as far as they were concerned. Others, like Doc Smith, recognized that a contamination problem existed and had already formed an environmental task force.

In those early years of the EPA, and Superfund in particular, community relations were an afterthought for the agency—if they were thought about at all. The project managers' job was to find the source of the contamination, engineer a solution, fix it, and move on. They had their bureaucratic steps to follow, and it was a report-intensive process. Over the years, Leadville and Lake County officials would be handed three-inch-thick binders filled with investigations, studies, reports, and plans that they then shoved into bookcases and piled on the floors of their offices. Residents didn't understand the jargon or the need for all of these interminable studies. The EPA was mandated by law to seek public input, but of the nine criteria used to decide how to fix the problem, public opinion was number nine. The residents were last on the list and that—at least—was obvious to them.

A year after the hearing in Judge Carrigan's courtroom, on a crisp, autumn Friday in 1986, after the willow bushes along the Arkansas River had turned a brilliant yellow, Carl Miller was working at his desk at the Lake County Courthouse, when one of the clerks, an old high school friend, came into his office shaking. When she'd gone home for lunch, she'd found a big, brown envelope in her mailbox from Colorado's Office of the Attorney General, CERCLA Litigation Section. She showed Carl the document she'd found inside. Carl read the top page:

DISTRICT COURT, LAKE COUNTY, COLORADO
Case No. 86CV48
NOTICE OF CLASS ACTION AND HEARING TO CONSIDER
CLASS CERTIFICATION AND PROPOSED SETTLEMENT
STATE OF COLORADO,
Plaintiff,
v.
ASARCO, INC.,
RESURRECTION MINING COMPANY,
RES-ASARCO JOINT VENTURE,
HECLA MINING COMPANY,
NEWMONT MINING CORPORATION,
LEADVILLE CORP.,

LEADVILLE, SILVER AND GOLD, INC.,
ROCK HILL MINES COMPANY,
DENVER and RIO GRANDE WESTERN RAILROAD COMPANY,
C AND H DEVELOPMENT COMPANY, and
ROBERT ELDER, individually, and
ATLAS MORTGAGE COMPANY individually and on behalf of all present owners (excluding the individually named defendants) of interests of any nature in real property from which surface water and/or ground water contaminated by hazardous substances flow and/or flowed into the Yak Tunnel and/or into the California Gulch Drainage, including tributaries to California Gulch,
Defendants.
THIS NOTICE MAY AFFECT YOUR RIGHTS. PLEASE READ CAREFULLY.

The document was more than thirty pages of baffling legal jargon. It included statements such as "The State of Colorado has brought suit against a class of which you may be a member"; "Defendants, by engaging in said ultra-hazardous activities, have caused and will continue to cause irreparable harm to the public health and welfare and the environment"; and "you may appear personally or enter an appearance through your own attorney."

Was she being sued? she asked Carl, horrified. What had she done? Carl tried to reassure his friend but he, too, wondered what was going on. He walked home to check his own mailbox and found a similar brown envelope. At that moment, 2,435 brown envelopes were being delivered to every owner whose property drained into California Gulch, including the entire town of Leadville, its mining district, and much of the surrounding area six miles down to the Arkansas River.

Carl Miller was livid. Colorado's attorney general, Duane Woodard, had—without warning—filed a reverse class action lawsuit, naming every property owner in Leadville as a defendant. The State of Colorado had sued Leadville. It was an incredible blunder. Now the problem wasn't just over in California Gulch, it was in everyone's backyard, and everyone appeared vulnerable. The attorney general had poked a hornet's nest.

That afternoon, Carl called the attorney general's office and demanded to speak to Duane Woodard. "I called him every name I could think of for what he was doing to our community." (Woodard later complained to Lake County's attorney that Carl had abused him.) It was a tension-filled weekend for Leadville residents. At least there was some comfort in numbers; everyone apparently had received the same ominous letter.

When the twice-weekly local newspaper appeared on Monday morning, the state's explanation for the lawsuit didn't clear it up much—join the class action or possibly be held liable for the California Gulch contamination and for the eventual cleanup costs, which were estimated to be in the tens of millions of dollars. Joining the class meant signing a legal agreement—a consent decree—giving the state access to their yards for soil sampling during the length of the cleanup. In exchange, owners would be freed from liability if the state found their yards contaminated with heavy metals. Boiled down, the sole purpose of the lawsuit was to gain access to everyone's property to test the soil. Instead of going to each homeowner individually for permission which, given the distrust mounting against the government was unlikely to be granted in many if not most cases, the attorney general's office had inexplicably decided that a blanket million-dollar threat would be more expedient. They intended for the residents to be represented by the Leadville law firm also representing Atlas Mortgage Company, a small company that owned a number of mining claims in the district. After returning home from a cruise in China, Peter Cosgriff, the designated Leadville lawyer, was surprised to learn that he apparently was now also representing 2,435 angry residents in a lawsuit. His secretary had been fielding phone calls for days. The attorney general's office expected Atlas Mortgage and the residents, through Cosgriff's law firm, to quietly sign the consent decree at a court hearing on October 22, one month away, so the state could get started drawing up their grids and testing the town for contaminants.

Nothing went as planned. Atlas Mortgage's owner, who lived in

California and had inherited the properties, refused to sign the consent decree or to represent the town. Residents were not about to let the government have unlimited access to their yards for years, and they were anything but quiet. Leadville's unemployment was a whopping 40 percent, and residents were afraid the lawsuit clouded their property titles, particularly if the state decided their yards were contaminated. They worried that they would be unable to sell their homes, causing residents to feel as though the state were holding them hostage in Leadville. "It gave the people a black eye," Carl Miller complained, and stigmatized Leadville as poisoned. Who would buy a house or move to Leadville with this threat hanging over the town? Carl organized a town meeting in the local high school auditorium and all but dared lawyers from the attorney general's office to appear.

A week later, a crowd of more than six hundred people at the auditorium spilled out the door. It was the biggest, most volatile town meeting Carl had ever witnessed. On stage sat two intrepid deputy attorney generals and the county's three commissioners. Carl was determined that the people would have their say, but he was also concerned about keeping the meeting under control. People were so upset he was afraid they might riot, so he posted sheriff deputies at the doors—just in case.

Carol Russell reluctantly drove to Leadville for the meeting. She expected it to be acrimonious and had brought her husband and a friend along for support, but she wasn't prepared for just how angry the crowd would be. People were shouting, pointing, raising their fists. "Let's hang the bastards." Carol decided she was not going to sit on the stage with the lawyers. It was their responsibility to explain the lawsuit to these people, not hers. "I feared for my life," she recalled later. "There were sheriffs at each one of the doors, with guns. It was awful. It was absolutely awful." After the meeting, and for several meetings that followed, police officers checked under the government cars for explosives.

During the three-and-a-half-hour meeting, Carl peppered the attorneys with questions. The men admitted that a cloud on the title might exist until the property was deemed safe, which could take up to five years. They apologized for the inconvenience, but emphasized that a public health problem existed in Leadville and must be fixed. All the state wanted was access to their properties.

"Is this America or Russia?" one Leadvillite had demanded in the local *Herald Democrat* in the days leading up to the meeting. Not only did the townsfolk feel the suit was an unwarranted invasion into their lives, but most remained unconvinced that a health threat existed or that their properties were contaminated. "Show me the casualty list." Families had been living in Leadville for generations, and they'd never seen any evidence that their community was unhealthy. "Will anyone get sick and die if the hazardous wastes aren't all cleaned up?" asked a resident, who said she had grown up playing in the tailing and dump piles and was just fine. If the contamination had been there for a hundred years, why pick on Leadville now that the town was hurting economically? "Who the hell is it bothering?" demanded a resident. "We will have to fight this tooth and nail," vowed another.

For more than a century, Leadvillites had been exposed to heavy metals and smelter fumes. Now the state was seeking to ensure the health of today's residents. But its ill-advised class action lawsuit misdirected the discussion away from health concerns and toward defending itself. The lawsuit gave residents a reason to direct their anger at the state—not at the mining companies, made rich off the local resources, that were now lobbying in Leadville and nationally to abandon mining towns and leave residents to deal with the environmental and health consequences themselves. Leadvillites, struggling since Climax had shut down, felt unfairly targeted by the state as the wrongdoers; they were paying the price merely for living in Leadville.

The attorney general's office was feeling the pressure. T-shirts were sold in town: "Up the Yak without a paddle. State of Colorado vs. Leadville." Editorials vilifying the state government filled the *Herald Democrat*. Some people worried that the judge wouldn't understand mining well enough to make the right decision. State politicians complained that Leadville was a "guinea pig" to test Superfund enforcement in mining sites.

The situation in Leadville was so volatile that the attorney general's office began to reconsider its tactic. If residents were not about to sign the consent decree giving the state access, could they really go through with a lawsuit against the entire town? On October 22, 1986, at a short, quiet hearing in the Lake County Courthouse, the state's attorney presented a motion to restrict the class named in the suit to just the mining district, thereby removing the town. But the state's contrition was too late. Judge Richard Hart denied the entire class action, and the lawsuit against Leadville was unceremoniously dropped.

The damage could not be so easily undone. Cooperation with the Leadville citizenry was now unthinkable. The attorney general's office had torpedoed not only its own case, but it had also wounded the EPA's Superfund efforts as well. In peoples' minds, the distinction between the state and federal governments was often confused. Workers for both governments were moving through the town taking samples, issuing incomprehensible reports, and telling Leadvillites that their proud mining heritage was now an environmental and public health hazard. To the townsfolk, both agencies were an equal threat and equally guilty. The state was either in cahoots with the EPA when it brought the lawsuit or had merely beaten the feds to the punch and sued first. Fifteen years later, many people still believed it was the EPA that had sued Leadville.

It was clear that a change was needed. The government agencies were not only not cooperating with one another, they were getting in each others' way. The state, battered by its skirmish with Leadville, was willing to take a backseat. In February 1987, Judge Carrigan consolidated the state's Natural Resource Damage claim and the EPA's Superfund lawsuit and put the EPA in charge of cleaning up California Gulch. The state would play a secondary role, monitoring the EPA's decisions and signing off on all aspects of the cleanup. The two agencies would still give each other headaches in the coming years, but at least they were traveling down the same road. Judge Carrigan knew he would not have time to chauffer every twist and turn in what would surely be a long haul as the PRPs, the EPA, and the state negotiated the uncharted territory of Superfund litigation. He appointed a "special master," his former student Richard Dana, to help mediate a settlement. "Let Dick ride herd over the lawyers and keep this from going to trial," Judge Carrigan had decided. The EPA was now formally in charge, but the Brown Envelope, as it came to be known, would continue to haunt them in the coming years.

Perhaps the two men with the longest memory were Carl Miller and Ken Chlouber. In Leadville, they're often referred to as one entity. Ken and Carl. Chlouber and Miller. On the surface, they couldn't seem more dissimilar—in dress, style, or politics. But the two men, best friends for thirty years, were united in their passionate hatred of the EPA. They had both worked for Climax—Miller as an underground electrician, Chlouber as a shift boss. Chlouber had followed Miller onto the Board of County Commissioners during the Climax years when running the county was an easy job. Miller weathered the layoffs of 1982 and continued working his two jobs, though both had gotten much harder. Chlouber was laid off that year and after his stint as county commissioner was up, he decided to pursue greater political power. In 1986, at forty-seven, he ran for a seat in the state House of Representatives and won. Ten years later, he would be a state senator, and this time Miller would follow Chlouber to Denver, taking Chlouber's seat in the house. Both men would be only too willing to wield their power as state legislators in an effort to get the government "the hell out of Leadville." Chlouber wasted no time striking back. Soon after the Brown Envelope debacle, as a rookie representative in the spring of 1987, Chlouber urged fellow legislators in an impassioned speech on the House floor to reduce the attorney general's requested budget of nearly $6 million for CERCLA enforcement to just $1. "The attorney general and his swarm of lawyers are to mining as locusts are to agriculture," he said. Ken Chlouber lost that argument and the attorney general's office kept its budget, but Chlouber would be more successful in the future.

Of the two friends, Chlouber was the flashy one who made sure he wasn't ignored. Everything about Ken Chlouber was over the top. An imposing six foot, two inches, he was impossible to overlook just walking into a room, dressed in western snap-button shirts, bolo ties, oversized belt buckle, snakeskin boots, heavy turquoise jewelry, and a big ol' cowboy hat over his thinning, shoulder-length hair. Over the years, he showed up at the state capital driving a Harley, a Corvette, and a 1998 Chevy half-ton pickup—black with yellow, red, and orange flames.

The son of a Baptist minister, Chlouber hailed from Shawnee, Oklahoma. He attended Oklahoma Baptist University before a brief stint in the army, married a schoolteacher named Pat, and sold tires for a time. In the late 1970s, Ken, Pat and their young son, Cole, migrated to Colorado where Chlouber eventually took a job at Climax. In Leadville, he raced with pack burros, took up bull riding, and ran impossibly long distances. In 1982, Chlouber founded Leadville's Trail 100, the highest-altitude ultramarathon in the country, and would complete it fourteen times.

As a legislator, Chlouber liked to quote Will Rogers, once marched a burro into the state capitol, and at times physically threatened fellow legislators. He was a Republican but was just as likely to argue for abortion rights, labor unions, and gay rights as he was to champion concealed weapons and the death penalty. Chlouber liked to think of himself as a hillbilly fighting for the little guy, but "grandstander" was the term most often used to describe Chlouber, even among his supporters. "He's got a great knack for getting his picture in the paper," was a typical comment. "He blows off steam without any real progress," was another. "He's a laughingstock," was yet another frequent characterization. Chlouber was hot tempered, intimidating, hostile, and he admitted that he "loves to pick fights with the big shots." But there was no political handwringing or second-guessing Chlouber's position on the issues, which some of his fellow legislators considered a refreshing change, even if melodramatically presented. And he continued to get reelected.

If Chlouber was hard angles, tall, and antagonistic, his friend Carl was soft roundness, short, and amiable. Carl Miller was considered pragmatic and quiet, although he could get worked up where the EPA was concerned. "If Chlouber stands up and shakes his fist, then Miller will shake his fist a little, too. He's a little more rational," one Leadvillite observed. Ken Chlouber made it personal. Carl Miller saw the people behind the job description and often joked with EPA project managers. (One day he put a sign on the door pretending to cancel a meeting after two EPA officials had traveled two hours in a snowstorm to get there. Momentarily horrified, they turned to see Carl laughing impishly behind them. Sharing the joke helped ease tensions in the meeting that followed.) "Individually they're very nice, collectively they're a bunch of bastards," Carl would explain later.

People liked Carl, "a man of integrity," even if they disagreed with him, because they knew he was sincere and deeply loved his community. Carl was a third-generation Leadvillite, which gave him a certain cachet in the community. He had grown up in Leadville and stayed, following his grandfathers and father into the mines—and into politics. His maternal grandparents—the lineage that gave Carl his red hair and mustache—had come to Leadville from Ireland in 1893, the year of the silver crash. His father's parents, Swedes, had settled on the other side of the Sawatch Range in the smaller mining town of Aspen just a few years earlier. Carl's father moved to Leadville to work in the mines, making the rounds through the Greenback, the Pyrenees, and the Wolftone. Both of Carl's grandfathers and his father died of silicosis by the time they were sixty. At seventeen, Carl didn't give it much thought. He went to work for ASARCO's Irene mine in 1956 for a year, spent two years in the army, and then returned home to work for Climax. He married another generational Leadvillite, from a Slovenian family, and raised two daughters a block from his old family home. In 1981, Carl lost his thumb in a mining accident that nearly killed him.

Carl was a Democrat—the family had converted in irritation after his grandfather had lost an election for county commissioner as a Republican in the 1930s—but like Chlouber, he was just as likely to vote alongside the opposite party as he was for his own. Despite their apparent differences (Carl drove a battered, tan 1970s Buick pickup and preferred sweatshirts and baseball caps), Carl insisted that the two were in lockstep, particularly where the EPA was concerned. As county commissioners, they had schemed to have EPA officials arrested the next time they showed up in Leadville—"just to show 'em we didn't want 'em messin' with our town"—but the county attorney had advised them against it. "Ken's the best friend I have in the world," Carl would say later. "Our approach is absolutely the same, only he will tell you in a more violent tone."

It was in the midst of the Brown Envelope fiasco that Carl was laid off from Climax after more than twenty-five years on the job. Six months later, in early March 1987, Climax closed for good, and Jim Martin too lost his job. After five years of watching the company shrink away, no one was surprised by the shutdown, but it dealt another blow to Leadville's economy. Town leaders like Ken and Carl considered tourism the key to immediate survival, but many in town believed Leadville's mining days would return. The editor of the *Herald Democrat* would proclaim mining still king. "Sorry folks, but mining *is* the backbone of our economy," he would write in a June 1989 editorial opposing those who would "line Harrison Avenue with boutiques. . . . Mining is not only Leadville's past, but also its present and future. Those promoting tourism here need to keep that in perspective." He needn't have worried. The enthusiasm of a few years earlier had already fizzled. The $10 million to renovate the Tabor Grand Hotel and other buildings along Harrison had never materialized. Officials wanted to entice a small industry of some sort to move in, but Leadville's remoteness, thin air, and climate worked against it. The unemployed Climax miners who had stayed in Leadville were now driving forty-five minutes "over the hill" to work for the ski resorts in Vail or Copper Mountain, earning sometimes $20 less an hour than they had as miners. Lower wages or no, Leadville's proximity to the wealthy ski resorts had saved the town.

Jim Martin had no desire to work at a menial, low-paying job at a resort. He was nearing sixty. His dark hair was nearly entirely gray now, his wiry frame was filling out, and he liked to joke about missing half his teeth. Corinne knew her husband wasn't ready to retire either, but about the last thing she expected Jim to say was that he wanted to run for mayor. He had spent five years on the school board, but Corinne had never heard him talk much about politics. He had even tossed his Brown Envelope in the garbage. "To hell with that," he had concluded, and refused even to attend the meetings, confident that Ken and Carl would take care of it. Corinne suspected that Jim's drinking buddies down at the Silver King had talked him into it. But that didn't matter; being a mayor's wife would be fine with her. Running for mayor in 1987 was a bit of a surprise for Jim also. The job paid only $400 a month, but Danny, their youngest, had just a few more years of college, and it was something to do. He campaigned that fall talking about tourism development and won the election. Jim Martin was about to be thrust into a flurry of scientific studies, EPA disputes, and more town meetings than he had ever thought possible.

7

Plugging the Yak

Elisabeth Evans, a petite woman with dark, curly hair in her late thirties, became the third Environmental Protection Agency (EPA) project manager to head to Leadville, in 1986, not long after the Brown Envelope had arrived in town. Mayor Martin remembered her as "pleasant, nice, pretty, smiling. She was a figurehead who didn't know diddly about science." Other Leadvillites considered her tenure "atrocious," but by that time finding a sympathetic audience in Leadville wasn't easy. She'd been warned that the town was "hostile" and that several local politicians had even threatened to arrest the next EPA official who showed up. Within the first ten days of her tenure, Evans was expected to convene a public meeting and complete the Record of Decision (ROD), a lengthy document, the culmination of a myriad of studies that announces and justifies how the EPA plans to remedy a problem. Instead, Liz got the chicken pox.

It was an inauspicious beginning to her Leadville tenure. The final ROD took, not ten days, but three years to complete, and it was a rancorous process. But Liz did hold a public meeting—her first ever—soon after she recovered. "I was scared to death. I was catatonic," she commented later. Her co-worker had to help her get dressed and prop her up in front of the fifty people who showed. But she got through it and soon public meetings were routine—although her national television appearances, when Leadville was again making the news, made her so nervous she couldn't watch.

Liz Evans understood hardworking small towns—she'd been raised in one in New Hampshire where residents worked for the local pulp mill—but it was true she didn't know much about either mining or environmental cleanup work. After earning a degree in anthropology, she'd headed west to Arizona to study urban planning and water administration, earning two master's degrees along the way. By the early 1980s she'd found herself in the EPA's Region 8 office in Denver working for Superfund, and when she was assigned to Leadville, she gave herself a crash course in mining.

With the town still seething over the state's lawsuit, Liz understood immediately that she needed to stay out of people's yards. Best to let emotions settle—at least for now. So she focused on the Yak Tunnel, which was proving controversial enough. Four years of studies had shown that a number of sources in the Leadville Mining District contributed to contamination of the Arkansas River, but 80 percent of it flowed out the Yak. Although the mines had long since been abandoned, the tunnel was still doing its job, draining hundreds of thousands of gallons of underground water into California Gulch every day. The acidic water picked up heavy metals as it coursed through the underground mine workings, each year unearthing nearly 200,000 pounds of zinc, 6,000 pounds of copper, 600 pounds of cadmium, and 120 pounds of lead—concentrations that far exceeded toxicity levels for aquatic life, some by thousands of times. Arsenic, manganese, and iron were also released in smaller amounts. In searching for life in the six-mile stretch of California Gulch between the Yak Tunnel and the Arkansas River, researchers found just two flies and a worm. Not surprisingly, they also found that metals, including arsenic, seeped into the groundwater; Stringtown residents who had been drinking well water for generations had since been put on the municipal water supply. Once the Yak discharge reached the Arkansas

River, some of the metals continued downstream and could be detected in the Pueblo Reservoir 150 miles away.

Though a few in town refused to believe that the Yak Tunnel was contaminating the Arkansas River at all and others felt that once the metals flowed out of the county it became someone else's problem, most agreed that the dead zone was real. Some of them realized that if a thriving fish population returned, the struggling county could dip into the millions of dollars recreational fishermen spent in Colorado each year. But that was as far as most in town were willing to go: fix the Yak and get the hell out. That was Liz Evan's intention. But when she announced how the EPA planned to do so, this extraordinarily attentive and vocal town said it would never work.

The EPA and its consultants had decided that the simplest and cheapest solution was essentially to plug up the holes. It was a remedy being implemented in other mining sites across the West. Once miners had bored miles and miles of tunnels, leaving a vast underground network of void space and drastically altering the Earth's geology and chemistry, the land could not be returned to its natural state. But the EPA believed that by strategically plugging tunnels and shafts, it could mimic the land's previous condition and prevent acid mine drainage from contaminating streams and groundwater.

In California Gulch, the EPA planned to install three concrete plugs along the four-mile stretch of tunnel. Two plugs would cut off the flow of water from large mine workings draining into the tunnel and another plug at the portal would immediately halt the discharge. Instead of running out the Yak, the water would fill up those holes, reaching a more natural equilibrium underground. It wasn't a perfect solution. But in her public meetings, Liz assured the town that by taking additional precautions—treating leakages, patching holes or faults that proved problematic, and monitoring the water through wells—the amount and whereabouts of any errant acid mine drainage could be controlled.

The citizenry was far from convinced. Ex-miners, like Jim Martin, thought plugging was a bad idea, and they had been telling the EPA that since it was first proposed years earlier. The acidic water was going to find its way through the countless fissures in the bedrock and possibly contaminate Leadville's city water supply, which travels from a high mountain lake untainted down Evans Gulch northeast of town. How, Mayor Martin and others asked repeatedly, was the EPA going to guarantee that that didn't happen?

It was clear, too, that this was not a walk-away solution. The treatment system would have to be maintained and operated, sludge disposed of, and wells monitored *in perpetuity*. "How do you describe that to someone?" Liz reflected years later. "How do you negotiate an agreement that deals with water treatment in perpetuity? What does that really mean? We're not talking ten years, twenty years; we're talking forever. It was a difficult concept for me to grasp." It was even harder to accept. It began to dawn on the Leadville citizens that the EPA was not about ready to "get the hell out of town." Not by a long shot. In 1983, the EPA had predicted two to four years, five years later the agency was talking about forever.

And what was going to happen to Leadville's mining future if the Yak were plugged? others demanded. Rumors that the next big mining outfit was on its way made the *Herald Democrat* regularly. In one of her public meetings, Liz noted that the future of mining would not be affected because the ore bodies had already been depleted. Many loudly disagreed. Mining was still king in Leadville, after all. "Contrary to recent reports of their deaths, the Leadville mines are not exhausted of their mineral wealth," a resident wrote in the *Herald Democrat*. "This is important to Leadville! . . . The Yak Tunnel still serves us all by serving Leadville's industry—mining."

Signs went up around town. "EPA—Yak Off" read one. At times during her three-year tenure, the community's strong emotions made Liz nervous, but she never felt truly threatened. ASARCO officials, however, were making her job difficult. As a "Potentially Responsible Party," the company was required to work with the EPA on studying and remedying the acid mine drainage, if not voluntarily than through court orders, but officials often stubbornly refused to do the work. At one point, Liz resorted to spray-painting the rocks and ground to show ASARCO employees exactly what to move and where. The Black Cloud manager at the time, a brusque, burly man in his thirties, often expressed his resentment of the EPA. "Intimidating" was the term EPA employees repeatedly used to characterize Mike Lee. Even an ASARCO co-worker agreed Lee was frequently offensive, though he believed it was unwitting. The miner just didn't have the temperament to finesse deals with the EPA. But the distrust and dislike worked both ways. During the early negotiations, each side tried to strong-arm the other—the EPA by threatening huge fines; ASARCO by forcing everyone into court for Judge Carrigan to sort things out.

Although Liz stressed in public meetings that the EPA was taking the town's concerns into account, saying it didn't make it so. The primary bone of contention—plugging—was going forward. Townsfolk were frustrated; public meetings were being held, it seemed obvious, just to go through the statutory motions. Officials in charge of the town's water supply wrote Liz complaining of the EPA's "cavalier treatment" of their concerns that plugging might contaminate Leadville's drinking water. Members of the Environmental Task Force, who had spent a great deal of time responding to the EPA's requests for information and suggesting alternatives to treat the water, felt dismissed and discouraged.

At the same time the EPA was reassuring the community that plugging was safe, thirty miles north of Leadville, on the way to Vail near the town of Minturn, regulators were dealing with the recently abandoned 750-acre Eagle Mine site where tons of toxic mine waste were contaminating the Eagle River. The dead zone extended a mile downstream, and fish populations were affected for another fifteen miles. Through a series of mergers and acquisitions, media giant Viacom International, a New York–based company, found itself responsible for this remote western mine. Unlike ASARCO and the Leadville citizenry, Viacom officials didn't want to argue, they just wanted to be rid of the problem, and in 1988, the EPA plugged the mine.

It wasn't long before the mountainside resembled a colander. As leaks popped out all over the mountain, zinc contamination in the Eagle River quadrupled. Plugging had worsened the problem, just as

Leadville's miners were forecasting would happen in their own community. Predicting the flow of water through the seeps, cracks, faults, and mine workings clearly was more difficult than first imagined, and more expensive: $50 million later, fish now swim past a water treatment plant that has revived the Eagle River.

It's easy to understand why the EPA refused to listen to communities in those early years. The highly educated scientists and engineers that make up the agency and the contractors it hires use sophisticated, state-of-the-art technology to help guide decisions. The miners were small-town laborers who wouldn't know the intricacies of geology, underground hydrology, and acid mine chemistry—or so the EPA seemed to assume. The EPA's scientists, focusing on their abstract charts and plans, dismissed the local knowledge gained from lifetimes spent working underground as muckers, geologists, and mining engineers. Public meetings, fact sheets, and soliciting public comment were simply part of the regulatory checklist, and dealing with the public was regarded as a taxing nuisance that got in the way of the "real" work. EPA officials seemed to believe that mollifying Leadville's cantankerous citizens would be accomplished, not by working with them to find a remedy together, but with more public meetings and fact sheets—a superficial gesture that did little to appease residents.

For the first seventeen years, the Region 8 EPA office in Denver had had just one community liaison officer for all of its projects, Superfund and otherwise, in its entire six-state region. Public relations was clearly a low priority. In 1988, Sonya Pennock, a Des Moines, Iowa–bred former public issues campaigner, became the second, hired specifically to deal with Leadville. Sonya joined Liz at her town meetings. Jim Martin found her pleasant and ineffectual but at least she knew all of the buzzwords. "I think Jim never got over thinking I was some slick spin artist. I would talk to him sometimes and he would say, 'Well, you put that very well.' I remember thinking, 'That may not be a compliment.' I was only on the end of his gruff style a few times. He didn't think much about the process at all, and he let us know."

Mayor Martin's explosive nature was legendary to EPA's succession of project managers. The man did not mince words, and he wasn't going to slide through his mayoral term. He spoke only when he had something to contribute, but when he did he came right to the point, usually punctuating it with a raised voice and red-faced with emotion. Jim could either increase the tension level with a frustrated bark or ease it with a good-natured jab at the EPA or a self-deprecating aside. "I try to get along with everybody. But you have opinions, you got to express them. I don't make it personal."

Jim wanted to see California Gulch cleaned up, but like nearly everyone in town, he disagreed with the EPA's plan. "If you plug the tunnel, instead of a point source of discharge, you'll have the crap coming out all over the place," he explained. It just didn't seem like rocket science to him. But the EPA seemed determined to go ahead regardless. A cartoon circulated through town of two miners hauling a wheelbarrow full of paper toward the Yak Tunnel. "Just a few more reports, by golly," says one miner, "and this tunnel will be plugged solid."

In 1989, however, the EPA and ASARCO had had a change of heart, almost certainly a result of the disaster taking place up at the Eagle Mine and not because of the community's persistence. Plugging now had developed a bad reputation in the Region 8 office, but according to EPA official James Hanley, ASARCO blinked first, fearing the liability that would result if disaster struck. ASARCO proposed a much more expensive option—a water treatment plant that would scrub the Yak water clean before sending it down the gulch. The plug would now be a "flow-through bulkhead" with a drain to control the water and prevent blowouts from turning Doc Smith's river red. The two upper plugs cutting off some mines draining into the Yak would still be installed, upsetting those who felt the plugs would curtail Leadville's mining prospects. With ASARCO and Newmont, co-owner of the Yak Tunnel, willing to spend $13 million for a better solution, the EPA readily agreed. The plant's $500,000 to nearly $1 million annual maintenance cost would be the companies' responsibility—in perpetuity.

It was the first serious chunk of change levied at the companies, and some in town didn't think targeting the only viable mining company left in Leadville was fair. The *Herald Democrat* observed that "all Americans have relished in the finer things that metals from the ground south of town have provided. . . . Now society owes it to Leadville—and to itself—to clean up the mess it has left behind." Mining benefited society, therefore society should foot the cleanup bill. No mention was made that mining also benefited the mining companies—billions of dollars worth, much of it royalty free on public land—for more than a century. ASARCO may have been the last company standing when the music stopped in Leadville, but for one hundred years around the globe, it and other mining corporations had bullied their way into places they were not welcome as they mined their way to larger profits.

Throughout the twentieth century, scientific evidence was irrefutably showing the health hazards associated with many aspects of the ongoing—unregulated—industrialization of the United States. It is well documented that companies and industry trade groups routinely manipulated and hid such information from the public, thereby avoiding any regulations that might have resulted. Even the scientists—industry grants largely funding research in those days (a practice that continues today)—were intimidated with threats to their funding, lawsuits, and in some cases physically. The strong-arm tactics industry and their political loyalists used for decades enabled companies to avoid making current practices safer and cleaning up old ones far longer than the scientific evidence warranted. If the price tag for stalling went up in the intervening decades, company officials could blame themselves—or look to their bank accounts for consolation.

In Leadville, eight years after Doc Smith had received his anonymous warning, residents watched the Yak Treatment Plant going up in California Gulch just upstream from the Apache Tailing Impoundment. Leadville residents couldn't help but wonder about the location. Clean water discharged from the treatment plant would pick up new metals just five hundred yards downstream. But no one was listening. The Yak Tunnel issue—80 percent of the acid mine drainage—was finally settled.

What about the other 20 percent? The EPA's studies had shown that acid mine drainage and heavy metals were also draining out of upper California Gulch and neighboring Stray Horse and Oregon gulches and into the Arkansas River. Should these pollution sources be treated as well, how much would that cost, and who was going to pay for it? There were plenty of people in town, most vocally Chlouber and Miller, who thought the EPA had already done enough—it was time to go.

But in the 1980s yet another government agency was beginning to make its presence felt in Leadville. The Centers for Disease Control and Prevention was taking a hard look at lead poisoning, particularly among children. For nearly one hundred years, smelter stacks had showered neighborhoods nationwide with lead and arsenic. When lead settles out of the air, it binds tightly to soil particles. Even though most of the smelters were either closed or their emissions now regulated, the lead in the surrounding yards stayed behind. A bigger storm was brewing in Leadville.

In January 1990, a reporter from a local Colorado public television station came to Leadville. Standing in front of the Yak Tunnel's crumbling timber frame on a cold, windy day, Liz Evans explained why the EPA was in Leadville. "We don't want to have dead bodies in the street before we take action." Townsfolk were aghast. Liz was merely echoing the EPA's long-standing emphasis on prevention to defend their actions, but it was a harbinger of the battle to come. She recognized that it was time for her to move on. "I knew that once we started invading people's yards to test for metal contamination, it was going to get extremely hard. If I had to do all of the soil sampling in people's yards, I don't know if I would have been any more successful than the person who followed me."

As the 1980s ground to a close, Mayor Martin was fighting to prevent the Tabor Grand Hotel, Horace Tabor's gift to Leadville nearly a century earlier, from being demolished to make room for a parking lot. An out-of-towner with a passion for Horace Tabor agreed to step in and restore the decaying hotel. The day after he signed a contract to purchase the building for $2.3 million, a pounding rainstorm collapsed the northwest corner of the hotel. Hundred-year-old bricks crashed down on cars parked below, exposing four stories of fuchsia and chartreuse-colored bedroom walls from a more flamboyant Leadville era.

8

The Lead in Leadville

Ken Wangerud came to Leadville a "starry-eyed scientist." Here was a
complex environmental problem he could get excited about. To
Leadville's newest EPA project manager, the town was a "sick patient
in a bad wreck" and he was the emergency room doctor assigned to
perform reconstructive surgery. He charted what seemed to him an
obvious, linear progression from sickness to health. First, he would
initiate diagnostic tests such as waste-pile characterization using elec-
tron microscopy and taking soil samples—seventeen thousand at
least—all over Leadville. Second, he would use the data to diagnose
the patient, identifying the contaminants, where they were located,
and the risk they posed to Leadville residents and the environment.
And third, he would prescribe a remedy. This course of action would
inevitably expand the Superfund site well beyond the Yak Tunnel, and
it would probably involve removing yards.

   In the summer of 1990, during his first months as project manager,
Ken Wangerud drove to Leadville to reveal his plan to the residents.
Standing at the front of the meeting room, Ken stood out in his suit
and tie, red hair, and stocky build. Residents would come to consider
his "casual preppy" look and "hundred-dollar designer jeans" all
wrong for Leadville. His presentations included detailed maps,

charts, and timelines. Not to worry, he sought to convey with his confident demeanor, Ken Wangerud had everything under control. The townsfolk, however, resented the implication that their community was somehow diseased, and they took an immediate dislike to this new government outsider and his condescending attempts to cure them.

Ken had been raised a town kid in a Norwegian farm community of a thousand people in the flat, cold Red River Valley in eastern North Dakota back before oil was discovered. His father had worked for the railroad; his grandfather had moved to the valley to sell axle grease and kerosene, traveling to ranch homes by horse and wagon for Standard Oil. By the time Ken hit high school in the mid-1960s, oil had been discovered underneath the farmers' fields, and oil pumps, the impassive, dogged metronomes of industry, had begun to pop up in the windswept wheat fields. The oil companies brought geologists with them, and Ken was captivated. He studied oil and gas geology at the University of North Dakota, where he met his wife.

Ken graduated in time to take advantage of the West's oil boom of the 1970s. He took a variety of jobs for coal mining and oil companies in North Dakota and in Denver, dabbling in oil speculation for a time. A decade later, the recession had collapsed the oil and coal industries, and Ken found himself among the thousands of unemployed geologists scrambling to find a job. He turned to the government, working for a time reclaiming coal-mining sites for the Department of the Interior, earning much less than he had for the oil companies. By the late 1980s, Ken realized he needed a bigger challenge.

In 1990, Superfund was expanding, and California Gulch needed a new project manager. Ken felt he was right for the job. He had worked for big oil and mining companies, and he wasn't going to be intimidated by the likes of ASARCO. "Give me guff and I'll take you on" was his attitude. Ken switched to the Environmental Protection Agency and headed to Leadville on his first Superfund assignment. "My God, what a baptism," he would say years later.

At that time, construction of the Yak Treatment Plant was under-way, and the EPA had turned its attention to the other 20 percent: the two thousand or so waste rock piles and half a dozen tailing ponds in California, Stray Horse, and Oregon gulches also contaminating the Arkansas River with acid mine drainage. The agency was also ready to wade back into the turbulent waters of determining the health risks of living in Leadville.

During the plugging debate of the late 1980s, the state's health department had raised the specter of metal poisoning of the town's residents, primarily lead and arsenic from one hundred years of smelter smoke. Despite the Brown Envelope fiasco, the state health department had pushed ahead with studies to test the area's soils and to determine if residents, particularly children, had dangerous levels of lead circulating in their blood. Folks bristled at the idea that living in their town posed a health hazard, and town officials were confident that the government's own results would prove otherwise. But the controversial results convinced the state that a serious health problem did exist in Leadville and ultimately prompted the EPA to expand the reach of its Superfund investigation.

More than two thousand years ago, Hippocrates suspected that lead caused neurological and other serious health problems in the slaves working in the lead mines. Evidence of the metal's use dates back more than eight thousand years, and the extent of lead mining climbed steadily as ancient civilizations found new uses for the soft, bluish-white metal. The Greeks and Romans were prolific users of lead, putting it in face powders, ingesting it as medicine or as a sweet-ener, and making pottery, wine vessels, and water pipes with it. Lead was so pervasive that scientists believe lead poisoning was endemic in Roman citizens and may account for the bizarre behavior of some of its leaders.

Romans recognized the hazards of lead, and the first complaints of smelter smoke were recorded during these ancient times. But they continued to eat it, drink it, and breathe it, as we do today. Over the centuries, as new uses of lead were discovered, doctors continued to observe the metal's adverse health effects. By the 1920s, as the Industrial Revolution rapidly accelerated the production of lead, lead poisoning—severe illness or death—was considered a "frequent" occurrence, particularly among children and industry workers. In those early years of the twentieth century, the malady was diagnosed by its overt symptoms, which could include everything from kidney damage to anemia, heart disease to retardation and dementia. In the 1940s, diagnostic tools proved that lead poisoning came not just from a single toxic dose of lead, but could accumulate in the body slowly over time.

By then, lead was thoroughly entrenched in modern society, used in construction materials, water pipes, plastics, batteries, insecticides, and as an additive in gasoline. Even as leaded gasoline proliferated, sending huge amounts of lead directly into the atmosphere, lead in paint was identified as the primary culprit of lead poisoning. Because leaded gasoline didn't cause the sudden, tragic consequences that occurred when children gnawed on the sweet-tasting paint chips in their homes, society viewed lead-based paint as the greater threat. Most European nations banned leaded paint in the 1920s, but it would take the United States another fifty years before it could bring itself to regulate the lead industry. By then, lead was more pervasive than ever, lining the walls of millions of homes nationwide and spewing from every automobile on the road.

One reason lead toxicity was permitted in American society throughout the twentieth century was the perception that it was limited to children in the ghetto. Lead poisoning, the logic went, was caused by bad parenting and poverty, therefore the cure was to educate poor, black mothers to pay better attention to their children. That racist attitude began to change somewhat by the 1960s as the environmental movement focused attention on the health risks of even low levels of toxins in the environment. At that time, only lead levels above 60 micrograms per deciliter, roughly the level at which outward toxic effects appear, were considered harmful. But evidence that even lower levels could cause harm, particularly to developing children, was mounting. In 1971, the Centers for Disease Control and

Prevention (CDC) lowered the threshold of allowable lead in children's blood from 60 micrograms to 40. That year, President Richard Nixon signed the first law regulating lead, the Lead-based Paint Poisoning Prevention Act, a first step that was limited to paint surfaces exposed to children in new housing built with federal assistance, but not in the estimated sixty million homes already contaminated with lead-based paints.

As scientists gained the ability to measure lead in the blood at increasingly lower levels, they found that remarkably small amounts affected children's mental development, measurably lowering IQs and contributing to behavioral problems. In 1978, the CDC reduced the blood lead threshold to 30 micrograms, and then to 25 micrograms in 1985. Each drop was weighted with political and social consequences as more and more children fell into the category of lead poisoned. Lead toxicity wasn't limited to black, inner-city children. Millions of children in neighborhoods nationwide were suffering varying degrees of lead's poisonous effects on their mental development and that required a political response. The CDC considered lead poisoning the most common—and preventable—health problem in children. It had been known for years that leaded gasoline was the primary contributor to America's endemic high blood lead levels.

In the early 1970s, the invention of the catalytic converter finally provided the economic reason the United States seemed to need to begin banning leaded gasoline; the lead additive ruined the new device developed to control carbon monoxide emissions. The government began taking tentative steps to reduce lead and by 1980, sales of leaded gasoline were down to half of all sales. That decade, President Reagan and his EPA administrator, Anne Gorsuch, considered the phase-down program one of those onerous regulations on industry and attempted to dismantle it. But as was happening with Superfund, public pressure forced the Reagan administration to reconsider.

Lead, once released from the Earth, doesn't go away. According to a 1993 National Academy of Sciences report, roughly half of the three hundred million metric tons of lead pulled out of the Earth in the last five thousand years has been, and continues to be, released into the environment, much of it into the atmosphere. The concentrations of lead in the bodies of modern Americans are three hundred to five hundred times that of preindustrial peoples.

Paint and leaded gasoline received most of the attention in the 1970s and 1980s, but the CDC and EPA also began addressing drinking water flowing through lead pipes, food stored in containers sealed with lead solder, and the lead found in soils contaminated by smelter emissions. As significant and pervasive as lead-based paint and gasoline were to the nation's overall lead risk, the EPA had deemed living near lead smelters as the single highest concentrated pathway of lead exposure to children, most commonly from playing in their own backyards. But the government had been equally reluctant to study and eliminate the impact of lead-contaminated soil. Though the Clean Air Act of 1970 and subsequent National Ambient Air Quality Standards set in 1978 were intended to limit smelter emissions, by 1990, most smelters and refineries still weren't meeting those standards. In 1980, Superfund at least gave the government a method for eliminating old sources of lead found in mining and smelter towns.

With a link between lead in the soil and lead in the blood of young children established, many questions remained. Educating parents and children to alter their behavior was one method of reducing lead's impact, but the federal government believed removing or capping the soils was the only way to effectively and permanently eliminate the risk. But how much lead had to be present to be harmful, what should the trigger point be for requiring yard removal, and how could it be determined efficiently at sites nationwide?

In the late 1980s, the EPA began the lengthy and expensive process of developing a computer model to estimate the risk of high blood lead levels in children under age seven. The Integrated Exposure Uptake/Biokinetic Model, or IEUBK, took site-specific information about an area's soil and dust lead concentrations and figured in assumptions about children's behavior. If exposure to 500 parts per million lead in the soil (a measure comparable to 5 gold marbles in a vat of 9,995 silver marbles) were predicted to elevate blood lead levels, then 500 parts per million was the "soil action level," the amount above which the soil must be removed or covered to ensure protection.

While the EPA was developing their model, Colorado turned its attention to understanding the health effects of living in the state's numerous mining towns. The idea that lead in the soil—mining's environmental pollution—correlated to a public health risk was untenable to many in the western towns built from mining, not just in Leadville but in places like East Helena, Montana; Triumph, Idaho; and Midvale, Utah. Few had ever looked at the health consequences of living in a historic mining town. Leadville, its numerous smelters well documented, would be one of the first. The Colorado health department tested the soil in 150 spots around Leadville and Stringtown. Not surprisingly, the results revealed high levels of cadmium, arsenic, and lead—the closer to the waste rock piles and former smelter sites, the higher the contamination. No one in town got worked up over the idea that there was a lot of lead in Leadville. As they liked to point out, the town was named for a reason. What did that have to do with their children's school grades?

To convince the town to cooperate in a blood-lead study, Carol Russell, the harried health department liaison, held meetings in Leadville to reassure the community that the department was conducting the test in its role as scientists, not regulators. At one well-attended meeting, Commissioner Carl Miller and the audience listened to an epidemiologist explain the subtle, but measurable effects of lead on mental and learning capacity and the risk to Leadville's children. When the scientist was done, Carl looked at the other commissioners and said, "Well, I didn't want to be a genius anyway." Carol suddenly realized that by raising the alarm for the kids today, they were also implying that their parents—generations of Leadvillites in fact—might themselves already be somehow mentally impaired. Even so, Carl Miller and the county's health officials encouraged residents to volunteer for the blood lead study; they were confident that the state would find no health problems. They had all played in Leadville's dirt as youngsters, after all, and they were just fine.

Leadville

In September 1987, 150 children between six months and six years had their blood tested for lead. Only a few children tested above the CDC's official acceptable level of 25 micrograms per deciliter. Fifteen percent had levels over 15, and 41 percent had blood lead levels over 10. The average was 10.1, lower than the researchers had expected. The CDC, however, was preparing to lower the acceptable threshold to 10 micrograms, in which case nearly half of Leadville's children would be considered "lead poisoned." The state considered that a health emergency.

Many of the citizens—and ASARCO—saw it differently. ASARCO won an injunction to prevent the EPA and the state from using the results of the blood-lead study in court. The methodology, while scientifically appropriate, had not followed the court's rigorous procedures for use as evidence. The results were controversial, not just because high blood leads had been found—they were being found in urban and rural communities across the nation—but because the study had found an association between the children's lead levels and the lead found in their backyards. Amounts as low as 500 parts per million—the amount found in 80 percent of yards—increased children's blood leads, the study concluded. Children whose parents were miners, bringing home lead dust on their shoes and clothes, also had higher blood lead levels. The study found no association between blood lead levels and lead-based paint found in the town's numerous historic houses. In Leadville, it seemed, it was indeed the town's mining past that was a public health risk.

By this time, the state had handed authority for California Gulch cleanup over to the feds. Health department officials began an education campaign to minimize children's exposure to lead, encouraging parents to teach their children to wash their hands often and to not play with toys in the dirt. A few parents were asked to replace the tailings they had used to fill their children's sandboxes. Many Leadville parents undoubtedly took the advice to heart, even while dismissing the results. Only a few children were above the CDC's current acceptable level, and they felt it was unfair to judge Leadville by a lower standard or implicate mining as the culprit when so many other causes could be to blame. Everyone knew the state of Colorado was out to get Leadville—the Brown Envelope had proven that.

Throughout the 1980s, most residents felt the government was kicking them while they were down. Climax had shut down for good just as the blood lead study had gotten underway. More than a quarter of the town was still unemployed and in a few years, the 1990 census would show that Lake County had lost half of its residents the previous decade—the largest drop in the entire nation. Sales tax from the dwindling number of stores was the town's primary source of income now, and town officials were searching for ways to attract tourists, so far without great success. The state, it seemed, had given Leadville a "black eye"—again.

National television coverage began with a relatively painless ten-minute segment on the MacNeil/Lehrer NewsHour in November 1988 that focused on the environmental damage in California Gulch. The reporter had stayed out of people's yards, and the segment didn't create much of a stir. But when Nova aired a program entitled "Poison in the Rockies" in January 1990, the town came unglued. The title itself was provocative, but even more so were the pictures beamed into homes across the nation showing gunky orange sludge oozing into crystal clear streams under a Rocky Mountain backdrop. Only four minutes of the hour-long program were devoted specifically to Leadville, but to the townsfolk, judging by their reaction, it must have seemed an eternity. As video footage of a skinny, blond girl digging a cave in the Hamm's Tailing Pile—the "sand dunes"—filled the screen, actor Peter Coyote said gravely, "There is widespread exposure to heavy metals in Leadville, particularly for children who are exposed to lead, cadmium, and arsenic and other metals at playgrounds, in their own backyards, and on unfenced tailing piles." He went on to recount the state's blood lead test results.

Editorials denouncing the program inundated the *Herald Democrat*. Mayor Jim Martin and the city council shot off a letter to Nova's producers. Residents felt unfairly singled out. (Aspen, a section of the historic mining town a Superfund site since 1986 because of high concentrations of metals, had gotten only a brief mention by comparison.) The documentary was "one-sided sensationalism" full of "innuendo, misinformation and fabrication through omission," wrote a local editorialist. Leadvillites had come off looking like mountain hillbillies, wrote another. One man described playing on the mine dumps as a child: "It is my pleasure to report that having grown up with Leadville's dirt on my hands and in my veins, my whiskers have not grown in green and my eyes do not phorphoresce [*sic*] in the dark from 'heavy metal poisoning.'" It was a common sentiment.

But there was a small minority, Doc and the other half dozen members of the Environmental Task Force for example, who felt Leadville needed to acknowledge the problems mining had left behind and help find a way to repair the damage. "The only true toxics seeping from Leadville now are denial and guilt laced with paranoia. . . . Now that the 'big provider' [Climax] has diminished, what saddens me most is that Leadville is still on a path of 'just say no,'" wrote one ex-Leadvillite in the *Herald Democrat*—from Arizona.

Living in Leadville takes a certain grit. The summers are short, the winters are long and harsh, the air is thin, and the amenities few. Leadvillites reveled in the resilient reputation their rugged existence afforded them. The only glamour to be found in Leadville came from the occasional bride and the coifed tourists, their soft city faces contrasting with the weathered Leadvillites, who tended to look older than their years, the year-round glare of sun and snow plowing deep crevices into their faces, the dry air cracking their calloused hands. It wasn't unheard of to find a man in his eighties wielding a sledgehammer or a ninety-year-old woman repairing fences. They viewed themselves as self-reliant westerners, descendants of that particularly tough and stubborn branch called miners. This remote mountain town had existed for more than a hundred years, and its residents felt they could take care of themselves.

These were not the sorts of folks the EPA was used to dealing with. The criticism normally leveled at the EPA came from communities protesting for greater protection. Globeville, the neighborhood surrounding ASARCO's Globe Plant in Denver was a typical community in this respect. Any molecule of arsenic or lead was too much as far as the smelter's neighbors were concerned. By contrast, "you go up to Leadville, and for a time I felt that they thought you could have it on your cereal," an EPA official said later. Leadville residents had spent their lives working with and surrounded by lead, zinc, and cadmium. Metals had given their families and the community an income and an identity spanning generations, and they felt comfortable—proud—to live amongst the waste and smelter piles that had made Leadville an important mining center for the nation. Metals sprang from nature and were as much a part of the Leadville backdrop as the majestic Rockies. In urban areas like Globeville, contemporary residents had never economically benefited from the smelter that had long ago contaminated their neighborhoods. Because their personal histories and identities were not associated with the smelters, the sense of security and acceptance of risk in those neighborhoods were much lower than in mining towns like Leadville. As an EPA official summed it up to a Denver reporter: "The problem in these mining communities is people have been used to living with this stuff for 100 years. It's not an acute toxicity problem—people getting cancer and dying—so they don't understand why there's a risk."

So while EPA officials were honing their sales pitch to the residents of places like Globeville—convincing them that some level of risk was acceptable—it was forced to adjust its tactics in mining communities like Leadville that were determined not to acknowledge that any health risk existed at all. Like an oversized bus, the lumbering bureaucracy needed a wide swath before it managed to reverse course.

Ken Wangerud kept a quote on his desk from President Theodore Roosevelt's Citizen of the Republic, or "man in the arena," speech given in Paris on April 23, 1910.

It is not the critic who counts; not the man who points out how the strong man stumbles, or where the doer of deeds could have done them better. The credit belongs to the man who is actually in the arena, whose face is marred by dust and sweat and blood; who strives valiantly; who errs, who comes short again and again, because there is no effort without error and shortcoming; but who does actually strive to do the deeds; who knows great enthusiasms, the great devotions; who spends himself in a worthy cause; who at the best knows in the end the triumph of high achievement, and who at the worst, if he fails, at least fails while daring greatly, so that his place shall never be with those cold and timid souls who neither know victory nor defeat.

"This is the arena," Ken said enthusiastically a dozen years later. "This is the pinnacle in engaging the environmental arena." In that arena, Ken faced many adversaries: the PRPs (potentially responsible parties), thirteen in all, but ASARCO was the snarling tiger to be tamed; his own headquarters in Washington; and of course the Leadvillites themselves who, underestimated at first, would come to seem like relentless piranhas. But Wangerud had allies in the arena as well, primarily the toxicologists in EPA's Region 8 office and the federal government's Department of Justice.

A few months after Nova aired in 1990, Wangerud received his orders: determine how far the contamination extended and assess just how dangerous it was to live in Leadville. EPA toxicologists had recently determined that, of Region 8's fifty-two mining sites now on Superfund's National Priority List, Leadville and East Helena, Montana, another ASARCO smelter site, were the two most hazardous to human health and required immediate attention. Wangerud started down Superfund's path, initiating fifteen different "remedial investigations"—on the water quality, waste rock piles, tailing piles, slag piles, and residential soils. The studies were to serve two purposes. They would set a process in motion that would eventually lead to cleaning up Leadville's hazardous waste, and they would dig up evidence for the Department of Justice, the agency that would argue the Superfund case if the PRPs refused to pay for the cleanup and the case went to trial. Ken felt the Justice Department's added muscle strengthened his position in the arena. He gathered the PRPs together during a series of meetings and asked them to divvy up the fifteen studies he had in mind.

From a PRP's point of view, the arena was a complicated mix of interchangeable adversaries and allies. Each one faced not only the federal government, but each other as well. Alliances between them could be made or broken, depending on the subject at hand. To complicate things further, the 1955 marriage of convenience between ASARCO and Newmont's Resurrection had soured years ago, but the two companies were now forever united by Superfund as the Res-ASARCO Joint Venture—PRP. The companies had disparate strategies. Newmont, which had only a few Superfund sites to contend with, wanted to settle and move on. ASARCO, on the other hand, had the government chasing it at dozens of sites all over the West and Midwest. It wanted to keep fighting. So while ASARCO and Newmont were squared off against each other, the two companies were reluctantly holding hands, negotiating with the government as a single entity as well. Their struggle for a united front may have been the most intriguing battle in the arena. Many lawyers spent years—billed hourly—strategizing their positions and planning their moves. Newmont quietly agreed to take on some of the studies, perhaps to enhance the evidence against ASARCO, the smelter company. ASARCO, however, maintained that no health problems existed and, for the most part, complied only after the EPA and Justice Department ordered them.

The summer of 1991 was a volatile time in the arena. Earlier that year, Ken Wangerud had announced the results of the IEUBK model's assessment of Leadville's health risk—and it was worthy of escalating Leadville's ongoing fury. The computer predicted that 41 percent of Leadville's children had blood lead levels over 10 micrograms, the same number the state's study had found four years earlier. Ken, along with the EPA toxicologist assigned to Leadville, a soft-spoken, bearded man named Chris Weis, stressed that the results were preliminary. As more data became available for analysis, it might alter the model's results. The community, however, was outraged. They weren't about to trust some computer in Denver to tell them how healthy—or unhealthy—they were, and they worried that the model's "soil lead action level" would be equally outrageous, calling for wholesale yard removal. At the same time, ASARCO countered with their own risk assessment that predicted *no* children had levels over 10 micrograms. The EPA was using "worst case scenarios," the company said, while ASARCO's assessment was based on "average case scenarios." In some respects, that was true. The EPA chose more conservative estimates to determine risk.

To support its position, ASARCO contracted Robert Bornschein, a respected lead health researcher from the University of Cincinnati, to conduct another blood lead study. ASARCO organizers emphasized that the EPA was not involved with the study, and they asked the Lake County Health Department to participate as well to give the study local endorsement and, they hoped, to encourage widespread participation.

The EPA was conducting additional studies of its own as well. Bill Brattin, a toxicologist hired as an EPA consultant, recalled that "the original arguments advanced by the mining companies, and particularly by their attorneys, were overly aggressive. They asserted that this material was simply and totally benign, absolutely no risk." The mining companies claimed that the lead was not absorbed in the body and therefore, even if swallowed, posed no health hazard. The toxicologists studying Leadville doubted that all lead was harmless, but believed the companies might have a valid point—though only in part. Lead comes in many forms. There are lead carbonates, lead oxides, lead sulfates, lead phosphates. Twenty types of lead were found in Leadville alone. Scientists suspected that not all lead types were absorbed equally and, thus, posed different health risks. If that were true, then the health risks probably were overestimated. So Weis, Brattin, and a team of scientists began a series of studies to determine the absorption rates of various lead compounds found in Leadville.

The researchers conducted their tests on young swine because they mimic the digestive systems of children. The connotation did not go over well. "All you've shown here is there may be a health risk to young pigs," said one resident. In a front-page article headlined "EPA's study is slammed by Leadville health officials," the *Herald Democrat* wrote, "The 'pig studies' which were performed by the EPA pumped massive amounts of ground lead directly into the stomachs of starving pigs. The EPA accepts the results of these tests in their data on humans." Even the *USA Today* got in on the fun in 1994, when it wrote, "For many, the last straw was when the EPA, unable to find high lead levels in children, began an experiment to force-feed pigs soil with lead in it." The "pig studies" became another source of resentment—and confusion—that has lasted for more than a decade.

"Did we study the toxicity of lead in swine? The answer is absolutely not," Brattin countered. "I went up there a number of times trying to explain this, and the message tends to get lost. We studied the absorption of lead, not the toxicity of lead. The doses were far below any sign of toxicity." The EPA did feed young pigs lead in amounts similar to what young children might ingest, but researchers were measuring how much of the substance was absorbed into the bloodstream, not how sick the pigs became or, by extension, the health of Leadville's children. To be absorbed into the blood, lead must dissolve in the gastrointestinal tract. The lead found in paint is highly soluble so most of that lead type is absorbed if swallowed, making lead-based paint toxic at low doses. But if the absorption rate for a lead compound found in a tailing pile is half that of paint's highly soluble form, then more of it must be ingested for lead to cause an equally toxic effect. The researchers were looking for that absorption rate— the "relative bioavailability"—to plug into the overall equation. The amount ingested required to cause toxicity was another measurement entirely. The "pig studies" were one of many that EPA toxicologists hoped would lead to more accurate model predictions. If the scientists were right, and not all lead was created equal, then a national one-size-fits-all standard for soil lead abatement was inappropriate.

In the spring of 1991, to determine how much and where the different types of lead were located, Ken Wangerud unveiled his plan to take seventeen thousand soil samples from Leadville's yards. The response was clear: "Take that trowel and shove it." Editorials denouncing the EPA again filled the *Herald Democrat*. Shop owners sold "EPA—Keep Off" signs in town for $1. The *Herald* ran a handy cutout version that read:

> The EPA and its Associates
> Do Not have permission to conduct
> Soil sampling research on this property.
> The Owner.

In October 1989, Chris Barnett, the new twenty-three-year-old voice of the *Herald Democrat*, had begun writing regular editorials extolling Leadvillites to keep up the pressure against the "Federales' Folly":

> Mining is our history, it is still our main industry, it is a way of life.
> It seems, however, as an EPA representative talks in a room filled with metal chairs, a room supported by steel beams, a presenter using an overhead projector, that somehow it's a problem of which is part of an ugly past.
> All of the effort here to promote business in the area takes a step back each time, as in the case of this week, the EPA cranks out a press release, this week's entitled, in capital letters, mind you, "SURGES OF METAL-LADEN WATER FROM THE YAK TUNNEL IN LEADVILLE WILL NO LONGER ENTER THE UPPER ARKANSAS RIVER WHEN A POND DESIGNED TO CONTAIN THE CONTAMINATED WATER BEGINS OPERATION TODAY."
> Ouch. This is the type of thing Denver and front range media types pick up without thinking twice. I don't know about you, but that intro conjures up pictures in my mind of wholescale destruction, sludge, dead things, etc., flowing down the Arkansas.

During the summer of 1991, while Barnett's editorials urged residents to post "Keep Off" signs, another reporter wrote that the EPA was violating residents' constitutional rights: that of individuals to own and protect private property and to be considered innocent until proven guilty. The weekly local rag had unwaveringly opposed the EPA since the beginning. The paper was generous enough to publish an occasional letter that ran against the town's riptide, but the reporters' biases over the years were obvious. ASARCO's paid sources were billed as experts presenting facts; the EPA's information—the contamination itself—was "alleged." Through the many long years, Leadville's reporters had few resources, little time, and even less inclination to dig behind the press releases and rhetoric coming from both sides. Their coverage often added to the hype and gave residents a slanted viewpoint from which to draw their own conclusions.

By the end of June, "Keep Off" signs outnumbered the tourists. Leadville's short summer season, when the yards were free of snow, leaves little time for work each year, and Ken was anxious to turn the situation around to avoid losing a year. In well-attended public meetings, he urged cooperation, but residents remained resolute. So Ken got tough. "The law is in our favor. We won't take anyone to court this year, but one way or another, we're going to get this thing done." If urging compliance didn't work, intimidation was even less effective. It incited people and was counterproductive, a town official warned Wangerud and his team of Justice Department lawyers.

Residents worried about liability and clouds on their titles. Ken spent hours trying to reassure the community that, no matter the results of the tests, the EPA would not sue homeowners. But the Brown Envelope loomed large. Wangerud sent a "letter of comfort" to the community, but years later acknowledged, "Why should people believe that when the state has already put all of those homeowners on notice that we might sue you?"

The Denver and national newspapers seemed to enjoy covering the western showdown between the federal government and the feisty mountain folks with their colorful comments. "Do I see deformed babies? People with hydrocephalic heads? No," one resident told a

Denver reporter. The EPA was "out of control," "growing like a cancer," "growing like weeds," "had come to town and declared Marshall Law," and "were ramming their solutions down our throats."

Although it was clear from the "Keep Off" signs around town and the anger expressed at public meetings that most residents were not about to give consent, an important few were willing to work with the EPA. Mayor Jim Martin didn't think there was a health risk in Leadville, and he certainly didn't appreciate the bad publicity programs like Nova's "Poison in the Rockies" heaped on Leadville. But he was concerned enough that he thought the EPA should be allowed to do their tests—just in case. "Who wants to destroy kids' minds?" he explained years later. At the other end of Harrison Avenue, Jim's good friend from the Climax days was a county commissioner. Together, they decided to let Wangerud test the town's alleys, roads and other city- and county-owned properties. It was a dicey move for their political careers—about the last thing either man considered. By July, they had convinced their respective boards to go along with their plans.

A grateful Wangerud took full advantage of the offer. He sampled to the very edge of the easement, which often included what people considered part of their backyards. "There were people who sure as heck weren't going to grant EPA permission to sample in their yard," Ken recalled later. "Then all of a sudden here comes a team sampling every twenty-five feet down the alleyways going right into their backyards. I'm sure they thought, 'Duplicitous bastards!'" But how well did samples collected in and near the roads and alleys—where Leadville had been spreading slag and waste rock as roadbed material off and on for a hundred years—correlate to residential yards?

To help answer that question another small group of citizens came forward. "When we'd drive up there for a public meeting and there would be a lot of shouting go on," Chris Weis remembered, "we'd be packing up our papers in the back of the room after everyone had cleared out, and a couple of moms would come in and say, 'I can't speak out in my own community, but I want to make sure my child is protected. What do I do?'" Wangerud was thus able to sample at least some residential yards—about 10 to 20 percent of the town cooperat-ed with the sampling study that summer, he estimated. But it was enough to compare residential yards to alleyways. The alleys were indeed higher, but not by much, and the EPA decided to use the alleys to determine residential contamination.

Ken scrounged up a few more samples through a court order requiring the local community college, sanitation and water districts, and other nonresidential entities to allow the EPA on their property. Between city and county access, court-ordered sampling, and cooper-ative residents, Ken had a total of 4,800 samples, far short of the 17,000 samples he needed to adequately map the contamination in town. So Ken "krieged," a technique that predicts values for areas between data points. Geologists use the method in exploration to estimate how much mineral is present. Other environmental sciences might kriege to estimate exposure levels to toxins in drinking water or air pollution. In Leadville, the EPA used it to draw a map of lead con-tamination in Leadville without the community's cooperation. When Ken showed up at a public meeting with his map, residents were stunned. "There were people who had not given access and here I'm coming out with a damn map, saying, 'Well, even though we didn't sample your yard, it looks like it's contaminated.'" Mayor Martin, who had taken the unpopular stand of giving the EPA access to city property, was furious. "That was completely illegitimate. This son of a buck was krieging the alleys and the shoulders and the roadways and drawing contamination lines. I said, 'This is baloney,' only I used stronger terms than that."

The results from the soil sampling found lead in nearly every yard in Leadville and Stringtown, the nearby smelter community. The yards averaged 2,000 parts per million, but reached as high as 31,700 parts per million. Nearly six hundred waste rock piles, holes from children playing visible in some, had averaged 4,500 parts per million lead, but could go as high as 66,400 parts per million. Leadville was proving to be an inordinately complex site. The rich variety of metals in this part of Colorado's mineral belt and the long history of mining that had placed Leadville among the nation's preeminent mining sites also made it one of the biggest and most challenging Superfund sites in the nation. The area had seen mining, milling, and smelting of gold, silver, lead, zinc, and copper for over a century. The variety of mining activity had laid down a wide mosaic of lead types. And over time, people had moved the waste around. The railroad had used the slag for railroad ballast; the town and state had used the slag on the roads; and waste had been used as construction fill. By the time Wangerud came along with his studies, one area could have a completely different contamination makeup than its neighbor, posing different health risks and requiring different levels of cleanup action.

Leadville may have been a difficult site to understand, but one thing was clear to the EPA: the sources of contamination extended well beyond the Yak Tunnel. Wangerud redrew the Superfund contamination boundaries to sixteen and a half square miles, including most of the Leadville Mining District. The new Superfund map excluded the Black Cloud Mine which, as an active mine, fell under different regulations, but it did include the entire town of Leadville. "Can anyone control you EPA eco-Nazis?" one man bellowed at a meeting.

Jim Martin's term as Leadville's mayor was up at the end of 1991. He took the following year off, but by the fall, Jim was running for county commissioner, alongside Bob Casey, a fourth-generation resident whose great-grandparents had arrived in the 1880s. In late 1992, Bob and Jim both won seats on the Board of County Commissioners.

After growing up the son of a Leadville lawyer and district court judge, Bob had left Leadville only long enough to go to college. When he returned, he took a job at Climax. But mining was not for Bob. He got a job at the local fire department, and after eleven years became a paralegal and investigator for the district attorney's office. Now he was a county commissioner alongside Jim Martin, a man he would come to admire for his honesty, dedication, and ability to get people's attention.

The two new commissioners decided a change was in order. "The Board of Commissioners needed to come to the table," recalled Casey, his shoulder-length hair now thinning and gray. "Past boards had decided that they didn't want to engage in any kind of proactive litigation for various reasons. One of them was that they didn't want to be named as a PRP." But Jim and Bob decided the greater risk was not having a say at all. They wanted to educate themselves on the Superfund issues and become more involved in the decisions being made in Denver that were affecting their town. So they asked around and found John Faught.

Jim remembered meeting him on a cold day in March on the seventeenth floor of an elegant suite of law offices overlooking Denver. He and Bob had put on their suits and ties for the trip to visit their prospective lawyer. John Faught's high-rise view may have stretched far, but it stopped short of his hometown, the tiny farming community of Elsie—just over the Nebraska border. Faught had a bachelor's degree in electrical engineering ("so he probably has a few good qualities about him," Jim decided), but ended up a lawyer in the Navy Judge Advocate General's Corps in Washington, D.C., for four years, serendipitously specializing in environmental law. He came to Denver in 1976 and six years later owned a large downtown law firm. When the two Leadville men walked into his office looking for someone to help their county, Faught, a shock of white hair accentuated by his penchant for wearing black, was in the midst of representing the Shattuck Chemical Company in another contentious Superfund case in Denver.

Over a "classy" lunch, Jim Martin and Bob Casey explained that they wanted to have a say as the decisions were being made. They would pay his fee out of the county's meager budget; it was that important, they had decided. John Faught sensed the two men's genuine concern for the environment and their community, and he agreed to represent the county.

After meeting with Faught, Jim and Bob drove back up the mountain to Leadville and stopped at the Silver King for a beer. A rich, pretty, young visitor approached Jim to ask him about Leadville's elevation. "I'm getting ready to tell her, and this jerk she was with comes up and grabs my tie and says, 'What are you doing with this girl?'"

Jim knocked the man's hands off his throat, and the fight was on. Bob, in his suit, joined in. Tables turned; drinks flew. When Jim saw the bartender go behind the bar to call the cops, "I walked the hell out and sat in the car—it's twenty below." No one was arrested—Bob did work for the district attorney's office, after all. After the dust had settled, Bob went outside and saw his friend's silhouette sitting in the car, waiting for someone to take him home. "We went from the seventeenth floor of this Denver high rise to the floor of the Silver King all in one day."

9

Stall, Stall, Stall

Lawyers. If there was one thing EPA project manager Ken Wangerud, ASARCO, and the people of Leadville could agree on, ten years after Leadville had been named a Superfund site, it was that the time had come to lose the lawyers, find a way to compromise, and start moving dirt.

Leadville had a long history with lawyers. They came on the heels of the miners after the silver boom in the 1870s. The laws regarding mining claims were straightforward: first come, first served. After striking a vein, the miner who recorded his claim first, owned the rights for the length of that vein. But the bedlam that usually resulted brought out both guns and lawyers. Until the site was surveyed and recorded, it was vulnerable to claim jumpers, and, even properly registered, the competition and get-rich-quick frenzy was so intense that owners had to maintain a constant vigil to protect their mines. Soon, the hills and gulches east of Leadville were a convoluted jumble of hundreds of overlapping claims running in all directions. With so much money at stake and little governmental oversight, conflicts were inevitable as miners dug into each other's claims. Mischief through trickery or use of guns was rampant. Early on, the guns settled many disagreements, but as the lawyers arrived and the disputes became

increasingly complex, more and more of them were settled in the
courts. In Leadville, the number of lawyers soon rivaled the number
of saloons, which said a lot in a mining camp, particularly one with
Leadville's sodden reputation. By 1879, more than a hundred and
twenty lawyers had hung a shingle in town.

One of them was George Elder, a twenty-two-year-old Quaker
who had studied law in the tradition of the day—by reading books in
his father's law office in Lewistown, Pennsylvania. George was drawn
to the West by the tremendous opportunity to earn a living untan-
gling mining claims. In January 1879, he headed for the "boomtown
of boomtowns" and set up his law practice in a small, rustic office in
the Quincy Block, a distinctive gray, brick building that still stands on
Harrison Avenue. The western mining camp's noise and disorder
came as a shock after George's genteel eastern upbringing, but the
young Quaker adapted and had no qualms carrying a gun to protect
himself. His practice flourished, and, like many lawyers of the day, he
was occasionally paid in mining shares, some of which brought in
extra income. By 1886, he felt secure enough to bring a bride home
from back East, and three years later the couple bought a large,
unadorned white house west of Harrison Avenue and an upright
piano for the young Mrs. Elder. Their son Robert was born in one of
the home's bedrooms a few years later.

Robert grew up to follow his father and grandfather into law.
During the Depression, he became a small-time mine promoter,
hoping that one of his ventures would pay off. Eventually, Robert
inherited the house, the piano, and the bits and pieces of mining
claims scattered about the mining district his father had been given.
By that time, Leadville's boom days were long over, and the claims
lay idle. But, like most townsfolk, Robert Elder believed mining
would flourish in Leadville again one day and those claims would be
worth something. Over the years, he tried to consolidate the frag-
mented pieces he already owned by buying claims that became available. He didn't get far.

Robert Elder never had much luck in mining, and he finally took a
job in his mid-fifties as an attorney for the Navy Department in

Arlington, Virginia. Robert had married late in life, and his only child, also named Robert, was just eight years old when the family moved to Arlington. Though young Bob was raised in an eastern big city, his summers spent at the family home in Leadville persuaded him to return West. In college he studied—not law as was the tradition among Elder males—but mine engineering. He attended the Colorado School of Mines in the 1950s and, after a brief stint in the army, worked in various Colorado and Wyoming mining camps before ending up at Climax in 1966. He bought a house in town, married a schoolteacher, and settled into raising his daughter.

In 1983, after his father and mother passed away, he and his family moved into the old family home to live surrounded by the Elder family belongings, antiques now, including the old upright piano bought in Leadville by young newlyweds a hundred years earlier. Bob also inherited the mining claims his grandfather had first earned helping miners too poor to pay in cash. His land totaled about 350 acres—a small amount compared to ASARCO's holdings—that were scattered among a hundred and fifty claims, fragments of no more than a few acres here and there.

In 1986, Bob, now in his fifties and laid off from Climax, was in the hospital with an ulcer when the certified letter from the Environmental Protection Agency arrived. On the news footage that was in Bob's future, he would appear as a soft-spoken, quiet man, tall and long-limbed, large glasses hiding his face. EPA officials would come to consider Bob a kind, intelligent, thoughtful "statesman." No one at the EPA who met him seemed to feel he deserved what happened, but somehow the bureaucracy had gotten Bob in its sights. Out of thirteen potentially responsible parties (PRPs) sued by the EPA, Bob Elder was the lone individual.

To Glenn Anderson's way of thinking, working on the Leadville Superfund project for ASARCO represented job security. In early 1990, four years after Bob Elder received his letter from the EPA and about the same time Ken Wangerud was settling into his new job at the EPA, Glenn was a superintendent at ASARCO's Coeur d'Alene mine in

Idaho's panhandle. As he worked on the mine's five-year plan, he realized the Coeur d'Alene didn't have five good years of ore reserves left—two, maybe three, tops. Then where would he end up?

Fortunately for him, ASARCO's mine manager at the Black Cloud, Mike Lee, had reached the end of his endurance at about the same time. For years, he had been overseeing the mine while running to Denver for lengthy meetings with lawyers at every turn. He could no longer manage both jobs, and Glenn Anderson seemed like the perfect man to take over ASARCO's Superfund fight with the EPA. It was said amongst the miners at the Black Cloud—men he'd begun his career with "diggin' in the piss ditch"—that when Glenn Anderson cut himself shaving, he bled baby blue, the company color.

Glenn was raised far from the labyrinth of Leadville's underground, on a Virginia farm where his father installed milking parlors for other farmers. When Glenn wasn't taking apart his family's radio, he liked to sit at the kitchen table in the evenings and put together pieces of his dad's milking contraptions. For a farm kid who preferred tinkering to milking cows, engineering was the obvious career choice.

At a friend's suggestion, Glenn headed to the Colorado School of Mines, but he quickly bailed; school was interfering with his social life. He took a job shoveling rock at the Black Cloud Mine. In the mid-1970s, Leadville was still a thriving mining town, full of bars and young men with big paychecks. Glenn had found his niche. Within a year, he was promoted to mucker, drilling and blasting in the tunnels. By 1982, now in his mid-twenties, Glenn was a shift boss at the Black Cloud, and he'd hit the rock ceiling. Without a college degree, he'd gone as far as he was going to go. He reenrolled at the Colorado School of Mines, studying engineering during the week and working at the Black Cloud on the weekends. During those frenetic four years, he managed to find time to marry a longtime friend from Virginia.

After Glenn graduated in 1986, ASARCO sent him to a mine in Montana, then to the Coeur d'Alene a few years after that. In early 1990, when the company asked him to oversee the California Gulch Superfund site, he recalled, "I got to thinkin', Jesus, two years worth of ore reserves here and then who knows what they'll do with me, or

Superfund in Leadville," which seemed to Glenn as if it would go on forever. Glenn, his wife, and their two young children moved back to Denver, where Glenn would spend most of his time in high-rise buildings talking to lawyers on behalf of ASARCO.

The practical-minded engineer had stepped into a quagmire full of lawyers, and he didn't like his own gaggle any more than he liked the EPA's. He was dealing not only with ASARCO's attorneys, but because ASARCO was the managing—and decidedly more aggressive partner—of the uneasy Res-ASARCO Joint Venture, he was also working with the Joint Venture's separate set of lawyers as well as with Newmont's. It didn't take Glenn long to realize that the lawyers were getting nowhere.

"ASARCO's first position [in response to the EPA's claims] was, 'Go to hell.' When you associate somebody's name with a Superfund site, the first thing they do is haul ass. You don't want any part of that. When they send you that 104e request letter that says 'Welcome to the party,' you hire a lawyer and look for somebody else. Everybody had tangible involvement. If it's $10 million to fix, getting ten people to pay instead of two is a lot cheaper. It's insane. The system is not geared to do dirt work and solve the problem. Superfund is set up to find responsible parties and to pick their pockets.

"The law firm that ASARCO hired was running the show," Glenn continued. "Everybody's objective was always stall, stall, stall. They were out of control. If I'm a law firm, I don't want this case to end. Then I have to find another one. If it goes on forever, I can send my kids to college and buy a ranch in Wyoming. ASARCO realized they had to deal with it. I was told specifically to go down there and ride shotgun on the [company] lawyers. There were lots of times I stood up and told the lawyers they were full of shit."

The absurdity of the situation hit home when Glenn was called upon to explain twelve years of Superfund disputes to newly hired lawyers from a prominent Denver law firm while at a baseball game. "We sat, three of us—me and two freakin' lawyers—and watched a Rockies game—in the family section where I couldn't even drink beer! I had to attempt to get them up to speed so they could represent us. That didn't sit well with me, and I fought from that moment on to get rid of them. It took me a while, but I got rid of them."

As negotiations with various parties continued, Glenn grew increasingly frustrated. In his estimation, three-quarters of the money—everybody's money: the EPA's, ASARCO's, the other PRPs'—was being spent in Denver when it should have been going toward cleanup work in Leadville. "For me as an engineer, I look at how I can move the most amount of dirt for the least amount of money. With Superfund, it was all paperwork. We, the PRP group in general, were spending a phenomenal amount of money on lawyers and consultants, bickering back and forth, doing studies, and trying to argue liability. The law was pretty clear. There's no argument to liability. Suck it up. You can spend everything you have battling that issue, and you'll never win. There's no precedent for it, and there's no out. My argument was: okay, accept the liability, lose the lawyers, and start doing the work."

ASARCO refused to acquiesce, however, despite Judge Carrigan's quick and unequivocal summary judgment against the PRPs in 1985. As the years dragged on, it became increasingly apparent that paying the lawyers to fight Superfund was costing ASARCO more than if it had just paid for the cleanup in the first place. The company occasionally won minor battles in court, forcing adjustments to the EPA's proposals, but it was certainly losing the war.

Even as officials continued to deny responsibility, the first hint of a willingness to compromise emerged in the early 1990s, and it came in the form of Glenn Anderson's efforts. Early in his tenure, he approached Ken Wangerud with a proposal. He wanted to appease his engineer's sensibility to construct something as the endless talk in Denver continued, but he also wanted to demonstrate to the town that ASARCO was the good guy—a responsible company actually doing something to help the town.

Fixing East 5th Street was the obvious choice. Lined with one-hundred-year-old houses, the street climbed up the hill away from Harrison Avenue. After a mile, the now dirt road curved upward along the contour of Stray Horse Gulch past Finntown, a ghost town since the last Finn was dragged down to Leadville in 1964, and into the heart of the mining district where the town's best-known waste dumps resided. For more than a hundred years, 5th Street had been a conduit for acid mine drainage that flowed off the dumps and traveled down Stray Horse Gulch into town. Early settlers had carved ditches—six feet wide and four feet deep—along both sides of the street to carry the orange sludge down the east side of Leadville. Fifth Street residents crossed small, wooden bridges to get to their homes and driveways. Most of the drainage was caught a few blocks east of Harrison Avenue by the Starr Ditch, which sent it south to California Gulch and the Arkansas River. During heavy rainstorms, though, the ditches overflowed, acid mine drainage spilling into the street and lawns and at times bypassing the Starr Ditch to continue on to Harrison Avenue, over the county courthouse lawn, and down the west side of town. Even when dry, the 5th Street and Starr ditches were stained the same rusty-orange that marked the path of acid mine drainage through California Gulch.

The 5th Street residents weren't worried about a health risk, but the bridges and overflows that damaged their lawns were a nuisance. They welcomed Glenn's plan to fill in the ditches and deliver the runoff to the Starr Ditch via underground pipes. For ASARCO, it was a simple, inexpensive, and popular fix. Ken Wangerud also endorsed the plan. The EPA had long been concerned about the drainage. Driving up the street, Wangerud sometimes saw toddlers playing in the orange-stained ditch in their front yards and bicycle tracks up and down Starr Ditch. For five years, proposals to enclose the Starr Ditch with a chain-link fence had been bantered about, but community opposition had been strong. Carl Miller feared the town would resemble a concentration camp if the fences were installed. Now, with ASARCO willing to cover the 5th Street ditches, Ken decided the time was right to deal with the Starr Ditch as well. "It was a no-brainer. Starr Ditch was sitting there chock loaded with fine-grain silt. You could see Tonka toys in that ditch. I mean, for God's sake, roll that into your risk assessment." ASARCO made it clear that it sided with the town against the fence. But the EPA ordered the company to put up a six-foot-high, chain-link fence along both sides of the Starr Ditch that cut across the east side of town.

The community uproar was instantaneous. The Denver newspapers and a few national ones rushed back to Leadville for more colorful quotes. "I used to wash my hair in that ditch when I was a girl, and I'm just fine," huffed one elderly resident. Someone hung a sign on the fence: "East Berlin Wall, EPA." It was an unexpected public relations coup for ASARCO. The company could shake its head in empathy. It wanted only to do right by the town and was fixing an obvious nuisance (not a health hazard); it was the EPA that had come along and invoked the town's ire yet again with an unnecessary eyesore.

Glenn Anderson insisted later that the company never egged the town on in its opposition to the EPA. "The PRPs didn't have to do anything to poke the town. They were already well-riled and could stay well-riled all on their own. I took some satisfaction in that. In the public meetings, we could just sit there and enjoy it." But the besieged Ken Wangerud felt ASARCO officials were helping to incite opposition, standing up in public meetings after he had spoken and announcing, "That's a crock."

ASARCO's information often contradicted the EPA's findings and conclusions. The company refused to accept the results of Wangerud's residential soil-sampling study because researchers had used field X-ray fluorescent spectrometry, a new, portable technique that could rapidly determine lead concentrations in the soil. A decade later, the technique's use was routine. ASARCO also hired consultants to talk to the residents. Within government circles, they were widely held as "hired guns told what to say by the lead industries," but their presentations were well attended by Leadville residents.

Merrill Coomes, who worked for one of ASARCO's consulting firms, was an occasional speaker. "EPA overstatement likely, advisor says," read the front-page headline in the *Herald Democrat* March 21, 1991. As the EPA prepared to release a health study, ASARCO paid Coomes to come to Leadville to dismiss the results before they were even announced. The "capacity crowd" watched *Big Fears, Little Risks*, a thirty-minute video on "how human health risks from chemical and metal exposure have been blown out of proportion nationally." In his presentation, Coomes dismissed the government's contention that a health risk existed in Leadville. Besides, he insisted, the EPA's plan to remove soils wouldn't work. Within a year, lead returns at the same level it was before, suggesting that background levels of lead are naturally occurring. The EPA, however, denied the assertion that lead migrates to the surface in soil.

In town a year later, Merrill Coomes equated 10 micrograms per deciliter of blood to one ounce of salt in 325,000 tons of french fries, implying that so little could not be harmful. "That is so ridiculous," Chris Weis, the EPA toxicologist, countered later in a rare burst of vexation. "It is so unethical to make that argument that I don't know how they can sleep at night. I can name dozens of toxicants that at 10 micrograms per deciliter would kill you easily. How much is there is not the issue; it's what kind of an effect it has on the central nervous system and how permanent is that effect."

In 1995, ASARCO sent Claire Ernhart to Leadville to further disparage the EPA view. Something of an anti-lead regulation celebrity and a well-known figure to the Centers for Disease Control and Prevention (CDC) and EPA, the psychologist had been one of many scientists hired by the International Lead Zinc Research Organization, an industry trade group, to discredit scientific studies—and the researchers—who were showing that even low levels of lead in young children were a health risk. Ernhart adhered to the poor parenting school of thought on lead poisoning, and for years, she had been an outspoken critic of national policies designed to reduce lead exposure and regulate the lead industry.

In her presentation at the National Mining Museum and Hall of Fame in Leadville, Ernhart and Henrietta Sachs, another opponent of national lead policies, were introduced as experts with thirty years of experience in early childhood development. Except for ASARCO's sponsorship of the public forum, no mention was made of Ernhart's ties to industry either at the meeting or in the three front-page newspaper articles dedicated to her opinions. "Both experts agreed that residents are being largely misled when they are told that child blood lead levels above 10 micrograms per deciliter (μg/dl) are cause for concern," the *Herald Democrat* reported. The two speakers had opposed the CDC's 1991 decision to lower the acceptable blood lead level from 25 to 10 micrograms. They cited studies that showed a significant drop in lead exposure levels nationwide, not because of the soil-treatment programs but because of the ban on leaded gasoline. Ernhart didn't mention that she had fought that ban as well. "The major lead problem today is bullets," Ernhart said, repeating her oft-used remark on her circuit through the western mining towns.

The public disparagement of the EPA provided the townsfolk with ammunition to question and to counter Wangerud's every move. "EPA meeting turns into a scrap," reported the front-page headline in the *Herald Democrat* on April 23, 1992. Residents had objected to the EPA's use of field X-ray fluorescent spectrometry. Ken didn't decry ASARCO's tactic to discredit him. The company was a heavyweight opponent in the arena, and Ken expected nothing less. Leadville residents appreciated ASARCO's alternative messages. They regarded it as a jury would a defense witness in a trial. They would decide for themselves which side was telling the truth—or if the truth lay somewhere in between.

By 1993 it looked as if lead—the ingested kind—was indeed a health problem, though not as prevalent as originally predicted. The results of Robert Bornschein's blood lead study of the town were in. More than three hundred children had participated, about 65 percent of Leadville's children, and the results found that 8.8 percent of them had blood lead levels over 10 micrograms per deciliter—not 41 percent as the IEUBK model had first predicted. On the east side of town, in Stringtown, and at the Lake Fork Trailer Park at the confluence of California Gulch and the Arkansas River the numbers reached 22 percent. The average blood lead level for the entire town was only 4.8 micrograms, and the highest blood lead hit just 16.7 micrograms. The EPA, ASARCO, and the town all claimed victory. Nine percent was much lower than the EPA's original prediction and the state's previous results, and Leadville felt vindicated. Their town wasn't the diseased community the EPA and the national media made it out to be. "This is nothing compared to what you see in the inner cities," a Lake County Health Department employee told the *USA Today* in 1994. "Of course there's no one to pay the bill there. The EPA sees a mining company with deep pockets here."

Leadville's blood lead levels were lower than the nation's inner cities, where lead paint was still prevalent. That Leadville wasn't as bad as the worst became a popular justification for getting the EPA to leave their yards alone, and it remained a common refrain a decade later. The EPA, however, preferred to make comparisons to the national average, and Leadville's total blood level average was 1 to 2 micrograms higher than that. For some, Bornschein's results proved that the state's 1987 study had been wrong. In fact, Leadville was following the national trend. The nation's blood lead levels had dropped as the use of leaded gasoline declined. America's average blood lead level was 15 micrograms in the late 1970s, but by the 1990s it was just 3.6 micrograms. Colorado's health department also pointed to the educational efforts it had implemented in Leadville and to a new day care center that had opened in 1988; with so many parents driving over the hill to work in the ski resorts, many children now spent much of their time in a lead-free environment at day care.

To the EPA, 9 percent was over the agency's 5 percent acceptable risk level, and 22 percent was cause for alarm. "Central nervous system poisoning in kids is not something we take lightly," Chris Weis told the *Rocky Mountain News*. "When 20 percent of the kids are at risk, that's high enough that we're required to address the situation. It's often painful, but that's got to take place. And that will take place whether or not we have critics." Townsfolk were worried. What did "address the situation" mean exactly?

In Midvale, Utah, outside Salt Lake City, it had meant replacing six hundred yards, cutting down trees, and uprooting rose bushes to lower the soil contamination from 1,500 parts per million lead to 500 parts per million. It was a drastic measure that had infuriated many of that mining town's residents. A subsequent study found that blood lead levels had dropped by only half a microgram, though some dispute the before-and-after blood lead studies as unequal measures.

Expensive and widespread soil lead removal programs were taking place in former mining and smelter towns throughout the nation.

Leadville residents knew what was taking place in Midvale—ASARCO had made sure of that—and they were adamant that their town would not suffer the same fate. To a great extent, what would happen in Leadville would depend on Ken Wangerud. As project manager he had tremendous authority over the remedies implemented in the town, and if he followed the EPA guidelines coming out of Washington, any yard with greater than 500 parts per million lead would have to be removed. Despite his unsavory reputation in Leadville, Ken didn't believe wholesale yard removal was necessary. If 500 parts per million were truly harmful in Leadville, the blood lead levels would be much higher. But the question remained: how much lead in the soil was dangerous? If not 500 parts per million, then what?

Judge Jim Carrigan was getting antsy. Ten years had passed since he had been handed some of the nation's first Superfund mining cases. He had found the PRPs liable in under half an hour and had been ruling on pieces of the Leadville case ever since. Now, the sixty-three-year-old judge was ready to retire. He, at least, was ready to wrap things up. Richard Dana, the "special master," continued trying to corral the lawyers into a settlement. Glenn Anderson had had it with the lawyers and, by this time, Ken Wangerud was ready to settle the lawsuit as well.

No one—not the EPA, not the PRPs, and not the Federal District Court system—wanted the case to go to trial, a tremendously expensive proposition that would tie up the courts for years. But ten years as a Superfund site, and all Leadville had to show for it was a new treatment plant, just coming on line, and the "East Berlin Wall." And the squabbling continued. Judge Carrigan decided some additional motivation was in order. He set a trial date for August 1993 and urged everyone to find a way to compromise before then, "unless you want to break in a new judge and start all over again," he warned.

Bob Elder was more than ready to settle. Six years had passed since he had lain in his hospital bed and felt the weight of the federal government bearing down on him. ASARCO had millions of dollars to fight its lawsuit. Bob was an unemployed ex-Climax engineer, married to a schoolteacher and raising a teenager in Leadville. He faced liability penalties worth millions that could wipe him out. His daughter had told a MacNeil/Lehrer NewsHour reporter that she worried about her own future when she inherited the land. Bob had become depressed and irritable. His peptic ulcer attacks had intensified, and the tension in Bob's marriage had mounted until he and his wife divorced in 1989.

All anyone who opposed Superfund, who felt its liability provisions were unfair, had to do was point to Bob Elder. To Leadville's residents, what happened to Bob represented what scared them most about Superfund and the federal government. He was one of them, a third-generation Leadvillite who had inherited a few worthless mining claims from his granddad, and the feds were putting him through hell. So when the state's attorney general office sued the town's residents and urged them to comply, or when Ken Wangerud offered a "letter of comfort" to assuage concerns about cooperating with the federal government, they thought of Bob.

After Bob had received the EPA's letter, he had driven to Denver to hire an attorney (his first Leadville lawyer had quickly realized he was in over his head), and the two began conferring with the EPA. They hired consultants to study Bob's claims and submit reports to the EPA. The whole thing was costing Bob tens of thousands of dollars. Much of the succeeding years were spent waiting, worrying, paying his attorney fees, and tending to his ulcers while the EPA figured out what it wanted to do with Bob Elder. His daughter grew up and moved away to college, and Bob remarried, to a woman he admired for her "ability to cope."

After six years as a PRP, Bob still didn't understand why he had been singled out. Hundreds of names popped up in the landowner records at the country courthouse. The Elder claims were fractured into hundreds of pieces and "Robert Elder" (that Bob shared his father's name may have contributed) appeared frequently. By 1992, results from Wangerud's blitz of studies showed that most of Bob's claims were either outside the Superfund area or were ultimately judged not harmless, leaving just the Big Chief, a mere two-and-a-half-acre claim in Stray Horse Gulch worth about $500. "The way my attorneys expressed it, they said the procedure was something like: ready, fire, aim," Bob would say later. "The 'aim' part was left out in determining who would be responsible parties."

With those results, together with Judge Carrigan holding everyone's feet to the fire with a court date, the EPA was finally ready to let Bob Elder go. In the end, all that the agency required was access to his property for cleanup work. "I would have done that in the first place," Bob murmured ten years later, looking down at his long fingers wrapped around a teacup ringed with roses. He was sitting in the parlor of his old family home, surrounded by his grandparent's furniture, his great-grandparents looking down from their portraits on the wall, and the old upright piano resting in the corner. Bob's inheritance had cost him $50,000 in legal fees, peace of mind, and a wife.

One might expect Bob Elder to feel bitterly about his episode with the federal government, but ten years after he had settled, Bob remained philosophical. "It's part of life experience. We don't always know why these things happen, but you just have to go through it. You have to look at the other peoples' perspective, too. They're just doing their job. You can't take it personally."

One Leadville man would say of Bob, "I asked Bob Elder one time, I said, 'How do you put up with all the problems that EPA has given you?' Because if you listen to what he had to go through, it was devastating to he and his family, a living hell. He says to me, 'What choice did I have? I couldn't stand up to 'em. I couldn't bury my nose in the sand. All I could do was work with them and try to get the best settlement I could out of 'em.' He's a remarkable man. When your business is mining, you expect risk a little bit more than you do when it's just your legacy."

10

"Beyond Denial"

As Judge Jim Carrigan's ultimatum approached, six of the smaller PRPs settled with the EPA one by one, primarily for small financial fines or access to their land. The holdouts were the Atlas Mortgage Company, whose tenacious owner in California would hold out to the bitter end before he, too, settled, and the big companies: Hecla Mining, Denver and Rio Grande Western Railroad, ASARCO, Resurrection and its parent company, Newmont, and the Res-ASARCO Joint Venture. Once or twice a month, for three or four days at a time, Richard Dana, the special master assigned to ride herd over the lawyers, would meet with his charges, and occasionally with technical types like Wangerud and Anderson, and divide them into a suite of conference rooms somewhere in downtown Denver. As the lawyers on each team discussed their position, Dana would go from room to room, maneuvering among them. "Judge Dana would engage in this Henry Kissinger–type shuttle diplomacy where he would try to sell an idea to each party," recalled Nancy Mangone, a diminutive, intrepid young EPA lawyer.

Richard Dana, "Dick," no longer had much twang left from his childhood spent in Borger in the Texas Panhandle, where his dad had been a geologist until the oil dried up and most of Borger along with it. Dick left his hometown for college and ended up a lawyer in Boulder, Colorado, where he married and raised his children. He started in the prosecutor's office and became a state judge by the age of thirty-one until, in his mid-forties, he opened the Judicial Arbiters Group, or JAG, with a colleague. In the mid-1980s, hiring mediators was common, but annexing it to the judicial process, as Judge Carrigan had done by hiring JAG to keep the Superfund case out of court, was relatively new. "I made a fortune, candidly, through these cases," Dana said later—a nice windfall that he considered a bad sign for Superfund. "Any law that invites this much litigation is poorly drafted. Why should you pass a law that is so complicated that everyone spends more on lawyers than they do on the technical side solving the problem? It should encourage people to clean things up. This law doesn't. This law encourages people to have lawsuits."

It was Judge Dana's job to get everyone past the lawsuit phase and accept that it was time to clean up the Leadville Mining District. But even as the mining companies came to accept that they would have to do something, arguments over the amount of responsibility ground on. "We got a lot done one day standing on a tailings pile with Judge Carrigan," Dana remembered. "That broke things loose a little bit. It's almost easier sometimes to get people to look at it and say, 'Could we do this? Could we do that?' To brainstorm it standing there."

But setbacks occurred. In August 1988, Colorado's Division of Wildlife, in attempting to kill off an introduced species in a nearby reservoir, unintentionally released the toxin into the upper Arkansas River and killed all of the fish. Though the trout were restocked in time for the Labor Day weekend, it confounded the negotiations. "So we're sitting here arguing about fish kills and fish counts and all of a sudden there aren't any fish for like twenty miles below Leadville," Dana recalled. "They're all dead courtesy of the wildlife service. It's very difficult to measure the metal loading in the fish population when there aren't any fish."

A bigger source of frustration came from the unfortunate Leadville

Mine Drainage Tunnel, built and abandoned by the federal Bureau of Mines during World War II and the Korean War. The tunnel, which started in the mining district and traveled to the north end of town, had been dumping more than two million gallons of contaminated groundwater into the Arkansas several miles upstream of the California Gulch confluence every day since it had been built. Soon after the war, the Bureau of Mines managed to unload the tunnel on the Bureau of Reclamation, which purchased it for $1, believing the water flowing out of the tunnel would supplement an extensive transmountain water diversion project the agency was planning. After it was completed in 1985, the Frying Pan-Arkansas Project, as it was called, carried irrigation and drinking water from Colorado's western mountains to the Front Range via the Arkansas River. But Reclamation's dollar was not the bargain it had seemed. By the time the project got underway in the late 1960s, the bureau learned that someone else had already purchased the rights to the water the Leadville Mine Drainage Tunnel contributed to the Arkansas, leaving the bureau with a useless tunnel. Worse yet, the water pouring out of the tunnel was contaminated with heavy metals, and new environmental regulations were requiring the bureau to clean it.

It took a Sierra Club lawsuit to force it, but the Bureau of Reclamation finally began designing a water treatment plant at the same time the EPA and the mining companies were negotiating the Yak Tunnel's treatment plant. Everyone could see that it would be cheaper to build just one facility, but Reclamation just wouldn't play ball. "We couldn't even get them to talk," Dana recalled. "They didn't want to get involved in the rest of the case, even though it made perfect economic sense to talk about it." One treatment plant, placed at the bottom of the gulch along the Arkansas River, would have caught contaminated water from both tunnels. Tens of millions might have been saved. But then, some in Leadville had been saying that for years. So as ASARCO was building its Yak Treatment Plant up in California Gulch, at the other end of Leadville, the Bureau of Reclamation was constructing its own facility. To Leadvillites, that the portal of the Bureau's tunnel remained outside the Superfund boundaries was evidence that ASAR-CO was being milked, while upstream, one government agency was back-patting another. "I was mad as hell about that," recalled Jim Martin. "You talk about prejudice." Evidence mounted when ASARCO claimed its plant cost $13 million while Reclamation's came in at just $6 million. But that accusation depended on where the lines were drawn around the accounting books and overlooked the differences in water that had to be treated. (Unlike the Yak, which drained through sulfidic-ore that generated acid, Reclamation's tunnel drained through carbonates, the water slightly basic by the time it reached the treatment plant.)

Despite the missteps, several novel concepts came out of the California Gulch negotiations. EPA engineers commonly created operable units, or OUs, to divide complex sites into manageable work areas. In California Gulch, the lawyers used the operable units already mapped to divvy up liability as well. The site as a whole had twelve operable units. California Gulch itself had three separate operable units, Stray Horse and Evans gulches together was another, the Apache Tailing Impoundment was another, and so on. Jim Martin would become adept at talking about his community in operable units.

Hecla Mining was the first of the big companies to find a way out of the Superfund negotiations. Its operations had been limited to a portion of Operable Unit 2, Malta Gulch, a small strip of land west of Leadville, and the company agreed to pay the EPA for its share of the contamination. The Denver and Rio Grande Western, which had purchased slag piles in the 1960s and 1980s to use for railroad ballast, also got out early. Studies had shown that intact slag, even when used as ballast, wasn't harmful. The railroad agreed to separate and contain the more hazardous crushed slag in its settlement with the EPA.

That left ASARCO, Resurrection, and the Res-ASARCO Joint Venture. "The OUs were a good idea," Glenn Anderson recalled, adding that they divided the site into negotiable pieces. "Something had to break. The stall tactic was becoming more costly than just getting on with it." To break the logjam, Glenn and Ken Wangerud were convinced they needed to come up with technical—not legal—solutions, and they began meeting with others technically inclined, including a few Leadville residents, like Jim Martin. "The lawyers were welcome to attend, but they had to sit in the back and not say anything. Of course, a lot of that was more joke than reality, but we generally ignored them," Glenn recalled.

"We said, 'Okay, we all have some responsibility,'" he continued. "Settling some of it was easy; other parts were more difficult . . . there were all of these arguments. The city built the alleys and subdivisions out of mine waste, for example. So we shuffled it all around. I'll suck up this one, if you suck up that one. We negotiated this goddamn thing for a long time, and it was not easy. But it all got settled."

Many agreed that the case was settled because the federal government was willing to take a big piece of the operable-unit puzzle, largely at the insistence of the forever-prodding Judge Dana. Stray Horse Gulch had been an important World War II mining area. A man named John Hamm had operated a mill in Stray Horse Gulch in the 1940s and left behind the "sand dunes" and other ruins after World War II. He was a "delightful seventy-eight-year-old man" living in California, remembered Nancy Mangone, the EPA lawyer. Hamm enjoyed telling stories of the mining fortunes he had made and lost over his lifetime, but now he was an old man, living on his retirement. "You can't get blood from a stone," Mangone explained. "He had no assets that we could or wanted to go after. This was, by the way, after the settlement with Bob Elder so our thinking on this stuff had evolved." With no responsible party, Stray Horse Gulch was an "orphan." Superfund sites were normally either designated as orphans, in which case the EPA used Superfund money to pay for the cleanup, or PRPs picked up the entire tab. In the past, the courts had apportioned orphans among the remaining PRPs. Dana wanted an exception. If the government accepted Stray Horse Gulch as an orphan, it would go a long way toward encouraging the PRPs to settle.

Eventually, the federal government relented. The EPA had sucked one up, and the others followed suit. The agreement set a precedent and required approval from EPA headquarters in Washington, D.C. Compared to the estimated $140 million in remediation work Newmont and ASARCO were agreeing to, Region 8 assured headquarters, Stray Horse Gulch was small-time. The implications of EPA's agreement extended to the state. Under Superfund, the state must pay 10 percent of the EPA's "orphan" costs and is responsible for maintaining the site once the EPA is gone. With Stray Horse Gulch, the state's stake in Leadville went up dramatically, but the settlement was an important one. Dana believed the key to success in Leadville was simply perseverance. "We just talked and talked and talked. You wear people out after fourteen years. They give up. Uncle. Don't call me anymore."

While Leadville's mining district was being divvied up among the PRPs, Operable Unit 9 — residential soils — remained a hotly contested issue. Many of the yards had been contaminated by smelter emissions, and there was no question — by now even to ASARCO itself — that the company would have to accept responsibility for Operable Unit 9 and clean up Leadville's soils. In the region's early history, smelters had surrounded the town. By the twentieth century, only ASARCO's Arkansas Valley Smelter, the giant complex southwest of Leadville, remained. The railroad had bought its black slag, but ASARCO was now responsible for what had spewed out of its smokestacks and settled over Leadville and Stringtown's yards and playgrounds for more than sixty years.

ASARCO officials, including Glenn Anderson, insisted that no health risk existed in Leadville from lead or arsenic in the soil. The EPA had not found arsenic in large-enough quantities to be a health risk (though the state would question that finding later). For now, lead was the metal du jour. With Judge Carrigan's deadline approaching, Anderson and Wangerud needed to find a way to settle. What they came up with is clearly laid out in the administrative record. How they got there is open to interpretation.

"Kids First was my idea," Wangerud asserted a decade later. "At some point, somebody's got to just get away and talk turkey. Glenn and I did that. We agreed that we've got to settle this because if we end up in court, each of us is forced to bet the ranch. It could all come down to one big showdown on main street in federal court. I was very candid with Glenn. I said, 'Look, I really don't give a crap about what is going on here, whether it's science or whether it's politics or whether it's blatant, self-interest public relations, but I believe to my core that there are kids at risk in Leadville, and if there is a mom in that town who believes she's got a kid at risk, I think ASARCO should take care of that kid first and start tomorrow.' That conversation turned into the Kids First program, and Glenn agreed to it, God bless him."

To EPA insiders, the Kids First program was either a creative solution or a dangerous precedent, but it was a first. Instead of wholesale yard removal, the program adopted a holistic approach, incorporating blood lead monitoring, education, and testing for lead from a variety of sources. The program would be voluntary, but it would include an energetic community awareness component and incentives as blatant as cash. If a child under seven or a pregnant or nursing woman had a blood lead level higher than 10 micrograms, then any and all lead sources would be identified and remedied whether it was in the soil, paint, or plumbing fixtures — right down to the mini-blinds and imported pottery. ASARCO also agreed to remove or cap any yards or playgrounds that tested above 2,000 parts per million lead.

Two thousand parts per million. Results from Wangerud's flurry of studies, the much-maligned pig studies and Bornschein's blood lead study were pointing the EPA's toxicologists toward a risk threshold substantially higher than EPA's guidance. The "pig studies" were proving that different lead types were absorbed in the body at differing amounts, though few, if any, caused no harm, as the mining companies insisted. But at a site like Leadville, with twenty different types of lead, removing all yards as if they contained the highly absorbable smelter soot was unnecessary as well. "As a biologist, I was happy to live with a wide range of risk values, although I'm sure it gave the project managers headaches," Chris Weis, the EPA toxicologist, recalled.

The EPA had accumulated enough information to design an intricately orchestrated cleanup plan with a variety of soil lead action levels, but the logistics would have been nightmarish. Instead of one argument over one action level, there would have been dozens. Ken Wangerud needed to take a number—that bright line above which yards would be replaced—to ASARCO, a number the toxicologists felt comfortable with and that ASARCO would agree to. "That value was basically negotiated based upon what we knew, the scientific story that we had woven together, coupled with political and financial realities of the overall cleanup," Weis said later.

The number was important, but the Kids First program was the critical element, ensuring that children with high blood lead levels were helped regardless of the level of lead in their backyards. Ken Wangerud considered it a "strategic surgery plan to only do remediation on those kinds of lead sites that really needed cleanup." Ken's version of the negotiations has him in a downtown Denver bar offering Glenn a choice, agree to 2,000 parts per million or fight it. That number was his bottom line. "Glenn and I had a great relationship," Ken recalled. "I thought Glenn was a straight-up guy, and I respected what he was doing. He and I could fight like hell. But at the end of the day, we could both say that we did a good job, let's go have a beer."

Glenn snorted at the suggestion that Ken muscled ASARCO. "We worked Wangerud. I disliked the guy from the very beginning. He was really big on all of this shit that didn't accomplish anything. Blood lead studies were showing that cleaning up residential soils made no difference. In fact, the act of cleaning up the soils made the risk greater than not doing anything. We couldn't make it go away, but we did make them see that the level for cleanup is an ambiguous line. If you have a kid with high lead, jump on it, figure out why, and take care of it." Because Kids First would extend indefinitely, ASARCO would cover the anticipated cleanup costs with an $8.6 million trust fund, another innovative idea that would prove vital to the program's success.

Regardless of the impetus behind Kids First, somehow through the haze of distrust and the egos, the EPA and ASARCO had finally reached across the arena and shaken hands. ASARCO would be legally required to remove any yards that exceeded 2,000 parts per million, but that number was far from solid. It was a legal trigger of sorts, not the final EPA-sanctioned "action level." If the EPA later decided that the action level should be below 2,000 parts per million, ASARCO could take them to court and make them prove it. That scenario was entirely possible. Kids First and 2,000 parts per million was a significant departure from the EPA's guidance, which maintained that the only way to ensure children's health was to cover or remove lead-contaminated soil down to at least 400–1,200 parts per million. To officials at EPA headquarters it seemed risky and to those in other regional offices, negotiating their own settlements, it was a precedent they didn't want repeated. "There were a lot of debates going on about soil action levels within the EPA," Wangerud recalled. "Me and my colleagues disagreed with the EPA's thresholds as vehemently as we disagreed with ASARCO's bullshit on the other end of the spectrum, and we were getting flailed."

Ken Wangerud expended considerable effort convincing officials at EPA headquarters to agree to Kids First and the higher action level, but Leadville residents were less than impressed with 2,000 parts per million as a threshold. Town officials had been kept in the dark during the negotiations despite their desire to be heard, and they would have something to say about 2,000 parts per million—a message they would deliver to EPA headquarters themselves.

Leadville's trust diminished further after EPA headquarters significantly lowered Ken's requested action levels for recreational and commercial zones—areas where children don't receive prolonged exposure. "Your credibility is shot," Bob Casey told Wangerud at a public meeting announcing the news.

In an internal memo, Wangerud reported the feelings in Leadville over the changed action levels. It was "another 'venting' of concerns and issues that we must obviously deal with. The . . . locals made it absolutely clear that they don't trust that Wangerud/Weis or Region 8 speak for EPA. . . . Given the perception (or is it reality) that HQ actually calls the shots on risk assessments, this must be addressed and resolved immediately." Wangerud continued with a resident's quote from a meeting: "'we can only conclude that EPA intends to drive a low enough residential risk number to cause widespread cleanup.' Perception is reality, and that pretty well sums up why heels are digging in on this risk assessment." The battle over soil action levels in Leadville was far from over, but the alliances would shift dramatically.

Using the operable units to divide up liability may have allowed those sitting in the conference rooms day after day, year after year a way to settle, but to the EPA managers that came later, the operable units were too rigid. On a map, operable units divided the Superfund site into color-coded puzzle pieces, but on the ground, the California Gulch watershed was an organic whole. Contamination didn't stop at operable-unit boundaries, but PRPs did. It created situations where orange-colored sludge from one operable unit flowed right past the remedy for sludge created in another operable unit, leaving Leadvillites and future project managers to scratch their heads.

The lawyers also left two operable units undecided. One was Operable Unit 11—the Arkansas Valley Floodplain—Doc's meadows, where everyone's mining waste eventually accumulated. No PRP had taken responsibility, and the operable unit was listed as a "Future Liability Determination." Eleven years had passed since Doc had first called in the cavalry and so far precious little attention had been paid to his metal-laden soils.

And then there was Operable Unit 12—water quality for the entire Superfund site. Just how clean was clean enough? "We were always having arguments about how clean is clean," recalled Dana. "How clean should it be? If you spend enough money, you can make it pristine, but is that practical? We've mucked it up so badly that we'll never know what the background level of lead was before mining." The lawyers decided that others could answer those questions another day. Instead of cleaning up each operable unit to meet specific standards, everyone would wait until all of the remedies were done, then decide if the Arkansas River was clean enough. To some, this was another case of ready, fire, aim. Years later, when the firing was done, who would decide if the cleanup had hit the target? How tempting would it be, particularly given the enormous costs and the predictable reaction to more years of Superfund, to inch the target closer to where the bullet had landed?

By 1994, all twelve operable units within Leadville's Superfund boundary had been assigned to a PRP, left as an orphan for the EPA to clean up, or deferred for future government and mining company officials to sort out. On August 26, Judge Carrigan signed the Consent Decree that outlined ASARCO's, Newmont's, and their Joint Venture's Superfund responsibilities. The Consent Decree ushered in a new era in Leadville's battle with the EPA, and the faces on the front lines would soon change. Ten years, eleven months, and eighteen days after the "fast track" Superfund program officially came to Leadville, the work could finally begin in earnest. Judge Carrigan gathered up his cartoons, his green pens, and his Groucho Marx glasses and retired to his home, his wife, and their grandchildren.

More than twenty years after the first Earth Day, ASARCO, the company born a century earlier as a conglomerate determined to control mining and smelting worldwide, was "beyond denial," the phrase company officials used to describe ASARCO's turnaround in its approach toward Superfund. The company didn't completely roll over at all of its sites nationwide—some, such as its struggle with the federal government at Coeur d'Alene, Idaho, would eventually go to trial—but it had come to accept that environmental concerns and the regulations they spawned would not go away no matter how many lawyers were put to the task, and it began negotiating with the EPA in earnest at a number of sites.

Leadville

The character of Superfund was changing as well. CERCLA, the Superfund law, was intended to be a "fast-track" solution to cleaning up the nation's hazardous waste sites. But despite the changes made through the Superfund Amendments and Reauthorization Act (SARA) of 1986, Superfund cleanup was still anything but fast for abandoned mining sites like Leadville. Of the handful of western mining sites listed alongside Leadville in 1983—places like Butte, Montana; Bunker Hill, Idaho; and Iron Mountain Mine near Redding, California—few, if any, had been cleaned up completely or removed from the National Priority List, and many more mining sites had joined their ranks. Superfund had been intended to bypass the courts, but fights over liability persisted. The RAND Institute for Social Justice estimated that about one-third of the $3 billion Superfund had dispersed in its first decade had gone to administrative and legal costs. The same was true of the $11 billion the private sector had spent. To speed up the process, the Clinton administration began a series of reforms to clarify liability and cleanup standards.

CERCLA (the Comprehensive Environmental Response, Compensation, and Liability Act) was also up for Congressional reauthorization. A decade earlier, SARA's passage had been a contentious battle spanning two years, and in 1995, industry supporters again lobbied to weaken CERCLA. This time, the Republican-led Congress complied and failed to reauthorize CERCLA. The law remained in force through ongoing resolutions, but the Superfund tax expired. Without the $1 billion-a-year income, the Superfund used to clean up the nation's most toxic waste sites would eventually run out.

While Congress argued over the law, in Leadville, as the weather warmed and the snows melted in the spring, the clear mountain water began its annual migration down the gulches, turning orange as it passed by the waste dumps and tailing piles on its way to the Arkansas River. With the Consent Decree imminent, a group of politicians, including the state's attorney general, Gale Norton, and the EPA's recently appointed Region 8 administrator, William Yellowtail, came to Leadville for a tour. The star attraction was the Yak Treatment

Plant, a corrugated, utilitarian building southeast of town, that had been operating for two years. The millions of gallons of acid mine drainage flowing out of the Yak Tunnel, its portal now a concrete reinforced entrance with steel doors, poured into a large red pond. Lime and other chemicals dropped the heavy metals out until clean, neutral water flowed out the other end. That it hit the Apache Tailing Impoundment several hundred feet later, picking up new metals on its way to the Arkansas River, was a problem for another day. For now, the treatment plant had already had an enormous impact on the river.

Fish were living longer and growing bigger, and there were more of them. The trout were even making it up to Doc Smith's stretch of the river—the "dead zone." The fish still weren't as big, as long-lived, or as dense as they were farther south, but wildlife officials predicted conditions would continue to improve. The river was doing so well that a new public access point just downstream of Leadville opened a few years later. Newspaper articles would encourage Colorado's fishermen to check out the upper Arkansas, assuring them it wouldn't "eat holes in your waders." "The U.S. Environmental Protection Agency deserves top credits," the *Rocky Mountain News* wrote. "Without the EPA's highly successful watershed cleanup efforts, any new public access would have been irrelevant." The EPA, Superfund, and Leadville were finally getting some good press.

After the tour that summer day in 1994, town residents aired their ongoing concerns. They didn't want "another ten years to go by" before the EPA left town for good. The new EPA regional administrator promised greater public participation. "I'm very impressed with your genuine commitment to environmental issues," Yellowtail told the audience, adding that he hoped the experiences gained in Leadville would help "break the old mold of how CERCLA operates."

Kids First was the program everyone was watching. That fall, it was officially unveiled in Leadville. Glenn Anderson and Ken Wangerud stood united, urging parents with young children to participate in this voluntary program. The town's reaction was mixed. Jim Martin and Bob Casey believed the program was an excellent compromise that would address the actual problems, not those identified by some computer in Denver. But others remained defiant, the adversarial stance too deeply entrenched. "It would be dealing with the enemy and bringing the EPA down on the neighborhoods," one resident stated. Another complained that people were enticed with incentives to enter the program.

A man with young children, still upset ten years later, said of Kids First, "I told them, 'You're not coming on my property to sample my soil. I don't want anyone on my property except for me and who I invite. But you had some poor people in town who said, 'Hey, this is great. We can have the EPA come in here and we can get a whole new grassy lawn. We can get our driveway paved.' Because you know they're going to find some lead in the soil because that's what they're looking for. ASARCO is spending millions of dollars to do something that doesn't need to be done. They use scare tactics with ads. Lead paint in houses—what does that have to do with the EPA, mining, and water quality?"

Despite the strong emotions of some, after eleven years spent fighting the EPA, Leadville's citizenry was tired. The previously well-attended meetings dwindled to mostly bureaucrats and town officials. "I went to all the meetings at first because it was very important that you keep knowledgeable," one energetic woman in her eighties would say later. "But, you know, you go on with your life. You can spend ten years, and then pretty soon you just say, 'Ah well, to heck with it.'" Just when the EPA wanted the town to pay attention—to volunteer for an innovative program that might prevent wholesale yard removal if enough families participated—people were tuning out. Jim Martin ruefully noted that no qualified parents had attended the Kids First unveiling. Even the Environmental Task Force, a hardworking, persistent voice for ten years, was limping along. Its membership had dropped precipitously and the group would soon call it quits.

While most of the town retreated, Jim and Bob Casey knew they were just getting started. Residents could soon expect to see bulldozers and caterpillars crawling around east of town. The Consent Decree had settled *who* would do the work, not *how* the cleanup would proceed. The commissioners had been left out of the Consent Decree negotiations, but they were determined that Leadvillites would have a say in what happened to their town.

While the commissioners dug in, convinced that working with the EPA was the quickest way to get them out, another pair of prominent residents were more determined than ever to undermine the EPA's Leadville work. To Ken Chlouber and Carl Miller, the Consent Decree only further entrenched the federal government in Leadville. Carl, now director of the National Mining Hall of Fame and Museum in Leadville and three years away from becoming a state representative, lamented that the mining companies had "caved in to those people."

By early 1994, state representative Ken Chlouber was ramping up the rhetoric. "The EPA, using our own tax dollars, said it is unhealthy to breathe the air and drink the water," he said at a public meeting. He might have at least gotten the facts straight; the EPA had, in fact, deemed the air healthy and the drinking water safe (unless Chlouber was referring to the orange sludge draining out the Yak.) But unlike commissioners Martin and Casey, his intention was demonstrably not constructive dialog with the EPA. He was on a mission, and his message was clear and unwavering: "My one aim, my one goal, is to get the EPA out of my community. The greatest catastrophe that has ever been visited on this community is the EPA," the laid-off Climax miner said at a public forum.

It was on May 9, 1994, that the vitriolic Chlouber proposed execution. Speaking at a national Republican Party conference in Denver, Chlouber stood in front of politicians from around the nation, and announced: "We're telling EPA: 'Get out of town.' My suggestion is to simply hang one at each end of town. In my community, that is the voice of moderation."

The newspapers reported this Wild West call to lynch federal government officials and would repeat it whenever Leadville's story was told to illustrate just how bad things had gotten. But now the articles were tempered by reports of fish in the upper Arkansas; some progress was being made. When Ken Wangerud, the EPA official at the top of Leadville's hit list, read Chlouber's statement in the *Denver Post*, he drove to Hugh Woods Hardware store. "I bought eighteen inches of rope and I made a hanging noose. I tied it on the side of my briefcase and carried it to meetings in Leadville. I jokingly said, 'Well look, if I'm going to hang, I'll bring the rope so it makes it easier for you.' I didn't feel threatened; that was just political posturing. I thought it was funnier than hell." Later that month, Wangerud sent Bill Yellowtail a memo about his meeting with Chlouber in Leadville: "At the end, I chided him by asking if, when we met again, I should bring a rope or a fifth of whisky. . . . He said, 'Don't worry. I've got plenty of rope.'"

Wangerud may have been amused, but his superiors were not. A year later, an EPA official, home sick with the flu, was watching news coverage of the Oklahoma City bombing of a federal building that killed 167 people when he read Chlouber's threat to federal employees repeated in the *Denver Post*. Deputy Regional Administrator Jack McGraw was then moved to write a letter to the editor: "This type of barbaric behavior is not a joking matter; it is not what Colorado deserves in its legislature. . . . If an elected lawmaker suggests hanging EPA employees for doing their jobs, can we be surprised if other zealots use car bombs?"

Commissioners Martin and Casey weren't advocating lynching, but they were eager to run Wangerud out of town. Jim Martin considered him personable, but "domineering and haughty. I thought he was a dodo. He's the son of a buck who's responsible for making this damn site so big. He went sampling everywhere." Others in town remember Wangerud as "a control freak" and "condescending," and observed that "he wanted to control things so much that nothing really got done because everybody had their back up" and that "he thought he was saving Leadville from itself."

The commissioners decided to take action. On a beautiful summer day, they invited Yellowtail back to Leadville for a public meeting.

People had another opportunity to air their complaints to the EPA regional administrator, but the meeting wasn't the reason for the visit. Afterward, Casey invited the fellow westerner for a ride in his pickup. As the two drove past spindly orange poppies spilling out of Leadville's yards, Casey laid it out. "I said, 'We can't work with Ken Wangerud. We need a clean slate, if we're going to get anything done.' He seemed to understand."

The town's appeal to the EPA's top regional boss coincided with Ken's own realization that his time in Leadville was up, and he asked to be reassigned. "You don't have the same general who fought the war come in and do the reconstruction afterwards. I'm sure there were plenty of people who were pretty damn tired of Wangerud by this time. I was not the person to carry on at Leadville."

Wangerud's departure made the front page of the *Herald Democrat*. Glenn Anderson was also reassigned—to Kamchatka in remote northeast Russia to work on a mining program that threatened salmon runs. (In 2000, the man who bled the color of ASARCO baby blue retired as the company's fortunes changed in the new century.)

Years later, Wangerud remained a vilified character to those who remember his tenure in the early 1990s. His demeanor infuriated the town. He was tenacious, process oriented, and stubborn, and he just couldn't understand why the town wasn't following the protocol. But he was also trying to make Superfund work in a western mining town. "Ken's the one who really put the bit in his mouth, put his head down, and negotiated a settlement on that case," Weis would say years later. Even an ASARCO employee who arrived long after the dust had settled considered Ken a "scapegoat." Wangerud and the town were caught in the middle of a wider EPA debate on lead hazards at a time when the CDC was pushing lead poisoning as a critical national issue.

Ken wouldn't hesitate to do it again. "I wasn't there to make friends. I was there to find out if there were kids at risk, and if there were, take care of them. I don't believe anybody ever caught on or believed that part of what I was trying to do was save their whole damn town from getting dug up. Leadville was unquestionably the high point of my career. I've never played poker like that before. It was kind of fun. I learned a lot about how one deals with the public. At the end of a hard-fought battle in the arena, if everybody is pissed off at me, short of being absolutely stupid and incompetent, I probably am where I ought to be. Me and my team had lots of people pissed off at us on both ends of the spectrum, and I view that as a good day's work."

11
A New Era

As soon as Bill Yellowtail walked into his new Denver office as EPA regional administrator in January 1994, Leadville became his biggest, most contentious challenge in the entire six-state region. A few weeks into his tenure, state representative Ken Chlouber fired an opening salvo across the new administrator's bow with an editorial in the *Herald Democrat*.

The EPA Must Get Out of Town

Once again, I'm asking you to join me in a cause—no, make that a crusade—by and for the people abiding in our great community today and tomorrow.

I'm asking that we unite as one, standing shoulder to shoulder, arm in arm, against a plague that has been attacking the very core of our community for over 12 years. The scourge is the Environmental Protection Agency. They must go and the[y] must go now!

The time for compromise is past. The time for negotiation is over. The time for action is now. We have tried compromise. It didn't work. We tried negotiation. It didn't work. . . . It's time the EPA gets out of town. . . .

Before starting this fight, I had to ask myself one question. Do we have a health risk in our community? The answer is we do not. What is at risk here is not only our way of life, but our quality of life. . . .

I have great hope that Mr. Yellowtail will move his troops where they are needed. He seems a good man and a fair man. Hopefully he will be sensitive to our cause [b]ecause of his rural background.

So again, I ask that we unite as one. Give support to our mayor and our county commissioners as they stand firm against those who seek only to destroy our community. Write our congressman and senators with a single message. We will stand for no more insults, intrusion or abuse of our Leadville.

EPA get out of town! I ask for your support in this fight. I have drawn the line. This is where I stand and what I stand for. And on this spot, you can count on me.

Chlouber went to work immediately setting up meeting after meeting with Yellowtail and various state and local politicians, giving everyone a forum to vent repeatedly to the EPA's new boss. Newspaper accounts and meeting notes suggest the theme was always the same. Chlouber didn't want to talk compromise; he would accept only one course of action: the EPA's unconditional surrender in Leadville. Perhaps he thought he could get somewhere with a fellow cowboy-boot-wearing, small-town westerner.

Bill Yellowtail, white-haired, tall, and husky, was a well-known figure in Montana—a success story straight out of one of the poorest areas in the nation—when President Bill Clinton appointed him to head the EPA's Region 8 office covering North Dakota, South Dakota, Montana, Wyoming, Utah, and Colorado. He had been raised on a cattle ranch with no electricity, running water, or telephone by a Crow father and white mother outside Wyola, Montana, on the Crow Reservation. His math smarts had earned him a scholarship to Dartmouth and after a rough adjustment to the Ivy League, he went on to become a cattle rancher and a popular Montana state senator from 1984 to 1993, praised as an environmental "champion," and a man who learned to "walk between two worlds," as he would later tell a reporter. He came to the EPA in 1994 a down-to-earth and charismatic forty-five-year-old, and he sought to use his small-town roots to make the EPA seem less like "jackbooted thugs" than a helpful neighbor. Several years later, Yellowtail's political life would hit the skids, much to Chlouber's open delight.

But in 1994, Yellowtail was a rookie, a political appointee, and trying to figure out what he could do for the troubled Leadville-EPA relations.

From the beginning, Chlouber was the biggest thorn in his side, but even a few months into his tenure, when Chlouber advocated hanging EPA officials at each end of town, Yellowtail wasn't too concerned. "Senator Chlouber was very enthusiastically anti-government, anti-Superfund, and hostile, flat-out hostile," Yellowtail remembered. "I had this image of this guy, Ken Chlouber, as some kind of minor political clown, so I must admit I did not take it seriously. But when the manner began to repeat itself and manifest itself in other forums and quite publicly, then it became clear that this man was serious."

Chlouber kept up the political pressure. In 1995, he introduced House Resolution 95-1011 that asked the U.S. Congress to compel the EPA to remove Leadville from the Superfund list. Colorado's House of Representatives passed the symbolic measure, though Congress didn't comply. The EPA was of course legally mandated to be there. Chlouber next began talking about turning responsibility of the cleanup over to the county and state. Jim Martin and Bob Casey blanched. The county didn't have the resources for such a massive undertaking. The commissioners had plenty of gripes against the EPA and Superfund, but they weren't ready to see the EPA leave just yet. The state wasn't eager to take Leadville on either, citing a lack of resources. Yellowtail was feeling the pressure though. HR 95-1011 may have been symbolic, but the House had gone along. And now Representative Chlouber was gunning for the state of Colorado's health department budget.

Yellowtail wanted to reassure the citizens of Leadville that the EPA's presence in town, now in its twelfth year as a Superfund site, was nearing the end. "Much to the chagrin of staff, I sat in a meeting and I listened to those folks and I said, 'We'll get out of town.' I suspect the staff wasn't happy with me for agreeing to a deadline, and they probably had a much better grasp of the gravity of the situation there and knew that it was going to take longer to get the whole thing done," Yellowtail admitted later. "But I fully expected it to happen."

On May 11, 1995, the region's top boss headed back to Leadville to announce the new schedule. "Yellowtail: EPA will be 'out of town' by 1997" read the front-page headline in the *Herald Democrat*. Leaving in two years was "very ambitious," Yellowtail admitted to the large audience, but he added that with the town's cooperation, it was possible. "I've made a commitment on this timeline and fully expect you to call us on the carpet if we fail to keep that commitment."

One member of the audience remembered Yellowtail's conference this way: "Ol' Bill Yellowtail comes in here with a big ol' hat on and a big belt buckle and boots, and he just looked like a good ol' boy. Chlouber was there, and those boys were just as happy as two clams in mud. But this Bill Yellowtail, he promised something he couldn't deliver. This guy was so out of touch with reality. That's when Ken Chlouber got mad. . . . [Yellowtail] should have never come out here and promised something like that, if he couldn't deliver." But Chlouber was already mad, and Bill Yellowtail had at least bought the EPA some breathing space from Chlouber's relentless insistence to get the hell out of town. It now fell to Leadville's new project managers to try to meet the EPA's admittedly unattainable deadline—or face Chlouber's renewed zeal in two years' time.

"If looks could kill," Mike Holmes remembered thinking as he stepped into the EPA's large conference room in a modern, high-rise office building in downtown Denver. Leadville's county commissioners were cordial, but the animosity was palpable. It brought to mind his first encounter with Leadville on an errand ten years earlier. Back then, he had been a young EPA official on his first Superfund assignment, driving to Leadville to hook up a Stringtown residence to the municipal water supply—a simple plumbing job. Mike, unassuming in his characteristic sweatshirt and work boots, had breezed up to

Leadville in a government-issue white sport utility vehicle ready to help. He had found the water district office right on the main street of the little Victorian mining town and stepped inside. Three scruffy ex-miners leaning against a counter stopped chatting and turned to look at Mike as he stepped forward. "Oh yea, we're just talkin' about ya," one man replied slowly. "We're just trying to decide if we want to tar and feather ya' or hang ya' in the street."

Mike had had no idea of the hostility that existed in Leadville toward the EPA. He had assumed, frankly, that he would be appreciated for helping out a local family. "Ah, I'm just here to hook up the water," Mike had told the three men and quickly got on with the job. Mike's naïveté about the impact Superfund had on mining communities had taken its first hit.

A decade later, Mike knew that the situation in the town had deteriorated dramatically in the intervening years—it regularly made the Denver newspapers. Turmoil over plugging the Yak Tunnel, the Brown Envelope, the emotional fight over yard sampling, the East Berlin Wall, and Wangerud's villainous reputation had all further enraged the town. Chlouber had made his infamous suggestion to lynch EPA officials who set foot in Leadville, and now, Mike's supervisors wanted him to return to Leadville for a few months, just long enough to get some dirt moving. The EPA had a new deadline, and it needed someone who could get things rolling fast. It was already June, and Leadville's summers were short. Bulldozing through the bureaucracy to get the "yellow iron" moving was known as Mike's forte.

For a man whom a supervisor would later describe as "the worst bureaucrat I have ever seen in my life," it was the EPA's bureaucracy that had awed him as a boy and drawn him to the agency as a young man. Mike Holmes grew up in Grundy Center, Iowa, a Newburyesque town of 2,500 that appears out of the cornfields seventy miles northeast of Des Moines. Until Wal-Mart arrived in the early 2000s, forcing local retail businesses to close, Mike's hometown had remained a time capsule from 1955, the year Mike was born. Its four-block-long, turn-of-the-century era downtown of red brick buildings housed a few banks, a couple of pharmacies, and a row of mom-and-pop shops. Folks were friendly, and the kids roamed free. The sixties and most of the seventies never reached Grundy Center.

Not that Mike noticed. He was outside with his friends, losing his shoes in the muddy stream banks, hunting, fishing, and working on the nearby farms. Mike and his younger sister grew up in a little ranch-style house on the edge of town. Mike was close to his affable, outgoing father, who was a well-known figure in town—he made farm loans. In a midwestern small town like Grundy Center, where the tradition of helping your neighbor ran deep and everyone was considered a neighbor, you learned to get along—a skill Mike's wife would later attribute to his success in Leadville, though he would point to the more exotic years spent in the Philippines.

In 1972, on a church-led field trip to Washington, D.C., while in high school, Mike visited the offices of the newly formed EPA. As he walked through the heavy, twin towers on the Waterside Mall, "Environmental Protection Agency" etched in gold paint over the front doors, the small-town farm boy who was always losing his shoes in the creek was awestruck by the size and energy of this new government agency. Soon after that trip, Mike's childhood ended. His parents had divorced, and after he graduated from high school, he followed his father to Colorado. He attended Colorado State University in Fort Collins to study agricultural economics—like his dad.

For Mike and Patty it wasn't necessarily love at first sight. "We were just good friends," Patty Holmes, a slim woman with short red hair and blue eyes, remembered. "We lived in the dorms, and then our group of friends dwindled down to four of us, and then three of us, and then . . . " she trailed off with a shy laugh. "We had so much in common. I spent a long time just getting to know him. The quality I admire most in Mike is his kindness. He's quiet, but he's in there. He's adventuresome. We were always doing really fun stuff."

But Mike's adventurous spirit was drawing him away from Colorado and Patty toward what many adventurous young people did in the 1970s—he joined the Peace Corps. After graduating from college, Mike flew to Costa Rica to train for his Peace Corps assignment, which was to take him to the jungles of Columbia. But it wasn't long before he called from Costa Rica to ask Patty to marry him. He would postpone the Peace Corps duty until she graduated and they could go together.

Two years later the reserved young woman from a Denver suburb found herself with Mike in a small town on Bohol, a tiny, remote island in the Philippines, eating fish, which she despised, working with the local midwives, which she enjoyed, and living in a little shack on a beautiful beach. Mike's job was to improve local farming practices. He climbed over mountain ranges to talk with subsistence farmers and town officials, sailed outrigger boats across the straits to talk with mayors on other islands, and traveled 425 miles and five islands north to Manila to talk with government officials and scientists. It was during the Marcos regime, and political corruption was particularly rampant. "I got a truck full of bagged fertilizer to deliver to one of our projects," Mike recalled. "The truck arrives, and here comes the mayor in his jeep, and he fills the back end of his jeep with the fertilizer. And I'm going nuts with my farmer buddies. 'Why are you letting the mayor take this fertilizer? He can't just take it.' 'Well, we would do the same thing if we were the mayor.' There was this attitude that if you're the mayor, it's part of the kudos of the job. You learned to bite your tongue and stay out of local politics. You just sit and drink coconut wine at the end of the day with the farmers."

Mike and Patty extended their Peace Corps stint to a third year and returned home to Denver only when Patty became pregnant toward the end of that last year. Mike had a particularly difficult time reentering life in Denver. In just three years, keypunch computers had become obsolete, replaced by ubiquitous desktops, and the agricultural economy had dived. "I thought, 'Oh, this is great. I have a pregnant wife, no job, and a degree that wasn't too promising.'" Mike scoured the classifieds. After three years on Bohol, he had learned the local language. "I put, 'I speak Cebuano' on my resume, but it doesn't really help you much." When a laboratory job opened at the EPA's Denver office, Mike jumped at the chance to get his foot in the door. "I still thought the EPA was a cool place, going back ten years before that."

Leadville

Two years later, Mike was an on-scene coordinator in Superfund's emergency response division, and he liked his fast-paced new life dealing with chemical spills, train wrecks, and other immediate environmental or public health hazards. In the 1980s, local authorities weren't yet equipped to handle hazardous material spills. Mike and his coworkers were on call twenty-four hours a day, responding to about 1,200 spills a year in the six-state northwestern region. Mike carried a beeper and was gone more than he was home.

Three years into his new job, Mike was sent to Butte, Montana, Jim Martin's old stomping ground that had once been a thriving copper mining town and had become a Superfund site the same time as Leadville. The contamination issues were similar as well. Acid mine drainage was contaminating the nearby river; mills had dumped fluvial tailings down the creek; and some of the yards in Butte and nearby Walkerville had been blanketed with heavy metals. Butte, with a population of thirty thousand, was much larger than Leadville and the residents more diverse in their reaction to Superfund. Some violently opposed residential cleanup while others looked forward to free landscaping. One woman was even caught "salting" her yard with mine waste because it had not tested high enough for removal—a trick from the old mining days when miners would "salt" a mine with gold or silver to trick potential investors.

"They weren't as resistant as in Leadville, but I still went through life-threatening public meetings," Mike recalled. "Those meetings toughened me up." The baseball field in Walkerville had been built on a mill site; home base had globs of mercury visible in the soil. Cleanup was not negotiable. "They would be yelling and screaming at me and threatening me. But I'd say, 'I'm sorry. This is a dumb place for a ball field. It has to go.' Then I'm worried about getting lynched after the meeting, and they're asking me to go across the street for a beer. I asked them about it, and they laughed and said, 'It's how we make a point.' That's just the way miners are. I learned that it was important to go have a beer and get to know people—not to be a pointy-headed bureaucrat. You need to listen to people and truly understand their concerns. You need to keep your eyes open to ways you can help the community."

After ten years of traveling, hotels, and being on call, Mike was tired. At the same time, his dad, with whom he'd always been so close, was starting to forget things. Mike's sixty-two-year-old father refused to believe the diagnosis despite watching his own father's slow decline from Alzheimer's disease. Mike also had a wife and three young children at home in Denver. When the opportunity arose to take on Leadville, just an hour and a half away, the thought of being home every night with his family was too appealing to pass up.

12

Moving Yellow Iron

Malta Gulch, a little gully filled with lodgepole pines and tailing piles, begins on the western edge of Leadville and slopes gently downhill for three miles before joining California Gulch near the Arkansas River. The placer miners had already combed the gulch searching for gold by the time Louis Pierre Bochatay had looked upon the small homestead of log structures at the bottom of the gulch and envisioned his future. In 1883, he left the sweltering charcoal kilns that supplied the smelter furnaces with fuel, moved his wife and six children to the little farm, plowed a kidney-shaped field of hay in the pine forest and went back to being a dairy farmer, as he had once been in his native Switzerland.

Unlike the pastoral setting of rural Switzerland, however, the Bochatay farm in the New World, situated on the edge of Malta, a railroad town destined to disappear in the coming century, was encircled by belching smelters and bordered by a railroad track. Nevertheless, Louis Bochatay was a farmer once again, selling milk to the miners in town like his neighbor Henry Smith a few miles down the valley. When Louis passed away less than twenty years later, his two sons ran the Pioneer Dairy until the early 1920s, when they too both died as relatively young men. The farm soon fell into disuse and the old farm buildings were vandalized and destroyed in the late 1930s, before the farmland was inherited by Ivy Rose, a granddaughter of Louis.

In 1943, the Ore and Chemical Company built a mill in Malta Gulch upstream of the Bochatay Farm. Under the noses of the United States government and the Leadville citizenry, the New York–based company, secretly run by Germans, began shipping molybdenum on the sly to Nazi Germany to help in the war against the Allies. In August 1946, the federal government shut down the Leadville operation and appropriated the company under the Trading with the Enemy Act. By that time, the mining company had deposited a huge amount of mill tailings behind a series of low berms that regularly collapsed, washing six hundred thousand tons of tailings down the gulch and across the Bochatay pasture.

Every year, when the tax bill arrived, Ivy and her husband, a moly miner, fought over their "damn worthless property," but for the next forty years, Ivy won the arguments, and she held onto the Bochatay Farm while the rest of Malta Gulch was bought and sold several times over. By the time the EPA arrived, much of the gulch had ended up with the Leadville Corporation, a small company run since the 1940s by Robert Risk, a dentist from Indiana. After the war, Leadville Corp's prospects collapsed and in 1974 they leased their claims, equipment, and mill to Day Mines, which in 1981 merged into the much larger Hecla Mining Company. The Hecla/Day operations left behind another 680,000 tons of tailings until it closed its operations and dropped its lease in 1984. A few years later, the Leadville Corp renewed operations and left its own mark with a cyanide leaching retrofit of the mill to more efficiently extract metals and another fifty thousand tons of tailings that added cyanide to the mix. Hecla Mining and Leadville Corp were two of the original potentially responsible parties the EPA had named in 1986. Hecla, in turn, countersued the United States government.

With its seizure almost half a century earlier of the German-owned company that had left the biggest stain on the gulch, the U.S. government became liable for the company's contamination. In its negotiations with the EPA, Hecla had agreed to pay $688,000 for its share of the cleanup costs. The Indiana dentist behind Leadville Corp, on the other hand, vehemently and unwaveringly disputed that his mining activities were his responsibility to clean up. Nancy Mangone, the EPA lawyer assigned in the early 1990s to reach a settlement agreement with Dr. Risk, by then in his mid-eighties, considered those negotiations more difficult and frustrating than those with ASARCO, Resurrection, and the Res-ASARCO Joint Venture combined. The doctor, obstinate to the bitter end, eventually settled with the government for $2.4 million—should the company ever become solvent.

Cleaning up Malta Gulch was Mike Holmes's first assignment in Leadville. When he arrived in autumn of 1995, the gulch contained six tailing piles, the concrete foundation and scrap metal of a World War II–era mill, and a downstream wash of cadmium, zinc, and up to 50,000 parts per million lead poisoning the Bochatay pasture. When Ivy died in 1990, her sons, Rohn and Dennis Herrick, continued their parents' argument over the "worthless land in Leadville." Rohn, a burly, good-natured man with a thick, white beard, had spent his life working as a junior high school science teacher and counselor in Denver. He liked the idea of owning land that had been in his family for a hundred years and over his lifetime had whiled away many hours in church dreaming about the home he would someday build there; Dennis, a more serious version of his older brother, didn't share Rohn's nostalgia, particularly when the tax bill arrived.

As Mike Holmes started the yellow iron crawling over Malta Gulch, scooping up contaminated soil on the old Bochatay Farm, the state changed the tax laws. The property was no longer considered agricultural. It was "vacant," and the brothers' tax bill jumped from hundreds of dollars each year to nearly $7,000. With a heavy heart, Rohn agreed to sell. Second homeowners, looking for their piece of mountain solitude, snatched up all but a small piece of the Bochatay Farm. A year after the EPA had finished removing the pasture's topsoil, boulders sprang up like weeds, loosed from the glacial moraine they had been buried in. Rohn's remaining little piece of pasture—his treasured lega-cy and dreamt-of home site—was a nearly impassible field of boulders.

Mike had taken his first steps in Leadville, but it went largely unnoticed in the little, out-of-the-way gulch. Jim Martin came by on occasion to see how things were going. He wasn't too impressed with the project—there were more important things to do on the east side of town—but he didn't mind seeing some dirt moving around. As work continued in Malta Gulch, Mike turned his attention to other hotspots on the EPA's hit list. From the relatively sedate beginning in Malta, the town's pressure would soon mount.

In town, residents sensed the change. They turned out for the EPA's meetings, curious to see the new EPA project managers, Mike Holmes and Rebecca Thomas. To recruit Rebecca, her boss had tracked her all the way to Salzburg, Austria, where she had been vacationing with her husband Stewart. The EPA was quickly assembling a new team for the Leadville site, and the county's attorney, John Faught, had specif-ically requested her, he told Rebecca. She hadn't understood the urgency, but Rebecca had accepted her new assignment over the tele-phone in Salzburg.

At the time, Rebecca had been cutting her teeth as a project man-ager working on the Shattuck site, a highly controversial and politi-cized radium Superfund site in Denver where incensed neighbors felt the EPA wasn't doing enough to protect them from environmental dangers, and the quiet and reserved woman found herself routinely quoted in the newspapers.

Rebecca had met Stewart, a fellow environmental scientist, at a lit-tle jazz club downtown called The Ruby, not long after she'd arrived in Denver. She'd marveled at Stewart's strong ties to the city; he'd lived there all his life and was surrounded by family and friends. Rebecca, on the other hand, had learned the concept of tramping, her earliest years spent as an air force brat in Georgia. She became a mid-westerner after her father retired and moved the family to Kansas, then Iowa, then back to Kansas, this time to a small college town in farm country called Manhattan.

Leadville

After spending a year in France during college, the romantic in Rebecca envisioned a life there, learning the language and finding a job. But her practical side won out, and she became an engineer like her brother, her nearest sibling sixteen years her senior. She took a job working at an EPA regional office in Kansas City, in part to be near her mother. But after her mother died of cancer while Rebecca was only in her mid-twenties, she headed to Denver in 1990 to join the Region 8 office and make a fresh start.

Rebecca and Leadville's county officials met for the first time in the EPA's conference room in Denver. Such a meeting was atypical; most local officials weren't involved enough to drive an hour and a half just to meet the new minions. Bill Yellowtail had been there and a few other EPA bigwigs, an ASARCO representative, and Rebecca's new partner, Mike Holmes. At the meeting, Jim Martin and Bob Casey had made it clear they were frustrated by the EPA's slow progress and were demanding action. They wanted to establish the ground rules early for the newcomers: get your work done, do it the way we want, and then get out of town.

Mike and Rebecca began making regular trips to Leadville. Standing before the citizenry, the two were a study in contrasts. The young woman was tall, reed thin with an elegant stature, delicate features, porcelain skin, and long, brown hair she always wore pulled up behind her head. Her cubicle back in Denver was equally tidy, everything filed, a row of papers labeled with Post-it notes neatly arranged on her desk. Martin thought she looked refined; Mike, on the other hand, "doesn't try to polish his image too much." It was hard to feel intimidated by Mike Holmes. He slouched into his short frame, buried his hands in his pockets, and coughed lightly when he spoke. His cubicle, crammed into a corner, threatened to pop, with reports and paper stacked on the floor and hanging precipitously from shelves. His desk was buried. Mike wore a small, straight mustache on his weathered face, his brown hair flattened to his forehead as if he had always just taken off a cap. It was hard to imagine Mike in a suit and tie. "He really has the Leadville look," a local said later, approvingly. "Work boots, work shirt, work pants. He fits in."

There was more to Mike that the mountain town could relate to than his "Leadville look." Like the miners, Mike worked hard and played hard. The Grundy Center kid who rarely came inside was equally difficult to find indoors as an adult, and he loved cold weather, a sentiment close to Leadville's heart. Mike rode his bike to work every day, merely bundling up in the winter. (Rebecca, too, rode her bike to work without fail.) He took his family camping, cross-country and downhill skiing, bicycling, or hiking nearly every weekend. Geography and maps were his passion. On family excursions, before the tent was up, Mike had the map out, planning the first hike. "I could spend a whole night with a cold beer staring at topographic maps. It's fascinating. I go on backpacking trips and for weeks ahead of time, I study the whole area and all of the contours. And then you go there and think, it's all here."

Like the pragmatic miners who had stuck with Leadville through the bust, Mike Holmes was practical, down to earth, and exceptionally frugal. "Duct tape and Mike are good friends," his wife confided. "He's got shoes that are years and years old. He duct tapes them together. He repairs everything with duct tape." What can't be gotten with duct tape, Mike will barter for his needs, a skill the economically conscious residents who had long complained of Superfund's "wasted" millions would come to appreciate. What Leadville residents may not have sensed was just how goofy Mike's sense of humor could be. It was the eye-rolling, silly kind that made him adored by children—like catching a moth, coughing into his hand and letting the moth go, or cherry pit fights in the kitchen. As his two sons and daughter turned into teenagers, Dad's antics could be embarrassing, at least in front of friends, but they still considered him "a pretty cool guy," as his oldest son, Paul, described him.

In Leadville, Mike and Rebecca made a good team. While Rebecca led the meetings, Mike worked the room, getting to know people and their concerns in sidebar conversations. Back in Denver, Rebecca didn't mind dealing with the bureaucratic details, the meetings and paperwork that Mike had long ago discovered were not his strong suit. "I try to get sites cleaned up despite our process," he liked to say. To that end, Mike abandoned the Superfund's "Community Involvement Plan." He stopped mass-mailing fact sheets, discontinued the EPA's monthly public meetings in Leadville where project managers were routinely "bashed and trashed," as an EPA official had noted, and gave the new *Herald Democrat* editor, who was continuing the tradition of negative, lopsided coverage, a tour of the proposed work. "You can do flowcharts and decision trees of the Superfund process for risk analysis and determination, but people look at that stuff and get nauseated." Instead, Mike sought to shield the town from the bureaucracy. As he had done with the Philippine farmers years earlier, Mike's "plan" involved going to the bar and having a beer. It seemed obvious to Mike that sitting down for informal discussions, getting to know the residents, and understanding their concerns was a better Community Involvement Plan than reams of reports and fact sheets.

Jim Martin appreciated Mike's pragmatic approach, and he understood the value of getting off on the right foot. He knew the EPA wasn't going to leave town, but unlike Chlouber, he didn't want them to. The Yak Treatment Plant was doing its job, but waste in the mining district was still contaminating the Arkansas River—he could see the orange sludge running down the hills every spring. The EPA had much to do yet, he realized. But Jim wanted to make sure the new project managers kept Leadville's needs in mind. Since Climax had closed, the historic remnants in the mining district had become a tourist attraction and an important part of Leadville's post-Climax economy. Jim wasn't going to allow the EPA to destroy Leadville's history. So while Chlouber revved up the rhetoric in Denver, Jim and Bob Casey invited Rebecca and Mike out for a beer and a Mexican dinner. At one point, it seemed to dawn on the two commissioners who they were eating with. Mike remembered the two belting out to their friends at the bar, "Hey, we're having a beer with the EPA. Come over here. Can you believe we're having a beer with the EPA?"

When the weather was warm, after her waitressing shift at the Golden Burro, Myrna Windorski would walk down Harrison Avenue toward home, a small building that ASARCO had once used as an office. Myrna's walk took her alongside the enormous Harrison slag pile at the end of the avenue, before she turned east and headed up the hill where her gray house crouched between the black slag and the Apache Tailing Impoundment.

Myrna, a short, plump, cheerful woman with large glasses that darkened automatically in Leadville's bright sunlight, had grown up in town, married a Climax miner, and raised four children literally under the shadow of Leadville's mining waste. To those passing through Leadville who looked up to gawk at the monstrous piles of waste, the little house might have appeared vulnerable in the midst of all of that industrial wreckage, but it didn't bother Myrna. It had been there longer than she had, and the slag pile made a nice windbreak. When her sons were young, she tried—as her mother had tried with her children—to keep them out the tailing ponds because they always got so dirty.

Myrna's roots in Leadville went back as far as they could go. Her mother had been a Starr and, except for the slag pile, Myrna would have been able to see her great-grandfather's ditch out her window. Her mother had been raised in California Gulch but in her later years had found it a lonely place now that the gulch was deserted and the buildings had fallen down. Myrna was glad her son and his young wife, a third-generation herself, planned to stay in Leadville and put up a home just a few hundred yards away. Since Climax had closed, so many of the young people moved away after graduation.

Myrna wasn't sure what to make of the EPA. She didn't think playing in the tailings had hurt her sons, but she didn't like that the waste ate away at the house's water pipes either. Doc Smith, her distant cousin, had raised the alarm about contamination all of those years ago, and maybe he was right. She just didn't know. Myrna went to the EPA's meetings but was content to let others work it out. Then, in the fall of 1996, the view out Myrna's windows changed dramatically. The Harrison Slag pile was shrinking daily as the Denver and Rio Grande Western, now the Southern Pacific, hauled the entire three acres of slag down the road to the Arkansas Valley slag pile. When they were done, Myrna had a grand view of Colorado's highest peaks but, truth to tell, she preferred the windbreak.

Now that residents were finally seeing changes in town, approval mixed with apprehension. Leadville may have been born from transience, but the Leadville mindset that had survived the booms and busts of the past 120 years was leery of change. The EPA's impact on the mining district's historic remnants had always been a concern to some. Back in 1984, when the railroad first suggested moving the slag pile, a local historic preservation group had protested, and in a town survey in 1986 residents voted Leadville's historic remains as its number one resource—higher even than the abundant fishing, hiking, and kayaking nearby. But it wasn't until tourism became Leadville's primary source of income that preserving its history took on greater urgency. As Mike and Rebecca outlined their proposals for Leadville's cleanup in town meetings, new questions and conflicts emerged. What was worth preserving? Were the World War II mills and tailing piles as valuable as the 1880s waste rock piles and timber headframes? How could preservation of the historic remains coincide with a healthy environment when it was the historical legacy that was causing the environmental damage?

The black slag had its admirers, but it was hard to find much sympathy for the tailing piles. No one, not even Carl Miller, objected to doing something with Apache—unquestionably the "ugliest spot in town" and the first sight to greet visitors. The Hamm's Tailing Pile up 5th Street—the sand dunes—was also on Mike and Rebecca's early hit list, and residents welcomed that too. On windy days, the fine sand-like tailings blew over the east side of town, and rainy days washed a slurry of the stuff down 5th Street. But the railroad was carting away the Harrison slag pile, and the EPA was talking about making changes to the Penrose as well.

Leadville wasn't much more than a decade old by the time the mines east of town had pulled out much of the high-grade ore. Shafts were sunk deeper and deeper to keep the metals coming. But the ores these deeper mines retrieved were of a poorer quality, mixed with sulfides and more difficult to smelt. Mine owners suspected that the metals didn't stop at the town boundaries. To prove it and to boost Leadville's mining, the Chamber of Commerce sunk a shaft—the Lucy B. Hussey—in 1889 amongst the houses east of Harrison Avenue and promptly struck a rich silver vein.

The Downtown District, with its mining complexes of buildings and shafts, became the new industrial center as the end of the nineteenth century neared. Those mines, too, closed some decades later. Over the next century, as the mine buildings from the once-prosperous Downtown District came down, the waste rock piles remained. From the Penrose Mine came a large brown pile stretching a block long and rising fifty feet out of residents' yards on East 4th Street. An adit (horizontal tunnel), its timber frame buckling, gaped toward the street. To some in town, it was an historic treasure. To the EPA, it was four acres of dirt contaminated with lead, arsenic, cadmium, and zinc right in people's yards.

Mike Holmes knew all eyes were on him as he negotiated the first project that directly affected the town. The EPA proposed moving the Penrose to the nearby Hamms, capping the resulting pile with a plastic liner and clean dirt to prevent the waste from moving, and seeding it with grass. The land under the Penrose could then be developed, which satisfied Commissioner Martin. But one man's nostalgia—or selfishness, depending on who is telling the story—resulted in a half measure that wound up pleasing no one, especially Jim Martin.

A portion of the Penrose was owned by a flatlander who agreed to sell to a man living in a mountain town eighty miles away who said he wanted to preserve a World War II era building sitting on top of the Penrose; others claimed he just wanted to use the building for storage. To avoid a federal "taking" of the property, Holmes agreed to remove only part of the waste dump, capping and vegetating the portion holding up the building where it was. As the yellow iron dug into the Penrose that summer, a group gathered around with their metal detectors, eagerly waiting for something to glisten in the sunlight.

Then, the Penrose sale fell through. The owner wanted the entire pile removed, but it was too late. The EPA had already fixed the contamination problem and wouldn't return, so the owner tore down the building. The land, now a much smaller mound, was no longer the historic Penrose nor was it available for development. So far, Jim Martin was not impressed. Mike Holmes would have to do better, and the real opposition had not yet organized.

The Penrose was just one of only thirty-eight so-called Downtown Dumps that Mike would have to contend with. They all had names—the Coronado, Midas, Gray Eagle, Lazy Bill, Starr—and they all had a history. Someone's great-grandfather or great-uncle had once worked in this mine or that. But the Downtown Dumps would have to meet the same lead-level standards as the residents' yards. Twenty-three of them had concentrations of lead greater than 2,000 parts per million, the level Wangerud and Anderson had agreed to in the Consent Decree two years earlier. ASARCO, responsible for residential cleanup, was talking about moving them. Opposition was mounting, but ASARCO would turn out to be far less pliable than the EPA.

In October 1996, a shudder rippled through Leadville when ASARCO announced it was shutting down Leadville's last active mine and laying off 120 miners. Lead and zinc prices by this time had fallen too low to operate the Black Cloud Mine profitably. The announcement shocked the town. Black Cloud miners represented 5 percent of Leadville's workforce, and residents worried about another economic hit to the still-struggling town. But more was at stake. As long as the Black Cloud continued to lower miners into the mountain east of town, Leadville was still a mining town. Townsfolk bombarded ASARCO headquarters in New York City with letters begging that the mine be kept open.

Ken Chlouber, now a newly elected state senator, sprang into action. He flew to New York to talk to the top brass and came "ready to draw guns" unless they agreed to reopen the mine, he told the *Herald Democrat*. Perhaps ASARCO officials had received a telegraph warning them that Chlouber was on his way, but that same day they agreed to resume operations, citing Leadville's convincing campaign. Chlouber could put away his guns, at least for the time being.

With the Black Cloud reopened, the holidays passed uneventfully in Leadville. As 1996 came to an end, however, Yellowtail's deadline quietly expired. It might have gone unnoticed in town. Mike and Rebecca had brought a new sense of progress. Things were happening. One person, however, was not going to let the opportunity pass. Ken Chlouber renewed his earlier crusade, and this time he could point to Yellowtail's broken promise. He was joined by his buddy, Carl Miller, a newly elected state representative. Now the EPA was telling the legislators it would be another two years. This time there was no appeasing Chlouber and Miller. That spring, the two sponsored a joint resolution demanding the EPA remove Leadville from the Superfund list and "allow the citizens of Lake County to regain control of their community, their lives, and their future." Like Chlouber's previous state house resolution, this resolution was not a law, but it was intended to send a message to Congress and the EPA. "Why is the EPA wasting taxpayers' dollars on a community that is clean and healthy?" Chlouber demanded.

In a small conference room at the mining museum in Leadville, Chlouber and Miller met Rebecca and Mike for the first time and accused the two of destroying Leadville. As in the past, the agenda was not compromise. "What can we do to stop you people?" Mike remembered Chlouber demanding. Mike suggested the senator let them get their work done, so they could get out.

Chlouber did not have power over the federal EPA, but he did wield control over state agencies. Two years earlier, Chlouber had made good on threats to cut the health department's budget, when he successfully eliminated the state's 10 percent share of the capital costs for the EPA's "orphan" areas in Leadville. "The only way we can get rid of this kind of cancer is to cut it out and trash it," Chlouber had said at the time.

The budget cut didn't deter the EPA, but it was an obstacle that could potentially slow down its work in Leadville as it worked out the financial alternatives to the state's share of the costs. Chlouber's actions, however, had a more damaging and far-reaching effect than working around a budget shortfall. It sent a distressing message to state agency employees working on the Leadville site to consider their actions or fear for their budgets. Though subtle, the impact was real. Bill Yellowtail, who had once been a state senator in Montana, considered Chlouber's action "old-fashioned politics at its worst—when a powerful committee chairman is willing to threaten, and not only threaten but exact revenge, on a state administrative department because they don't toe his mark."

Cutting the health department budget in 1995 had not stopped the EPA so Chlouber, at his meeting with Mike and Rebecca two years later, asked them which state agencies work with the EPA. Chlouber was looking for more ammunition, and he found it in Mike's answer: the State Historic Preservation Office.

13

Stray Horse Gulch

Mike's meeting with Senator Chlouber in the summer of 1997 marked the end of his second year in Leadville. His six-month stint had gone too well to replace Mike so soon, and he had agreed to stay on to tackle the EPA's other, larger responsibility from the Consent Decree: Operable Unit 6, or Stray Horse Gulch. The EPA's unique situation as both regulator and potentially responsible party in Leadville made the agency's job more challenging as it juggled multiple roles. But under Mike's direction there were unanticipated benefits as well. Mike, the frugal barterer, could step out of his role as regulator and sit beside the mining companies as a fellow PRP. Meetings included discussions about engineering techniques, sharing materials and equipment, and figuring out the best approach to problems. If Mike had excess rock or clean dirt, and ASARCO or the community was looking for some, he offered it. He negotiated with the Leadville Corp to use dolomite, a "clean" rock free of sulfides, that the company had in abundance at a nearby mine in exchange for reducing the company's debt. He also encouraged the EPA's contractors to hire local workers.

Mike was building respect. It was a grudging respect for those who wanted to hold onto the bitter feelings of the past twelve years, but Mike clearly wanted to get work going, and if he could help out a fellow team member in the process, he jumped at the opportunity. As Mike had done in the Philippines and in Montana, he sought to build trust by looking for opportunities to help the community, and his efforts in Leadville were helping to thaw the relationship between the EPA, the mining companies, and the town. His efforts on behalf of the Mineral Belt Trail, in particular, had won a lot of converts.

One of them was Howard Tritz, a lanky, earnest, fourth-generation, ex-Climax employee whose passion for Leadville's mining history led him to envision a bike trail through the mining district, and another was Mike Conlin, who made it happen. In the early 1990s, after ASARCO's public relations success filling in the 5th Street ditches, the mining company had hired Conlin to figure out how to make Superfund benefit the community. "They needed a white hat and they needed it bad," remembered Conlin, the silver-bearded owner of Conlin Associates Resource Planners. Like many nonnatives, Conlin had come to Leadville in the early 1970s as a ski bum, but as the years passed he had found other reasons to stay in the little mountain town. In the early 1980s, Conlin started his own business coordinating development and environmental projects for ski resorts and municipalities throughout Colorado and Wyoming.

Conlin sensed in ASARCO's challenge an opportunity right in his own backyard to turn an adversarial and contentious situation into something beneficial for the community, the federal government, and the mining companies. It was during the volatile Wangerud era. Life in the arena was growing wearisome, and finding something the town could work toward cooperatively and look forward to could be a way to buoy the town's spirits. In 1993 Conlin, alongside Howard Tritz, helped form the Lake County Liaison Committee that was charged with going out into the community to determine what residents wanted most. The committee advertised in the local newspapers and put suggestion boxes around town. The ideas residents contributed ranged from building a bobsled run, or a visitor center at the Yak Treatment Plant, to an athletic recreation center. Tritz noticed how popular bicycling was becoming. A bike trail through the mining district might draw recreationists and history buffs, generating income for the town through tourism, and its very presence would emphasize the need to preserve the historic mining district. Just as importantly, a trail would directly benefit the locals, not just the tourists.

Tritz's bike trail was the runaway winner. "The community said we have some of the most significant scenery and history in the state of Colorado. We want the best bike trail that we can possibly conceive of and build," remembered Conlin. "Big order for a small community."

Conlin began shaping the idea into a specific plan. To pull it off, he knew the bike trail would require the cooperation of the EPA, the mining companies, the railroad, and the community. It seemed an impossible task. At the time, each of those entities saw the others as adversaries. To be successful, they would have to learn to see each other as partners. "The bike trail was a means of building partnerships that could be extended out beyond the litigation tables so that people could work together instead of constantly squabbling and answering their questions through the lawyers," Conlin said later. "Our philosophy is good partnerships are built around a common cause, but they stay together and work because of proprietary interests." To get everyone invested in the bike trail, Conlin promoted the benefits for each group. Lake County's interest was the trail's economic value. For the EPA and the PRPs, the trail was a feel-good project that could improve the working relationship with the community. The benefits might even ripple out to the rest of the Superfund project.

Most residents, including Jim Martin, recognized the opportunities a bike trail would bring to Leadville through increased tourism. Not everyone in town got on board, however. Some landowners ultimately had to be paid for right-of-way access on their land and the trail rerouted around properties when other owners still refused. Snowmobile and three-wheeler enthusiasts were upset because motorized vehicles wouldn't be allowed on the trail. When Conlin approached the local snowmobile club for their support, "I wasn't told 'no,' I was told 'hell no,'" he recalled. "I was told by one of the members that he had a shotgun and the first time someone got busted for running a snowmobile on it, he was going to station himself up there and make sure that the cross-country skiers knew that they weren't welcome on it either." Another contingency didn't agree with spending money—even if it was someone else's—on a paved bike trail while the potholes in Leadville's streets grew worse daily. But the idea of attracting more tourists—and the deeper issue of Leadville's evolving identity—also came to the fore. No one kept track of how many visitors came to Leadville annually, but judging by Harrison Avenue in the summertime, tourists were finding Leadville in greater numbers. Just how far the town was willing to go to cater to them, and thus encourage more outsiders to come, was an ongoing debate. Many regarded the bike trail as another step closer to becoming touristy like Vail or Breckenridge, a comparison often evoked as a fate worse than becoming a ghost town. Nearly every resident shared that view, but strong disagreements over what constituted "becoming Vail" erupted frequently in town meetings.

Community opposition wasn't the only obstacle. Conlin designed the trail to run along old railroad beds through California, Stray Horse, and Evans gulches in a twelve-mile loop around Leadville—a much more elaborate project than Tritz had even envisioned. It would pass through a Superfund site, a National Historic Landmark District, wetlands, forests, private property in town, and dozens of overlapping claims handed down through the generations still on the books in the mining district. While Howard Tritz, who also happened to be the county assessor, began calling claim owners, Conlin waded into a bureaucratic maze, navigating through numerous government and state agencies that included several historic preservation offices, the Army Corp of Engineers, state and federal forest services, the EPA, and the Bureau of Reclamation. Each agency needed to give its permission for the Mineral Belt Trail.

ASARCO, Resurrection, and the Union Pacific Railroad donated substantial amounts of land, money, equipment, and time toward the project. From early on, it was the EPA that had threatened to derail the entire project. Meetings where scenarios such as the potential liability of a pregnant woman using the trail or people stopping for lunch were discussed. EPA lawyers in Denver talked about unacceptable lead levels, chain-link fences, and patrols needed to monitor the trail. The EPA wanted to point to the bike trail as a Superfund benefit, but the agency's restrictions would have made it impractical. Conlin considered the EPA's stance adversarial, and a few years into the project he had hit an impasse. Just as Conlin wasn't sure he wanted to bang his head against another barrier, "everything turned around with Mike." Conlin credited both Mike and Rebecca, the new project managers, for approaching the community with a cooperative, open-minded attitude. They were looking for solutions rather than obstacles.

Mike was willing to incorporate the bike trail, which was to run straight through Stray Horse Gulch and the cleanup, into the EPA's plans. It was an example of his results-oriented approach to finding solutions that got the yellow iron moving quickly. Leadville noticed—and approved. "Mike Holmes was the only guy who was trying to work the problem. He doesn't have any ego about it," recalled one resident. "What a difference!" summed up another.

"Nobody thought out of the box," Mike explained of his approach. "When they named it a Superfund site, you start with your remedial investigation, and your feasibility study, and your proposed plan, and your record of decision, and your remedial design, and then your remedial action, which is when it all happens." To speed up that lengthy process, Mike initiated a series of "removal actions," Superfund's method for dealing with immediate dangers learned from his days in the Emergency Response program. It was a way to shortcut the usual years of studies and reports under the normal "remedial" process as long as the final result achieved the same cleanup goals. For Mike, it was a way to get the obvious problems resolved right away without getting bound up in endless reports. By the time the final Record of Decision, or ROD (the document that normally initiates the action for an operable unit) was published, the preferred alternative was often "No Action." It had already been done.

"We bureaucrats get wrapped up in our process and sometimes we have to think how is that helping the end result or reducing the pounds of metals going into the Arkansas River," Mike explained.

"There's comfort in the bureaucracy and the process. There's too many people in government that serve the process and not the public. They can go to bed each night and think, 'Well, I followed the process so I'm good.' I can't operate that way." Mike's willingness to get things moving while finding remedies that met the town's needs, such as the bike trail, proved invaluable as he sat down with town officials to deal with contamination in Stray Horse Gulch, which would prove much more controversial than the Penrose waste dump.

To many, the entire Leadville Mining District was sacrosanct. Any change, particularly to Stray Horse Gulch where their grandfathers had worked in the Wolftone, the Pyrenees, and the Greenback, was tantamount to grave desecration. But others thought the gulch looked like "the other side of the moon." During World War II, John Hamm and others had attacked the cone-shaped waste rock piles the nineteenth-century miners had left behind, scraping them away to extract their metals. After the war, they had abandoned the ravaged piles and mills, which had deteriorated into a landscape of scrap metal, old timbers, and shrunken, misshapen mounds of waste rock. In the succeeding decades, Stray Horse Gulch became the local—unauthorized—trash dump. Abandoned cars, tires, and refuse added to the rubble. If reverence existed for the neglected gulch before the EPA's arrival, it was hard to discern.

But Stray Horse Gulch, just a mile up the hill from Harrison Avenue, was the most visible reminder—aside from the Downtown Dumps—of Leadville's mining heritage. Every pile had a name and a unique history. EPA scientists also recognized each pile's unique qualities—as a contributor to acid mine drainage and heavy metal contamination. The waste rock piles ranged from nontoxic to a significant polluter, like the Wolftone and the R.A.M. Over the next few years, when Mike Holmes came under fire, critics would question why the EPA insisted on "fixing" one waste pile while leaving a nearby pile alone—surely it was evidence of the federal government's ineptitude. But each pile's contribution depended on the type of ore it contained, its metal concentrations, and the amount of erosion taking place. The geology of the area varied. As its name suggested, Carbonate Hill, southeast of town, was mostly carbonates, a neutral limestone. Farther east, the piles contained more of the sulfur that generated sulfuric acid. Typically, the more colorful the pile—like the R.A.M. with its bright yellows, oranges, and reds, the more metals it leached; the brown-streaked piles generated less acid, although those located in residential areas were subjected to greater, health-related restrictions.

High up in Stray Horse Gulch, at the ghost town site of Adelaide Park, now a pretty spot of wetlands and pines, the water was a healthy 6.5 pH. By the time it flowed down the hill, past the R.A.M., the Wolftone, the Highland Mary, the Robert Emmet, and into ASARCO's 5th Street culverts and out to the Starr Ditch, it was a very unhealthy 2.5, the acidity of vinegar, and rusty orange with metals. Identifying which piles were guilty of acid mine drainage normally involved the low-tech but lengthy procedure of taking water samples above and below each pile to measure the change in acidity. In the summer of 1995, the federal government tested a new, high-tech approach on Leadville. A converted U-2 spy plane, traveling five hundred miles per hour, flew twelve miles above the town and mining district. Instead of a spy camera, NASA's jet was outfitted with a spectrometer that could distinguish acid mine drainage and minerals by measuring how the various materials absorbed or reflected light. From the data, the government generated maps showing the sources of contamination, right down to exactly which piles contributed to acid mine drainage. When the jet flew over Leadville, it was the first time the technique had been tried for such a purpose. The event went largely unnoticed in Leadville, but it was newsworthy enough to make the *New York Times*. It also shaved a year of studies off the timeline.

While the EPA worked out the science of Stray Horse, the town considered what it wanted for the long-neglected gulch. Underneath the debris, remnants of Leadville's boom days still existed. Some of the piles remained untouched, here and there an old timber building, cribwall, or headframe still stood. The town's residents were divided. Most didn't care what happened to the gulch; to them, the area was either a town eyesore to be avoided or a convenient dumping ground.

To the nostalgic, it represented Leadville's glorious years as the Silver Queen, and to the more business inclined, it was an attraction to be mined for tourist dollars. Jim Martin believed the EPA's presence, particularly given Mike's supportive attitude, was an opportunity for the cash-strapped county to use the federal government to turn Stray Horse Gulch into an asset. In the mid-1990s, town officials created a Lake County Historic Preservation Advisory Board to evaluate historical assets and develop a plan for preserving them. Bob Elder and Carl Miller were founding members. The county also hired, at their attorney John Faught's suggestion, a technical advisor to help them make sense of the EPA's reports. The county commissioners knew that to be taken seriously as a legitimate voice, they had to come to the table prepared.

Jim and Mike agreed that any action taken in the gulch would require a compromise: preserving what the town considered to be historically important but at the same time remedying what the EPA had determined contributed to acid mine drainage. Leadville and the EPA were essentially searching for a balance between the townspeople's desires and the EPA's science—something Superfund was supposed to do in theory, but rarely, if ever, accomplished or even attempted. For two years, Mike and Rebecca drove to Leadville two or three times a week to meet with the county commissioners, the Historic Preservation Advisory Board, and the public, attending meetings and informal discussions to hammer out a plan for Stray Horse Gulch that was historically sensitive, incorporated a bike trail, and protected the Arkansas River.

What had been done to the Hamm's Tailing Pile the year before represented conventional mine reclamation. The pile had been flattened and contoured with gentle slopes, covered—or capped—with a plastic liner to prevent water from seeping into the pile and topped with clean dirt and then seeded so that, within a few years, the mound would be covered in a thin blanket of scraggly grass. For Stray Horse Gulch's waste rock piles, the EPA proposed something else. Spy planes and water sampling had identified eleven areas as the primary sources of contamination including the Wolftone, Maid of Erin, Mahala, the

Adelaide, Mikados, and Highland Mary. Instead of removing the piles or creating grassy knolls more reminiscent of the Nebraska Sandhills than a mountain mining site, the EPA decided it would try to mimic pre–World War II conditions by consolidating the offending piles and surrounding waste into seven large cone-shaped waste rock piles and capping them with dolomite, the Leadville Corp's nearby "clean" rock that would neutralize any water that seeped into the piles. Using historic photographs, the EPA mapped the future piles to match precisely Leadville in the 1880s. Though the EPA was trying to re-create a piece of Leadville's boom days appearance, the plan still called for destroying a number of prominent waste dumps.

In exchange, Holmes agreed to preserve other areas the town deemed historically significant—the relatively untouched Pyrenees, the colorful R.A.M., and the Greenback waste dumps. These piles also contributed to acid mine drainage, but instead of capping them, clean runoff would be diverted around the piles and the contamination caught in holding ponds to prevent it from washing down the gulch. The bike trail would follow an old railroad bed right through the middle of it all. In an added gesture, Mike put carpenters on the headframes, mine buildings, and cribwalls, the timber walls holding up the piles, to shore up some of the remaining structures. To Bob Elder, it was "a bit like locking the barn door after the horse is gone," so much had been lost to time already. But he also knew that if the EPA didn't do it, the county couldn't afford to and soon it would all be lost. After two years of negotiating, community officials and the EPA had a compromise both could live with. Mike Holmes began lining up $7 million in contracts to get the work going.

On July 31, 1997, as the bulldozers were rolling into Stray Horse Gulch, Ken Chlouber and Carl Miller published a long editorial—a renewed call to arms—in the *Herald Democrat*. An abbreviated version ran in the *Denver Post* two weeks later. "About the time you will be reading this letter we will be meeting with Gov. Romer, asking for his immediate support in preventing the EPA from destroying our mining heritage and history and ultimately his help in getting the EPA out of our community once and for all." The two then laid out the "facts": no health risk exists in Leadville and any environmental problems were solved years ago by the Yak Treatment Plant.

> So what's left for the EPA? What excuse are they using for wanting to destroy our history, remove or cover up many of our historic mine dumps?
>
> They contend the rain and melting snow adversely affects the water quality of the river. Friends and neighbors, that just doesn't make sense and the EPA knows it.
>
> Over 70 percent of our runoff occurs in a six-week period. The runoff on those 14 mine dumps they intend to immediately destroy couldn't possibly affect the water chemistry considering the millions of acres that contribute to the runoff water on the Upper Arkansas. . . .
>
> EPA's personal insults are many and ongoing; everything from digging on private property without permission to feeding pigs Leadville soil and equating that to Leadville citizens.
>
> *For 15 years, we've tried to negotiate, tried to compromise, tried to work with this federal agency in every conceivable way. Nothing has worked* [italics added]. . . .
>
> A call or letter to Gov. Romer, our congressional delegation and the State Historical Society would certainly be appreciated and help us in our campaign to save our mining district.
>
> With your help and the help of all our elected officials, we can and must win this battle. Our Leadville best to you each and every day.
>
> > State Sen. Ken Chlouber
> > State Rep. Carl Miller
> > Leadville

No one could recall Senator Chlouber or Representative Miller at a single public or private meeting to discuss Stray Horse Gulch. But now that millions of dollars in contracts were in place and bulldozers were on the move, and just a few weeks after the legislators had met with Holmes and Rebecca and heard the words "State Historic

Preservation Office," the two suddenly announced that they feared for Leadville's historic mining district. At their meeting with the governor, Roy Romer promised to look into it, but the real ammunition lay with the state's historic preservationists.

Thirty years earlier, in 1966, as concern for historic preservation grew around the nation, Congress enacted the National Historic Preservation Act. The act created the National Register of Historic Places maintained by the National Park Service; established a new federal agency, the Advisory Council on Historic Preservation, to review actions that affect historic properties; and required federal agencies, such as the EPA, to identify and consider preservation when planning activities that affected historic properties. In situations where the property cannot be preserved, the history must be documented, the law stated. The new legislation required each state to designate a Historic Preservation Officer responsible for administering the law at the state level, including reviewing federal activities.

Earlier, in the 1950s, Leadville had been designated a National Historic Landmark District and therefore automatically became a charter member of the National Register of Historic Places. In those early years, preservationists limited their focus to the grand, architectural gems. In the mining towns, the areas deemed historically valuable were often confined to the downtown corridors, and in Leadville, that narrow view limited the town's historic designation to Harrison Avenue, leaving out the gritty mining district surrounding it. By the late twentieth century, "cultural landscapes" were the buzz in preservation circles, and the mining districts with their waste dumps, rough-hewn timber headframes, and cribwalls were increasingly recognized as important elements in telling the story of American society and were worthy of preservation alongside the Tabor Grand Hotel.

To comply with the National Historic Preservation Act, the EPA had been conducting cultural surveys on Leadville's historical remains and sending the reports to the state's historic preservation officer. In Colorado, that person was the president of the Colorado Historical Society, but most of the work and decisions passed to two deputy preservation officers and their staff. In 1990, the EPA and State Historic Preservation Office, or SHPO, signed a Programmatic Agreement, outlining the two agencies' working relationship and procedures for California Gulch. Under the agreement, SHPO would review the reports and make recommendations to the EPA within a certain time frame. With the arrival of Mike Holmes and Rebecca Thomas, the reports submitted to SHPO switched from benign history lessons to discussing actual work about to take place in the Leadville Mining District.

By nearly everyone's account the State Historic Preservation Office was ill equipped to handle the job. On September 24, 1996, SHPO signed off on the Hamm's/Penrose project without visiting the site or perhaps, as some claimed, even understanding the reports. Later, when things "went political" and SHPO was scrambling, preservationists around the state blamed the EPA for issuing "incomprehensible reports" and for not giving the state's preservation officers enough time to respond. But no one in the preservation office attempted to solve that problem or request help, and the agency had agreed to the time frame. Now that the EPA was under pressure to begin the work, encouraging SHPO scrutiny was not a priority. Before the spotlight turned on it, the state's historic preservation office seemed content to let the EPA go about its work unimpeded. In 1997, as Mike Holmes prepared to send the bulldozers into Stray Horse Gulch, two reports sat on a SHPO employee's desk, unread.

As soon as Senator Chlouber learned of this weak link, he pounced. On July 17, 1997, soon after talking with Mike Holmes, Chlouber called the Colorado Historical Society and spoke with a preservation office employee, who took notes of the conversation. The EPA was damaging waste piles before consulting with SHPO, and the senator was determined to save the town's mining history, he told her. The EPA was only there because "Leadville is just a beautiful place to spend the summer," she quoted the senator as saying. He "wants to help us do our job."

That initial phone call prompted a flurry of activity. A week later, both Senator Chlouber and Representative Miller spoke with another

employee whose notes of the conversation document the two legislators' continuing "battle" with the EPA. They expected SHPO to pick
up the gauntlet Chlouber and Miller were throwing at their feet to
stop the EPA "in their tracks." The employee's notes follow him
through his next few harried days. There were "two reports not yet
reviewed," he informed his boss, deputy SHPO Susan Collins. After
leaving messages with four EPA employees, he spoke with Mike
Holmes later that day, who explained the Stray Horse Gulch project
and its intention to mimic Leadville's pre–World War II condition.
Mike invited him to Leadville to see the site for himself.

The next day, the beleaguered employee drove to Leadville and
recorded what he saw from the EPA's trailer on 5th Street: "Earth-
moving is proceeding outside the window. Actually it is a huge pile
and a small bulldozer, but nevertheless . . . I have no idea whether
this work has been reviewed or not." That "huge pile" was the
Hamm's Tailing Pile—the sand dunes—whose capping the State Historic Preservation Office had approved less than a year earlier. Now
that work was nearly complete, there was nothing to be done to stop
the capping of Hamm's or the Penrose. But the bulldozers were just
getting started in Stray Horse Gulch.

14
Give and Take

A week and a half later, Mike Holmes sat at a small table in the cramped construction office trailer parked up 5th Street near Hamm's, drinking coffee and getting a morning briefing over the radio from the work foreman. Yellow iron had been on the move in Stray Horse Gulch for about a week. This morning, bulldozers were pushing waste rock piles and a convoy of thirty-five-ton trucks were on their way, hauling rocks over the narrow, steep roads. The foreman's voice crackled into the radio. A television crew had just shown up. They were setting up a camera on the haul road. Senator Chlouber was with them.

Mike told the foreman to stop the equipment, then he jumped up and was out the door. Mike rushed up the hill in his government-issue sport utility vehicle he had dubbed the "Lead Sled." Standing in the road was an NBC Nightly News television crew: a soundman, cameraman, producer, and Roger O'Neil, preparing to interview Senator Chlouber about the atrocities to historic preservation the EPA was committing against his struggling mountain town. Mike would come to consider this "the worst day of my EPA career."

Four days earlier, on August 1, 1997, the State Historic Preservation Office (SHPO) held a meeting at the Colorado Historical Society across from the state capitol in downtown Denver to discuss this new problem in Stray Horse Gulch. The state agency was caught in the middle of a fierce debate. Not everyone agreed with Senator Chlouber's call to arms, and SHPO was getting angry calls and letters from both the EPA's fans and its critics. At the meeting, seven members of the SHPO staff were joined by Mike and Rebecca, Chlouber and Miller, the three county commissioners, Leadville's mayor, and Bob Elder, representing Leadville's Historic Preservation Advisory Board; their attorney, John Faught, was also there as was an EPA lawyer and representatives from ASARCO, the National Trust for Historic Preservation, Colorado Preservation Inc., Senator Wayne Allard's office, and other organizations and individuals now also interested in the fate of Leadville's mining district. Hovering in the background was an NBC camera crew.

At the three-hour meeting, Senator Chlouber and Representative Miller were adamant that SHPO force the EPA to stop the Stray Horse Gulch project that day. They claimed that the EPA's project would do little to control acid mine drainage or alter the water chemistry of the Arkansas River. Instead, the government's actions would obliterate the town's heritage, drive away tourists, and ultimately destroy Leadville. The community can't "stand up to EPA," Miller was quoted as saying by a SHPO employee, who took extensive notes of the meeting, or offer public comments that disagree with a federal agency.

Jim Martin, Bob Elder, and the other town officials who had driven down the mountain from Leadville told a different story. They agreed that the EPA had been in town far too long and they, like the legislators, worried that the soil lead action levels that were still to be set would be onerous. But they and others interested in historic preservation had, in fact, been working diligently with the EPA for nearly two years. They praised Mike Holmes and Rebecca Thomas for keeping the best interests of the community in mind as the two sides sought remedies that would benefit both the town and the environment. Martin and the other officials who had poured over many years of reports with their lawyer remained convinced that Stray Horse Gulch contributed to contamination of the Arkansas River. How, the commissioners asked Senator Chlouber, was the county to deal with this contamination problem, if the EPA were forced to leave?

Chlouber appeared unimpressed by the town officials' support of the EPA or the trust and cooperation they had developed with the new project managers. Despite his warning, Chlouber said, Jim Martin and the others had let the EPA divide Leadville. Now, he wanted SHPO to slow the federal agency down until he could reunite the community and appeal to Congress to get the EPA out of Leadville for good.

The historic preservationists in attendance from Colorado Preservation Inc. and the National Trust for Historic Preservation sided with Chlouber and Miller. The mining landscape of an important national historic landmark would be irreparably altered if the EPA were allowed to continue, they said. The two deputy SHPO officers in attendance acknowledged that the Colorado Historical Society could not stop the EPA, but they could work with the agency to minimize its impact on Leadville's historic remains. But the SHPO officers remained noncommittal. They needed to step back and look at the big picture, they said, and suggested delaying the project until they could "get a handle on what's happening and where we are."

It was already August 1. Any delay would mean the loss of another work season. Contracts had been signed, and the contractors would get paid whether or not they were moving dirt. Neither the EPA nor the Leadville men wanted the bulldozers stopped now. When the meeting adjourned three hours after it had begun, nothing had been decided.

Four days later, Chlouber and Miller were back in Leadville complaining to the county commissioners for making a deal with the EPA. The commissioners countered that they were being realistic and explained the compromise to the legislators. Before the meeting ended, Senator Chlouber had to leave. NBC was waiting for him.

When Mike Holmes, racing up Stray Horse Gulch in the "Lead Sled," reached Roger O'Neil and the NBC camera crew standing in the road with Senator Chlouber that morning, he had visions of thirty-five-ton trucks loaded with rocks bearing down on them. He asked the crew to move, stressing not the presence of hazardous materials but the danger of being in a construction zone. Chlouber, with his blond, curly-haired teenage son at his side, was already talking to the camera, however. "He talked about how he and his son used to go walking up there together, and they would never be able to do that again," Mike recalled. "I think he actually had crocodile tears in his eyes."

A week later, NBC Nightly News aired its story to the nation. As footage rolled of bulldozers moving dirt, haul trucks driving past timber mine ruins, and Leadville nestled against the Rocky Mountains, Roger O'Neil began: "High in the Colorado mountains, in Leadville, the legacy of man's rush to strike it rich litters the landscape. Now the Environmental Protection Agency is digging up one of the world's greatest mining camps. But like the old miners who fought to preserve their claims, a state senator is fighting to preserve Leadville's history."

Chlouber appeared on the screen in front of a haul truck, towering over Mike Holmes and pointing a finger at him. "You know what you're doing to my community is wrong, and I'm here to stop you."

Mike Holmes, a hand buried in his pocket, grimaced and looked askance.

"Leadville's always been a boom and bust kind of place," O'Neil continued as he walked up to an old Finntown building, the Robert Emmet headframe in the background. "First gold, then silver. During the war, it was zinc and lead that came out of here. Those days are long gone and now Leadville's past may be its only hope for a future. It's called tourism."

O'Neil's voice-over continued as a group of parents and children, the blues and pinks of their jackets shining against the earth-toned surroundings, peered down the Tabor's Matchless mine shaft: "While mines like the Matchless will stay, the EPA has targeted more than fifty other old mine dumps to clean up and make worthless as tourist attractions. The Penrose Mine is already gone, and they're working on the Hamm's now. The agency says the dumps must go because water from melting snow turns to acid when it washes over the mines' waste piles."

The scene changed. Mike Holmes sat pinned to his chair by a camera pointed down at him after the SHPO meeting a few days earlier. His eyes dart away from the camera nervously. "If we don't address the water quality coming out of that drainage than it's goi—cough— then it's going to continue to go downhill," Mike stumbled, unconvincingly.

"The EPA has spent fourteen years in Leadville and $50 million trying to figure that out," O'Neil continued as footage rolled of Senator Chlouber walking somberly past a timber mine ruin, an arm around his son's shoulder. "Critics wonder if this isn't a bureaucracy run amuck. Chlouber says the EPA plan is as empty as the old mines, and there are less destructive and far less expensive ways to take care of some dirty water."

"It just breaks my heart when I talk to these people. And I say, 'Can't you see what you're doing? Can't you see what you're doing to us?'" It's Chlouber again, talking plaintively into the camera.

"The government's big machines strip away in a day what took the old miners shovel after shovel and years to create—the history of mines like Nugget Gulch and Coronado. Roger O'Neil, NBC News, Leadville."

The message was clear: the EPA—Mike Holmes—was obliterating Leadville's famous heritage and forever destroying the blue-collar town's opportunity for a future. And all because of "some dirty water." But state Senator Ken Chlouber was there, valiantly standing up to the federal government to rescue his town.

"That night I had long-lost high school friends call me. 'Hey, I saw you on TV,'" Mike remembered and shuddered. "Senator Chlouber as a polished politician was able to get sound bites. He's very good with sound bites, and I'm not. I'm not a polished person in front of the camera. I'm a project manager." Even Jim Martin empathized:

"Chlouber rode poor old Mike Holmes so badly. I felt sorry for Holmes on that one." Jim chuckled at the memory.

Local television stations trotted up the mountain for their own colorful reactions, and a few Leadville residents obliged with the old standbys: "You don't see people walking around with three arms and three legs . . . I've been playing on the mine dumps since I was a kid, digging bottles and all kinds of stuff, and I seem perfectly healthy," one woman said into the news camera.

On August 13, the day after NBC's coverage aired, U.S. Senator Ben Nighthorse Campbell visited Leadville. Over the years, Colorado's politicians had occasionally entered the fray, visiting the town to assure their support or sending letters to EPA officials to support the town's desire. But except for a few symbolic demonstrations of support, neither the state nor Colorado's congressional leaders had ever made a serious effort to undermine the EPA in Leadville, despite Senator Chlouber's efforts to rally the big guns. Now, Chlouber again was seeking to get Congress to act on what he said was Leadville's behalf, but Nighthorse Campbell found a divided town. At the public meeting, Chlouber and Miller repeated their calls for the EPA to get out of town while the commissioners countered that the feds needed to stay and finish the job. Nighthorse Campbell concluded that he would not be called into action. "If the community is divided, I don't want to be the bludgeon for one side or the other. There has to be an understanding in the community so I know who to attack."

Years later, Miller lamented that the commissioners had "given in" to the EPA and had misrepresented residents' wishes. Some, such as Chlouber, have also claimed that Jim Martin had "changed his tune" regarding the EPA. To those with a single-minded agenda of getting the EPA to leave town, Jim may have appeared to flip-flop with Mike Holmes's arrival. But the commissioner had consistently denied that a health risk existed in town, and just as consistently acknowledged that acid mine drainage contaminated the Arkansas River. Jim seemed never to have played politics with the EPA. If he agreed with the agency, he said so. If he disagreed, he said so—with red-faced gusto.

"I don't care what people think about what I do," Jim would say later. "I do what I think is right."

If efforts to unite the town against the EPA were unsuccessful, Chlouber's campaign within the state government was gaining momentum and threatened to topple the balance the EPA and town officials had created in nearly two years of constant negotiations. SHPO was now on the case, prodded into action by political forces. The state health department, which had previously signed off on the project, was also waffling. It seemed clear to onlookers that with Senator Chlouber threatening to cut budgets—and after already making good on that threat once—the two state agencies feared for their budgets. Mike was overseeing $7 million in contract work, dirt was moving, dolomite was rolling in, and now some powerful forces were clamoring for the work to be halted.

A flurry of letters and meetings ensued. On August 7, deputy SHPO Susan Collins wrote Rebecca Thomas asking the EPA to stop: "Unfortunately, we have been looking at this project in very small slices, and this has hampered our ability to provide comments that reflect a full understanding of the anticipated effects on this highly significant cultural landscape. We must pause and consider where we stand in regard to the actions that are now occurring in Operable Unit 6. We recognize that the 1997 construction season is short and slipping away, but we must balance that consideration with our mandate to consider historic properties before they are gone."

After an intense few weeks of negotiations, John Faught brokered a deal. The EPA would finish capping the Wolftone, Mahala, and Maid of Erin, three piles already damaged by John Hamm during his World War II mining of the old waste rock piles. But the agency would find an alternative for the four other areas farther up the gulch. In an August 14 letter to Susan Collins, Rebecca explained that some of the work would continue, emphasizing that there had "been little to no controversy" to the proposed plan prior to the August 1 meeting. SHPO, the EPA maintained, had let an early opportunity to participate go by and now it was too late to completely undo the work. Mike went back to the contractor to renegotiate the $7 million "contract from hell." He managed to get about half of the government's money back for the four areas put on hold—a feat he's not sure how he accomplished—but the government paid hefty damages to the contractors for backing out.

As the bulldozers dug into the Wolftone, Mahala, and Maid of Erin in the short season remaining, the EPA, county commissioners, John Faught, and their technical advisor went back to the drawing board. By the end of January, Mike was ready to present new plans to the rest of Leadville. "It's quite a bit different than the typical work EPA does at mining sites," he told residents at a public meeting. Instead of capping the piles to prevent rain and snow runoff from reaching the contamination, essentially preventing it from forming in the first place, the EPA would manage the acidic water after it was created. The EPA's plan called for holding ponds below the piles to capture the acidic water and a series of diversion ditches that would divert clean water around them. This water management approach was much more technically challenging. The engineers had to know how big to make the ponds, where the water flowed naturally, and what to do with the contaminated water once it was captured.

The ramifications for this new solution were numerous. Consolidating and capping requires little maintenance, only an occasional inspection once completed. Water management, however, entails constant attention. Holding ponds must be dredged of sediments, repaired regularly, and monitored for spills; contaminated water must be treated; and safety issues associated with open acid ponds addressed. It was an expensive solution that would require maintenance *in perpetuity*. Most of that burden would fall to the state and its taxpayers after the site was delisted and the EPA was gone. Had the EPA been allowed to consolidate and cap everything, it would have been done within the year. The new plans ensured that the agency would be there for years to come. "Basically, Senator Chlouber trying to get the EPA out of town has actually caused more delay, more added layers to work on because now we have to manage the water," Mike Holmes would say later.

On August 28, 1997, just a few weeks after the SHPO meeting, Senator Chlouber would again direct his hostility at the EPA, and this time Bill Yellowtail would take action. When Yellowtail's announced deadline for the EPA's departure had passed at the end of 1996, just before the controversy at Stray Horse Gulch had erupted, he was no longer working for the EPA. In March of 1996, he had gone back to Montana to run what would become a soul-searching campaign for a U.S. senate seat. For the first few months, Yellowtail's campaign had cruised along with many predicting victory in November. Then in May, just before the Democratic primary, it all seemed to unravel. An anonymous source had leaked information about Yellowtail's past to the press. As a depressed and lonely sophomore at Dartmouth trying to fit in with his affluent classmates, the kid from the Crow reservation was caught stealing from a nearby camera store and was kicked out of school (Yellowtail was later readmitted and became a counselor to other Indian students); as a young man he was once accused of slapping his first wife so hard she needed medical care; and later, he had fallen behind on child-support payments when the family ranch nearly went under.

Democrats were stunned. But they were more surprised by what Yellowtail did next. He repented. "Those events are a contradiction of everything I was taught by my parents, and they run counter to everything this community instilled in me. I cannot justify what I did and will not try to. All I ask is forgiveness," he told a reporter. Instead of abandoning Yellowtail, people scampered to his defense, including his first wife and twenty-six-year-old daughter, and he won the Democratic primary, beating three other candidates with 56 percent of the vote. Yellowtail then faced a prominent insurance salesman and developer in the general election, a millionaire named Rick Hill. Despite being out-financed and running as a Democrat in a conservative state, Yellowtail continued leading in the polls. It remained a tight race to election day, and many were stunned when Yellowtail lost his 1996 bid for a U.S. senate seat.

Yellowtail didn't look back. "I didn't win, and it's a darn good thing I didn't. There are some mornings I wake up and thank the good citizens of Montana for not banishing me to Washington," Yellowtail reflected years later from his quiet Montana ranch. Running for the senate "was a darn fool thing to do. That's where Ken Chlouber got all his ammunition."

Yellowtail had emerged from the elections jobless, but the wheels of government were turning so slowly that his old job was still vacant. Yellowtail was back at his administrator's desk in Denver's Region 8 high-rise in time for a showdown with Ken Chlouber in the summer of 1997 that would turn ugly and personal. Editorialists in Denver were not amused either. Later that year, on November 2, Mark Obmascik of the *Denver Post* reported the scuffle in a column:

Chlouber Talks Toxic

In a confrontation with EPA bureaucrats, Chlouber spewed one of the ugliest political screeds heard in Colorado in years. But when the EPA responded, the elected official from Leadville really came unglued.

He said the agency's Denver office was being run by a thieving and cheating wife-beater.

The verbal assault by one of the state's senior elected officials has bystanders scrambling for flak jackets. Though this fight has no clear winner, the undisputed loser is anyone who believes government is supposed to solve problems, not create them.

Somehow this all resulted from a dull meeting of an obscure state board, the Interim Legislative Committee on Air Quality Issues. Before the Aug. 28 meeting in Fort Collins, EPA air pollution official Larry Svoboda decided to shake hands with one of the panel members, Ken Chlouber.

Big mistake.

"The senator looked me in the eye and said, 'You scum-sucking low-life. You're one of the lowest life forms on the planet,'" Svoboda recalled.

The EPA worker was startled. It was the first time he ever had met this politician, and somehow he expected a more civil greeting.

Chlouber said his insults were misinterpreted.

"I did say EPA is a scum-sucking low-life and one of the lowest life forms on the planet, because that is the truth," Chlouber said. "But I did not say the person was a scum-sucking low-life. I said EPA was. Maybe he took it personally. . . ."

When Chlouber insulted another worker at the meeting, EPA regional director Bill Yellowtail had enough. So he wrote a letter to the senator with a simple message: Knock it off.

"I was brought up understanding that as a matter of personal honor and integrity you did not attack people who could not fight back, nor did you go after the 'working hands' when your beef was with the organization or the boss," the EPA director wrote to Chlouber. "You obviously do not subscribe to that Western value."

In response, Chlouber fumed.

"In the simplest terms, Mr. Yellowtail," Chlouber wrote back last month, "I am unlikely to accept admonishments concerning my conduct from an individual who has admitted beating his wife, was convicted of stealing merchandise and of felony burglary and of failing to pay child support." With his letter, Chlouber attached newspaper clippings from Yellowtail's losing 1996 congressional campaign in his native Montana in which the EPA director admitted stealing cameras in 1967, slapping his wife in 1976 and ducking child support payments in the mid-1980s.

And to make sure everyone got the message, Chlouber sent copies of his letter and newspaper clips to Colorado's entire congressional delegation.

The irony is that all this nastiness is in the shadow of Denver's federal courthouse, where the bomb trials of Timothy McVeigh and Terry Nichols remind us daily of the danger of unchecked anti-government venom.

"When the scum-sucking low-life meeting happened, within hours, my employees came back to me and reported that they felt quite threatened," Yellowtail remembered. "Senator Chlouber, when he gets enthusiastic, is an imposing and threatening force. On the strength of that behavior and the famous other quote where he promised to hang an EPA person from each end of main street as a reminder that feds were not welcome in Leadville, I actually asked the Federal Protective Service to admonish Senator Chlouber and to provide protection for personnel who were working at the Superfund site. . . . Senator Chlouber huffed and puffed and he got mad at me and he wrote a nasty, personnel letter about me, but pretty much the rhetoric dried up, so it had the desired effect."

While Chlouber and Yellowtail tangled in Denver, the bulldozers went to work in Stray Horse Gulch. It wouldn't take long to change its "moonscape" appearance, but just what the gulch resembled next was hotly debated. And, with additional sources of contamination left to clean up, more battles were yet to come.

15

Saving Oro City

On a beautiful July day in 1998, the group that had gathered along the roadside in upper California Gulch watched as Ed Raines, a heavy, lumbering man, pick up a fistful of rust-colored dirt and shoved it toward Resurrection's project manager. "Do you know what this is?" he demanded. Rez's man, wearing a cowboy hat and a patch over one eye, grabbed his own handful of dirt and thrust it back in Raines's face.

As the two men stood there, angrily shoving fistfuls of dirt in each other's faces, Mike Holmes stood in the back of the crowd wondering why "this was the hill to die for among the preservation folks." To the EPA and Newmont's Resurrection, the company charged with remediating upper California Gulch, there was nothing here except the rust-colored dirt Ed Raines seemed to covet—fluvial tailings, the finely ground mill waste dumped into streams that accumulated along the banks and streambed. Up here, the tailings weren't generating much acid runoff, but the mineralized ground didn't support vegetation either, leaving most of the ground barren and allowing soil to erode down the gulch.

To Ed Raines, a board member of Colorado Preservation Inc., a nonprofit historic preservation group based in Denver, they were standing on all that was left of Oro City, the mining camp that had spawned Leadville more than a century earlier. Farther down the gulch heading toward Leadville, some structures still stood, including a few dilapidated remains of Meyer Guggenheim's Minnie mine and a long stretch of old cribbing threatening to topple onto County Road 2 that winds up California Gulch past the Yak Treatment Plant and the Oro City site before ending at ASARCO's Black Cloud Mine. "This is Colorado's premier frontier mining district," Raines told the group. In this case, history must trump the environment. "This *is* the environment now," he insisted.

The EPA tour of Leadville's mining district for a group of historic preservationists, Chlouber and Miller, and the county commissioners was threatening to become a repeat of the previous year's confrontation in Stray Horse Gulch—minus the television cameras. Back in January, Resurrection had announced its plan to finish cleaning up Operable Unit 4, upper California Gulch. Studies had found 131 waste rock piles in the gulch and its tributaries, 20 of which contributed to acid mine drainage into the Arkansas, and more than one hundred thousand cubic yards of fluvial tailings in what was once Oro City. Resurrection and the EPA proposed a combination of consolidating and capping waste rock piles—on the hit list were the North Mike, Mab, Little Winnie, and Printer Girl—and creating diversion ditches to route water around toxic but historically significant areas such as Guggenheim's Minnie. To contain erosion of the fluvial tailings strewn along the gulch, Resurrection planned a series of channels—modern flumes made of concrete—shallow basins, and an acre of wetlands. ("I don't think this will look like the remains of a mining district, but like the hanging gardens of Babylon," Raines had complained.) The entire project would cost just over $4 million. The only public comments the EPA had received were inquisitive, not disapproving. Chlouber, Miller, and the historic preservationists were absent during the winter that was spent planning the California Gulch remedy. Jim Martin and his two fellow commissioners approved of the plan.

One of those commissioners was Jim Morrison, who had beaten

Bob Casey in the 1996 elections. Jim was fourth-generation Leadville. His great-grandfather had been a blacksmith for the Oro City miners, and he and his wife had made their home in the coarse little mining camp before it had disappeared in the 1920s and the family had moved down to Leadville. Jim's grandfather grew up to become a mechanic at Climax, and his father a Climax accountant. After graduating from high school, Jim left Leadville for college. He wasn't gone long—Jim had dreams of owning a hardware store in town—but when his plans fell through, he found himself driving up the hill past Oro City to work above ground for ASARCO at the Black Cloud. Despite his family connection to Oro City—he had once taken his great-grandmother on an unsuccessful quest to find the old home site—he considered the barren stretch of ground a "mud bog half the year." Jim Martin had once been Jim Morrison's Little League coach. Now Morrison, nearing forty, his white hair pulled back into a short ponytail, had joined his former coach at the commissioners' table just six months before Chlouber had called in the historic preservationists and stopped the work in Stray Horse Gulch. Morrison had resented Chlouber's interference last summer—he thought Stray Horse Gulch looked like a trash dump—and he didn't appreciate it this summer now that bulldozers were ready to go into California Gulch.

This new plea had its genesis the previous winter. While Resurrection, the EPA, and the county commissioners were debating Operable Unit 4, Colorado Preservation Inc., or CPI, was looking for the state's most endangered historic places. Chlouber and Miller didn't hesitate to nominate their hometown, citing "the devastation being done by the EPA in the mining district." That February, when CPI announced its inaugural list of Colorado's Most Endangered Places—places that are "about to be lost forever"—out of sixty nominations, Leadville was number two on the list. "It was clear in everybody's mind that this was an incredible nomination," recalled Monta Lee Dakin, then CPI's executive director. "We quickly recognized that Leadville needed help. It was basically fighting a behemoth that is the EPA, a federal agency, and what small town can fight back a federal agency. It's very, very tough."

Leadville's officials didn't see it that way. Unaware that their town had been nominated and never asked for their opinion, the local politicians went ballistic. ("We were looking for objectivity," Dakin said at the time, explaining the agency's reason for not talking to local officials. Chlouber and Miller, she would add later, understood the "broader context" that the local officials were missing.) Chlouber and Miller themselves, as one might expect, felt vindicated by the CPI designation. "Our county commissioners at that time, which some people think may have been in bed with the EPA to a certain degree, were madder than hell," recalled Miller. "Senator Chlouber and I both said, 'Hey, this proves our point. Here's people from all around the state backing our theory that this historic mining district was being destroyed.'"

CPI's press release was provocative and overstated: "The mining district of Leadville was where famous Coloradoans like Meyer Guggenheim and Horace Tabor made their fortunes. Nearly 120 years later, the Environmental Protection Agency has decided that Leadville's historic tailings and mining structures pose a public health threat. Many experts feel the EPA's wholesale leveling of this historic mining landscape is not necessary and that the public's health can be protected without obliterating Leadville's history." In the mining district, the concern was actually acid mine drainage and heavy metal loading in the Arkansas River, not a "public health threat," a term that still rankled many Leadvillites, and CPI's "many experts" turned out to be Ed Raines, a geologist and mining history enthusiast.

"It was really Ed's take on Leadville that informed us all because he understood things that nobody else could understand," former director Dakin would say later. "He and another volunteer pinpointed the fact that the EPA was doing shoddy science." When asked if Ed Raines was qualified to make that judgment, Dakin hesitated. "We felt that he made sense," she said finally.

A year had passed since Chlouber had staged his standoff with Mike Holmes for NBC News. The EPA had finished consolidating and capping the Wolftone, the Maid of Erin, and the Mahala. The result was three towering, monochromatic piles, tier-shaped and covered with gray dolomite. The town had dubbed them "The Wedding Cakes." Despite the EPA's efforts to re-create the boom days, the Wedding Cakes bore only a vague resemblance to the multihued waste rock piles around them. But was it acceptable? On this, the town was divided. Jim Martin agreed that the Wedding Cakes didn't look natural. "You can see it from Safeway, for God's sake. You look up here, and you wonder, 'What the hell is that?' But you could never make them look like the real thing." (Jim complained to Mike about the gray color. So Mike sprinkled a bit of brown rock around, which made the Wedding Cakes look like gray piles with a bit of brown rock sprinkled around.) But the EPA had also carried out truckloads of trash and evened out the muddy quagmires. "This goddamned place was one hell of an ugly area before they got here," Jim insisted at the time, convinced that the EPA's work had made Stray Horse Gulch more tourist friendly, not less so as Chlouber, Miller, and the preservationists were contending. "People don't care if the pile is upside down or backwards; what you need is signage with pictures and explanations," said one ex-miner helping to promote tourism. Many in town didn't care one way or the other. Myrna Windorski, getting used to changes in her own neighboring waste piles, didn't think it looked so bad, not that she would have said so publicly. Bob Elder, who could name every waste rock pile in the district, also thought the EPA had done a good job, leaving most of the historically significant areas intact.

But others in town expressed outrage, and CPI agreed. "The Wedding Cake was such a travesty," Dakin insisted later. "The EPA was single-handedly ruining Leadville. They were destroying the one thing that was a draw for that town." It was too late for Stray Horse, but the organization was determined not to let the same thing happen in Oro City.

"We fought them all the way," Ed Raines said several years later. "SHPO didn't have the manpower to go through it, and the people they had didn't have the technical knowledge to interpret it. CPI and I felt like SHPO, as a regulatory agency, should be just as hardnosed as the EPA was on the other side. There were places where EPA was falling far short of what was required."

To Jim Martin and others working with the EPA, perhaps the most frustrating aspect of CPI's involvement was the outsider's attitude that Leadville was incapable of handling it themselves. "This was a lose-lose situation for Leadville," Dakin would say. "The EPA basically overwhelmed that town with information. They couldn't figure out what the EPA was doing. I don't know if that was calculated or not. People didn't realize where the stumbling blocks were until CPI got involved and opened up the doors and started analyzing everything and realizing where the problems were. The county commissioners might not have understood all of the complexities. It's true that we were not working on the issue on a daily basis. But on another level, they did not have the benefit of some of the experts that we had pulled in. They didn't always seem receptive because we were the fly in their ointment."

For the average citizen, understanding the nuances of EPA's remedies would have required more effort than most were willing to commit. But five years previously, their elected officials had hired a high-rise Denver attorney to help them sort through and understand the EPA's documents, negotiate with the federal government, and hire a technical consultant when necessary. Though John Faught was now paid by a state grant, for several years the county had paid the lawyer's bills from the county's paltry budget.

"CPI was brought in as a hammer instead of as a partner," said Mike Conlin, still working with the EPA on the bike trail. "They got bludgeoned because they were put in a position of being adversaries. They were an outside group coming in and telling Lake County that they were poor stewards of their land and their historical resources, and as poor stewards they were going to come in and fix it for us."

Dakin acknowledged that the organization didn't like entering communities as the outsider, but she felt that Chlouber and Miller had provided the entrée they needed. What CPI believed was a welcoming gesture into Leadville from the two legislators, others saw as yet another political ploy.

As with the concerns over Stray Horse Gulch the previous year, the state's historic preservationists had a legitimate concern and a right to participate. With their input, remedies could be devised to minimize the impact to the historic district. What frustrated local leaders, the preservation board, and the EPA was the chronic eleventh-hour appearances orchestrated by Chlouber and Miller. At that late date, the preservationists were perceived as hammers, regardless of their good intentions or their ultimate contributions.

Mayor Pete Moore, a newcomer, told the *Rocky Mountain News* that CPI had been fed information that was "totally untrue, misleading and inflammatory. We've lost more buildings to vandalism over the years than the EPA has touched." Friction between Chlouber and Miller and town officials mounted. As Martin and Morrison admonished the legislators in subsequent meetings for making comments without having all of the facts, down in Denver the preservationists were preparing for another round with the EPA.

Leadville had always been proud of its history. Numerous books, historic photographs, and annual events celebrated the town's boom days. But before the EPA shined its light on the mining district, very few in Leadville had taken any steps to preserve what was left. After mining had all but ceased in the hills east of Leadville in the 1950s, residents could still look up and see numerous timber headframes and mine buildings. But every year, more and more of those structures disappeared. By the 1960s, old weathered wood had become fashionable, and a large portion of Leadville's history was carted off in the back of trucks destined for mantels in Denver. As a young man working in a hardware store in the early 1970s, commissioner Jim Morrison remembered selling wood stoves to the "hippies," their trucks piled with lumber that had once been an old mining structure. Owners also routinely knocked down the old buildings to avoid paying taxes on them. It became a tradition to use "Devil's Night," the night before Halloween, as an "excuse for drunks to go burn something," as one resident recalled.

By the 1980s, what the vandals didn't get, the weather did. The structures had been subjected to rain, snow, and freezing weather for more than a hundred years, the average life span for a timber mountain building. All over Colorado, what wasn't being actively reinforced in the old mining districts was toppling over in greater numbers, and Leadville was no exception. Just as the EPA started crawling around on the east side of town, fewer and fewer structures were surviving Leadville's winters. By the late 1990s, relatively few structures remained, and the federal government became a handy scapegoat for those crying foul. Now that so little remained, more people were awakened to the importance of saving what was left.

The county had had plenty of opportunity to restore its historic structures back when it was awash in Climax money—when Chlouber and Miller had been county commissioners. Instead of spending money to stabilize the structures, the county had torn some of them down because of safety and liability concerns. Even the ornate buildings along Harrison Avenue were left to decay. After Climax closed and the county coffers tanked, merely preserving the roads and schools became overwhelming. The divisiveness that was to strike Leadville after the tranquil Climax days had more to do with preserving what some saw as the distinctive *character* of the mining town than with preserving its structures, and that argument centered around tourism.

By the late 1990s, the town of Leadville had changed considerably since the EPA had first driven into town. ASARCO's Black Cloud Mine was still sending miners below ground, but the operation had been teetering on the edge since its brief stall in 1996. More than fifteen years had passed since Climax had closed. Enough time for almost an entire generation of children to grow up and move away. After Lake County's population had plummeted to just 6,000 in the 1980s, it began climbing back up in the 1990s. Throughout Leadville's existence, the population had ebbed and flowed as the miners tramped a step behind the booms and busts, but this time the newcomers weren't miners. Most of them came to get in on the recreation boom going on just over the hill in the ski towns. They didn't have the emotional ties to Leadville's history or even to mining that the old families had.

Most of the anguish over Leadville's changing landscape came from outside the community. Editorials in the local papers denouncing the changes in the Leadville Mining District often came from people who had grown up in Leadville and moved away, or had been brought there as children by parents or grandparents who had once lived in the Magic City. Coming back on summer vacations, they wanted to embrace their childhood home as they had known it. They didn't see Leadville as a living, breathing town, but as a memory laminated in time. Most Americans don't have the luxury of halting a favorite place in the time frame of their choosing. But Leadville was a highly memorialized town and its poor economy had helped prevent significant changes for two decades. The expectations of finding Leadville as it once was—as it had always been—were tangible.

The other contingent consisted of those passionate about historic preservation. A few were newcomers, even fewer were old-timers. The majority were members of organizations down in Denver: the Colorado Historical Society, National Trust for Historic Preservation, and Colorado Preservation Inc. Ed Raines was right. Leadville was a "premier frontier mining district." Its riches had fueled the East's industrial machine. "Some places are significant locally or to the state. Others are a chapter out of our nation's history book. That's Leadville. It's that important," said a National Trust employee from her office in downtown Denver. Once rallied to the call, the historic preservationists seemed sincerely to fear for Leadville's past. (Though one Colorado historian wouldn't grant the preservationists even their sincerity: They "didn't care about Leadville;" they were more interested in tourism-friendly places like Georgetown, Silverton, and Telluride.)

But in Leadville, mining was still a way of life, not its history. Most of the historic preservation fervor Chlouber and Miller mustered in

Leadville was a smokescreen—a way to stick it to the federal government. With fish now swimming in the upper Arkansas, many residents now recognized that the EPA was doing some good. Any residual recalcitrance toward the EPA by the late 1990s was rooted in the West's particular brand of independence. Nothing undermines the perception of autonomy as having a federal agency parked in town.

"Leadville has always been complacent when it comes to historical issues," reflected one man, a newcomer with bushy muttonchops reminiscent of old Meyer Guggenheim. Few people attended the preservation board's meetings, including Chlouber and Miller. Though Miller was a board member for a number of years, legislative duties in Denver limited his attendance after the mid-1990s. "Leadville is a part of the mining community, and the thing about mining towns is they change, and they change in a drastic way," Muttonchops continued. "So somebody knocks down a headframe. Well, it's all in the name of progress. But if the EPA started pushing its weight around, that's different. That wasn't destruction for the good of progress. That was destruction because a federal agency said this was the way you were going to do it. That is one thing that Leadville does not like. If you say yes, they say no. If you say right, they say left. This is not a conforming community." Folks initially just didn't want a bunch of feds telling them what to do. But after fifteen years, the town was not nearly so united against the EPA. A lot of residents had just gotten used it. To its younger citizens, Leadville had always been a Superfund site; what's the big deal? And to most of the newcomers, their new home's Superfund status was background noise—if they even knew of Leadville's long-standing distinction.

Chlouber and Miller were beginning to seem "out of touch" with this changing Leadville. Were the two politicians sincere about historic preservation? That their sudden passion to preserve the mining district followed immediately upon learning of the EPA's relationship with the State Historic Preservation Office suggests that getting the EPA out of town remained their real focus. An article in *High Country News*, a biweekly newspaper covering the West's environmental issues, concluded a 1998 article about the historical significance of mining waste by saying, "Reading between the lines, it's apparent people like Miller are fed up with how long the cleanup is taking, how much it's costing and the bad publicity the town is getting, and they look for any ground upon which they can oppose the EPA." Even to the folks paying attention in Leadville, it smelled of politics. Nothing wrong with that, thought some: "You use whatever angle you can to get your point across. Don't we all to do that? And if we can piggyback onto history, well then, by golly let's piggyback onto history. Let's get these guys stuck," said the muttonchops newcomer.

Carl Miller may have been genuinely distressed by the changes he was witnessing in Stray Horse and California gulches and may have believed it would hurt tourism, which was growing but was still limited. As a Lake County commissioner for twelve years, some of them during the difficult years after Climax closed, Miller had embraced tourism as Leadville's best chance at survival. Later, he had been instrumental in convincing the National Mining Hall of Fame to locate its museum celebrating mining in Leadville's former high school and had been the museum's first director. He had also served on the Historic Preservation Advisory Board. Many in town believed Miller's commitment to the community was genuine and remained genuine even after he began spending more time in the halls of Denver's capitol than on the streets of Leadville. Whether they agreed that his actions were actually helping the town was something else.

Chlouber, however, seemed to be riding on pure politics, a number of Leadville residents had come to feel. He had spent his entire legislative career vilifying the EPA. Early on, when the community feared the EPA and was angered by the agency's "high-handedness," Chlouber's ability to grab the headlines was appreciated. But by the mid-1990s, when the "new era of cooperation"—as a new local paper, the *Leadville Chronicle*, had proclaimed in 1998—had emerged with Mike Holmes and Rebecca Thomas, some in town believed that Chlouber's posturing was hurting Leadville. The EPA was legally mandated to clean up the pollution. The federal government wasn't going to leave until the work was done, and by popping in to hinder the work—cutting the health department's budget, threatening other state budgets, and calling in the preservationists—his actions only slowed the cleanup and prolonged the EPA's presence in town. "It's good copy to be the guy who ran the EPA out of town. A politician can get quite a bit of mileage 'cause people say, 'Boy, that guy's brave,' and then they vote for him. But the more familiar you are with the situation, the more you feel it really isn't helpful," one resident, an old-timer, would say. A newcomer even speculated that Chlouber actually *wanted* the EPA to remain in Leadville because it served as such a good foil for him.

Jim Martin and Jim Morrison particularly resented Chlouber's meddling. "Chlouber didn't participate in the preliminary work; he just showed up with the TV cameras when the bulldozers came out. It's a show, a circus act. The commissioners were getting the work done, and Chlouber used it as a political springboard to stomp all over everyone. He's a bully. He rules by intimidation," Morrison said later. The commissioner was not one to back down either, and the two sparked each other regularly. Martin thought Chlouber was a grandstander: "He sure as hell didn't converse with us very much," Jim remembered. "I've always thought it was a very good way to get your name before the public and the press. He hates the EPA on principle."

It was a view that seemed to be supported by Ken Chlouber himself. "I'm not a historical radical either," Chlouber said in an interview in 2001. "I think the primary driving motivation is simply to be left alone, not being attacked by your own government. You leave 'em long enough they'd build a building here. They'd put their offices up here—a training center for the EPA radical environmentalist recruits. . . . There are well over two thousand mine dumps. And so out of the two thousand, they've eliminated the Penrose, the Morning Star, the Evening Star, the—oh, what's the name of that real famous mine where they had the underground diner?" Chlouber turned to his neighbor, struggling to remember. "Blacktone?" she offered. "Wolftone. Wolftone," Chlouber suddenly remembered. "They're gone."

In a 1994 meeting at Chlouber's home in Leadville with Ken

Wangerud and a state health department official, the three discussed the possibility of having the state take the lead on some of the cleanup to expedite the process. In a memo to Bill Yellowtail, Wangerud reported Chlouber's response: "I don't care if it takes twice as long, just so EPA's name isn't in our newspapers." Chlouber's sole concern, it seemed, was getting the federal government out of town, even if doing so might harm Leadville with a longer, more protracted cleanup.

After the tour in Oro City when Ed Raines "went absolutely bananas over California Gulch," as Jim Martin remembered it, Mike and Rebecca were reluctant to change the plans. Contracts had been signed, and yellow iron was ready to go. But the State Historic Preservation Office was adding its voice to CPI's and asking the EPA to hold off on Oro City. So that summer, as Resurrection began consolidating piles and digging channels, Mike steered the bulldozers away from Oro City, at least for the time being.

The following winter, Chlouber saw a new opportunity to raise the political bar. In January 1999, Ken Salazar became the state's new attorney general and Jane Norton the newly appointed executive director of the health department. They soon found themselves facing Chlouber and Miller who were demanding they stop the EPA. (The previous year, Chlouber had taken another swipe at the state's budget, this time targeting the attorney general's office when Gale Norton was still the boss. Chlouber had successfully amended the state's budget, cutting $2.7 million from the budget of the attorney general's office because of its liaison with the EPA, a move that would have laid off fifteen lawyers. Three days later, Chlouber asked the Senate to reinstate the money, admitting that the shortfall would have hurt other programs besides Superfund. But his ability to punish state agencies for working with the EPA had been made clear.) After their meeting with Chlouber and Miller, the two state officials appealed to the EPA, asking for a moratorium on California Gulch work until the two had had a chance to see the site and weigh in.

It was another beautiful day, this time in late May 1999, when a group of more than fifty people headed up the mountain to Leadville. Many of the same preservationists were back for round two, but this year Ken Salazar and Jane Norton were the heavy hitters. In a cavernous room at the mining museum, Chlouber and Miller repeated their unwavering condemnation of the EPA. Salazar and Norton agreed to help find an "exit strategy" for the feds, announcing plans to create "a small group that can resolve disputes before they become monumental issues." (The "Oversight Committee" met five or six times over the next year but was dropped by the state after the political winds had died down.)

The EPA had important announcements as well that day. Rebecca Thomas stepped to the front of the room; the EPA had agreed not to touch Oro City—at least for now, she said. Instead, they would monitor the water quality coming out of the gulch and decide later, as work in other areas was completed, if Oro City contributed enough contamination to warrant remediation.

Over the past several years, remediating Leadville's mining district had become a complicated balancing act: the historic preservationists' wishes; the town's interests of tourism, bike paths, and development; the state's stewardship responsibilities; and the mining companies' interests of keeping costs low balanced against the environmental task of preventing too much acid mine drainage from reaching the Arkansas River. This balancing act gave the appearance that Rebecca and Mike were arbitrarily choosing what to clean up. If they agreed to leave this area alone, why not that one? Acid mine drainage was coming from hundreds of sources in the mining district. The EPA had to cut off enough of those sources to protect the Arkansas River. Too many nods to historic preservation, the town, or the mining companies and the Arkansas River would remain contaminated—though how much acid mine drainage was too much had yet to be determined.

At the meeting, Rebecca also announced a new timeline: in the next few years, some aspects of the work would be completed and the EPA could start removing areas from the Superfund designation. By the end of 2004, the EPA should be done with everything in Leadville but monitoring the water quality—the results of the balancing act. "I presented this schedule that Mike and I had trumped up in about ten minutes on the way home from Leadville the night before. Honestly, that's as much as we spent on it. I was going through this schedule and trying to outline some of the highlights of that. Carl grabbed the schedule, shook it over his head, and said 'This is the New Testament. You shall do this or else!'" Like all of the other timelines announced in Leadville, the "New Testament" had little chance of coming to pass.

16

The Hydrologic Center of the Earth

Leadville's "gateway" at the south end of Harrison Avenue was eighteen acres of tailings roughly shaped into four massive, undulating piles, scattered with scrap metal, wooden cribbing, and the concrete foundation of a World War II milling operation. If the waste rock piles up on the hills—the R.A.M., the Pyrenees, the Denver City—were considered things of "beauty" and worthy of preservation, the Apache Tailing Impoundment was widely considered a "blight on the community."

Mike Holmes called it the "hydrologic center of the Earth"—Operable Unit 7—the spot where acid mine drainage from upper California Gulch and the Starr Ditch, relaying contamination from Stray Horse Gulch, flowed together. With cleanup progressing in the gulches above, Apache, sitting squat in the middle of California Gulch and under the shadow of the $13 million Yak Treatment Plant, was now the biggest single source of metals contaminating the Arkansas River.

Apache's ownership was difficult to unravel. ASARCO had operated a mill there during World War II and still owned a portion of the land. Apache Energy and Minerals Company itself had operated a mill there in the 1970s as well, but its land was sold off for back taxes. Over the years, ownership had bounced around and was unclear by the time the EPA arrived in town. ASARCO, as the sole surviving entity associated with Apache, was the PRP, the potentially responsible party, that had taken responsibility for it in the 1994 Consent Decree, and the company had been studying and planning how to satisfy cleanup requirements ever since.

Engineers may have considered Apache a contamination hot spot, but it was also the local poster child of Superfund inefficiency. Even after Newmont had capped piles and added channels, the ditches escorting the contamination down California Gulch were soon stained a rusty orange. Residents could stand on Harrison Avenue (and Myrna could look out her window) and see the rocky flume bypass the Yak Treatment Plant, slope steeply downhill past Apache, where the water picked up seventy pounds of zinc each day before continuing on its way to the Arkansas River.

Perplexingly, the contamination not caught by Newmont's remedies in California Gulch slid right past Res-ASARCO's treatment plant and picked up more toxic strength at ASARCO's Apache tailings piles before heading downhill. The treatment plant, built upstream of the hydrologic center, had only enough capacity to handle the drainage coming from the Yak Tunnel, particularly during the heavy spring runoff. Had a higher-capacity treatment plant originally been built even a few hundred yards downstream on the other side of Apache, the "hydrologic center," it could have treated nearly all of the acid mine drainage in the mining district. "All I can say is lawyers," Mike Holmes explained. The operable-unit boundaries had been sanctified by the Consent Decree, and the mining companies, Newmont in particular, were unwilling to deviate. From the EPA's point of view, the two mining companies had reversed roles. Once ASARCO decided they were "beyond denial," working with the subsequent project managers had been a more collaborative process, sharing resources and ideas, than anyone who had dealt with the company earlier could have imagined. Newmont had become the company less willing to work out more synergistic remedies.

Though everyone agreed that Apache was a "blight," coming to a consensus on the best plan to remediate it had not been easy—nothing ever was at this Superfund site. Early on, ASARCO had wanted to consolidate and cap the tailing piles in place. Some worried it would look like a giant gray Wedding Cake right at the entrance to town, but ASARCO planned a Sandhills remedy: cover it up with a plastic liner and clean dirt and plant a hardy grass over the top. For ASARCO, it was simple and inexpensive, just $4 million, and it met all of the EPA's criteria, except the last one—community acceptance.

Residents—those paying attention anyway—wanted the heap removed. Sulfates and other minerals might leach into the groundwater; the acreage, right on Leadville's main street, was also prime real estate and capping would limit the land's usefulness. Any development would not be allowed to breach the cap, making future construction difficult and costly. Removing the pile, however, was expensive. There was a convenient repository nearby—Newmont's Oregon Gulch where another large tailing pond, capped and seeded, lay hidden from view behind the trees. But moving tailings, a slurry, is more challenging than the hard rock of the waste dumps. ASARCO estimated it would cost $12 million to move Apache, three times as much as capping it would cost, and the company was unwilling to pay the extra expense. The tailing piles would stay where they were. Eager to keep Superfund moving, Jim Martin and the county commissioners got behind the project.

For once, as bulldozers were ready to roll, everyone was in agreement—Leadville, ASARCO, and the EPA were ready to watch the town eyesore disappear under a grassy mound. Remarkably, in a repeat of the previous three years, yet another demand to stop the work erupted. This time, the request wasn't coming from Chlouber and Miller or the historic preservationists. This time, it came from an Ohio dentist and Michael the Archangel of Aspen.

The history of mining records the booms, the busts, the Meyer Guggenheims and Horace Tabors who struck it rich, and even the

John Jones hoisted to heaven in the mine shafts. But hovering around the edges were the schemers and dreamers. The snake-oil salesmen hawking their latest mining inventions and the alchemists tinkering in their workshops, trying to turn lead into gold. The get-rich-quick mentality of mining created a subculture still found today among the numerous weekend gold panners—and among those with more elaborate dreams.

In the fall of 1999, as the EPA and ASARCO were finalizing plans to cap Apache, Richard Magovich, the Ohio dentist, stepped forward to claim ownership. He had his own idea for the piles. Instead of capping, Magovich wanted to reprocess the tailings for the pyrite, zinc, lead, and other metals still there, which would also remove the piles and leave the land available for development. He would use the money from the metals to finance his dream—a one-thousand-bed hotel honoring Elvis. The gateway to Leadville would become a tribute to The King, he announced. "I want the new mayor to sing 'Hound Dog' on opening night at the Heartbreak Hotel."

Michael the Archangel had still other plans. Michael Layne, the owner of Aspen-based MTAA Limited (the acronym for Michael the Archangel of Aspen), had also declared ownership of Apache. Layne, too, wanted to reprocess the tailings, but he planned an athletic training facility for the site, complete with condos, a health spa, medical clinic, a hotel complex, and an Olympic village. Layne was eventually deemed Apache's owner, but he told a local reporter that the dentist's plan was "not incompatible" with his own, and the two formed a partnership.

"I think they're both a couple of red herrings," Rebecca Thomas told the *Leadville Chronicle*. But the EPA wasn't opposed to reprocessing the piles as long as the project was technically sound, achieved the cleanup goals, and the men had the financial backing to carry it out. It was another eleventh-hour complication that threatened to sideline the work, but Rebecca invited Layne to submit a proposal. She gave him a deadline.

Instead, Michael Layne, despite his angelic alias, went on the attack, determined to stop ASARCO from capping Apache. In public meetings and in the newspapers, he tried to convince the community to oppose ASARCO and the EPA. Layne's plan should have been compatible with a number of normally disparate viewpoints in town—the mining-is-king club, the pro-development faction, and those worried about leaching groundwater—but Michael the Archangel just couldn't muster any support. His aggressive stance—"they want to cap death at your front door then walk away"—hit the wrong note in this mining town and, a city councilman warned, threatened to polarize the community.

Jim Martin made his feelings about Layne's tactics known. At a meeting, following Layne's presentation, Jim confronted him, saying he had "never heard such absurd statements in my life." In response, Layne asked Jim, nearly seventy years old now, if he'd spent any time at the site. Jim was apoplectic. "I have spent the last goddam twelve years of my life overseeing this Superfund site," he bellowed.

At the end of March, MTAA finally submitted its long-awaited proposal, but the EPA quickly determined the proposal was too sketchy to evaluate. Rebecca, anxious not to miss another construction season, scheduled a public meeting in Leadville on April 13, 2000, to give Layne an opportunity to present the missing technical information. About thirty people filed into the small auditorium in Leadville's mining museum. It was a comfortable room, one Mike and Rebecca knew well, with tiered, cushioned seating arranged in an arc. Sitting next to the two EPA officials in the front row, ASARCO's newest project manager, Bob Litle, stretched out his long legs, and down the row sat two representatives from the state. The Leadvillites, including Jim Martin, fanned out behind the officials.

Michael Layne, sitting in the middle of a long table at the front of the room, was a brawny, middle-aged man. His bright blond hair, gelled back around his ears, hung to his broad shoulders, and a swath of white flowers on his short-sleeved blue shirt stretched across his barrel chest. His tropical appearance seemed out of place in the old mining town. He was flanked by two men, mining experts meant to bolster his proposal.

Layne opened the meeting with Churchillian determination: "We will never give up," he began. The three-hour long meeting itself would be a test of endurance. Layne was aggressive, complaining repeatedly that he needed more time to complete tests. He accused Rebecca of a "rush to judgment" and threatened to go to court if the capping proceeded.

Rebecca, sitting upright, her hair pulled neatly up behind her head, continued to request more specific information while Mike, leaning forward with his head in his hands much of the meeting, appealed for sympathy. In a slow, halting voice, he explained his predicament with Leadville's short construction season and asked Layne not to hold up the Apache project another year.

Nearly three hours into the meeting, Jim Martin spoke up for the first time. "Where are the economics, sir? There might be $2 million worth of junk in there that you'll spend $5 million getting. I don't believe that."

"Why does that concern you?" Layne demanded.

"Because I don't think it's a viable project unless economics are involved," Jim answered.

"Well, I'm glad that you're the overall genius that has gotten the information from all of us, and your opinion is respected," replied Layne, though his harsh tone said otherwise.

The two men flanking Michael Layne throughout the meeting looked increasingly uncomfortable. One man kept his eyes on the table, a frown creased his face; the other, a younger man with a long ponytail and glasses, played with his pen. They answered generic technical questions when asked, but had no specific information to offer regarding Apache. They had just met Layne for the first time that evening.

Immediately following the meeting, both men disavowed any association with Michael the Archangel. "I have never been so embarrassed in my professional career," the frowner wrote in a letter to Rebecca the next day. He had been brought to Leadville "under false and misleading circumstances." The younger man was equally appalled. "It was disrespectful to a lot of professionals and citizens who should have been commended for their concern instead of humiliated in public," he told the *Herald Democrat*.

Layne remained defiant. "This will not be capped," he vowed. The only public comment to MTAA's proposal came from the county commissioners who considered it "highly questionable and, in part, ludicrous." Without additional information, Rebecca told Layne, the EPA would reject his proposal and capping would proceed that summer. Despite Layne's promise to provide the necessary information in a month's time, Michael the Archangel and the Elvis-loving dentist from Ohio disappeared, but they would be back.

ASARCO's Bob Litle had only been in Leadville for a few years when he faced Michael Layne over Apache. The engineer agreed with the company that Superfund was unfair. To him, it was like making citizens responsible for driving cars using lead-based gasoline before it became illegal. But the good-natured man with a ready smile wasn't in Leadville to argue about it. The company had moved on. "Mining companies were dinosaurs in the early days. They weren't proactive about the environment. We were in denial about the whole concept. But every company grows. Environmental issues were something that all mining companies had to learn to deal with."

In his nearly thirty years with the company, Litle had moved around a lot—from sites in Missouri, to El Paso, Texas, to a smelter in Omaha, Nebraska—before landing in Denver. He was in Omaha in the early 1990s when the company shut down the smelter after more than a century in operation. Litle switched to the "environmental side" of mining, which eventually brought him to Denver—and Leadville.

When Litle had arrived in 1997, the decision on the residential lead action level had not yet been decided, but of the nearly forty so-called Downtown Dumps, the cone-shaped waste cascading out of the gulches and into the east-side neighborhood, fourteen of them contained lead levels over 3,500 parts per million and would have to be capped or removed regardless. On the hit list were the Bison/Gray Eagle, Pocahontas, Star/Lazy Bill, Wolcott, Luzerne, and the Coronado.

In 1896, the Coronado had been a large mining operation just six blocks east of Harrison Avenue between 7th and 8th streets. That year had begun with promise. Leadville was getting back on its feet after the silver crash three years earlier, thanks largely to its downtown mines. But the Coronado was the scene of a controversy that turned violent and, some have argued, altered the course of western labor relations.

Miners were a hard group to unionize. They tramped often, spoke different languages, and often favored nationalistic ties over labor cohesion. But in 1896, Leadville's union was holding together with a few thousand members. When the union requested that all of Leadville's mines pay $3 a day—some were only paying $2.50—the miners faced an aggressive coalition of mine owners who understood the power of banding together.

Just twenty years after miners had rushed to the upper Arkansas Valley, nearly all of the mines were owned by corporations. Few owners had ever dug a hole or mucked in a tunnel. They were Eastern entrepreneurs who rarely ventured West, and they didn't understand what it meant to be a hardrock miner. But they did know how to win a power struggle. When the miners struck against the thirteen mines refusing to pay the extra fifty cents a day, the mine owners shut down all the mines, throwing more than two thousand miners out of work. The battle was joined.

The miners armed themselves and sat outside of town, intimidating strikebreakers into turning around. Instead of capitulating, the owners pulled the pumps on some downtown mines, like the Penrose, allowing the tunnels to flood, and reopened three others—the Coronado, Robert Emmet, and Maid of Erin—with miners willing to break the strike. The mines became wooden garrisons with high fences, guard towers, and rifles poking out of gun ports.

Many of the details are unknown, but on September 20, the families of miners living near the Coronado were awakened and warned to leave. On that moonlit night, the Coronado was attacked with gunfire and dynamite and was soon ablaze. All of the men defending the mine made it to safety. But when fireman Jerry O'Keefe tried to hook up a water hose, he was shot to death. When the fire spread to nearby houses, armed Leadvillites rushed up the hill to the Coronado and forced the unionists to disperse so the firemen could prevent the fire from destroying Leadville.

By morning, the town had been spared, but the Coronado was destroyed. An estimated five strikers had died, and Jerry O'Keefe received a hero's funeral. The union disavowed any connection to the violence, but the events of that night had turned the town against the strike. The governor ordered the state militia to Leadville, and four days later sixty-five miners from Missouri hopped off the train ready to take the strikers' jobs. With the militia standing guard with rifles, there was nothing the union could do to prevent the mines from reopening. The strike limped along for five more months, but the union was losing members as miners slowly went back to work. After nearly nine months, the holdouts voted to end the strike.

It took years for Leadville to recover. Businesses had closed and both miners and nonminers had fled during the economically troubled strike. The pumps in the downtown mines started back up, but it would take two years to dewater them and shovel out the silt that had accumulated in the tunnels. With a decisive victory, the mine owners were more powerful than ever, and the bitterness between the two camps lasted well into the next century.

A hundred years after the Coronado burned, ASARCO and the EPA were threatening two of its three waste dumps and twelve others with bulldozers. Miller and Chlouber were the most vocally opposed to removing the Coronado. "One of the nation's great struggles in which people died occurred there," Chlouber lamented to the *Leadville Chronicle*. "To remove it for no public good is just another EPA slap in the face, but this will last a long time because it will be gone forever. They're hauling our history away in the back of a truck."

Jim Martin wasn't nearly as impressed. "It was a pile of dirt. So you had a strike back then and somebody got shot," he said later with a shrug. Jim and the preservation board had worked hard to preserve what they felt was historically significant, but some of the Downtown Dumps were loaded with lead, and they literally climbed straight out of people's backyards. Jim didn't believe EPA officials were spending tens of millions of dollars in Leadville because they enjoyed summer-time in the mountains (one of Chlouber's favorite retorts). "If they're savable, I'd like them saved because they give a flavor to the town. But if it's got to go, it's got to go." Residents living near the Downtown Dumps agreed. Like the Apache Tailing Pile, most residents wanted them gone.

While the fate of the Downtown Dumps and Apache hung in the bal-ance, Mike Holmes was sitting in the EPA's trailer on 5th Street one day in November 1999, when a couple of men knocked on his door. They had an "EPA-endorsed" product that was just what Holmes needed, they told him. Spray it on and eliminate acid mine drainage. Problem solved. Mike was skeptical. "We don't endorse anything, like the Good Housekeeping Seal," he told them. But Mike agreed to let them spray the Ponsardine, a waste rock pile generating acid mine drainage at the edge of town, with their "pixie-dust."

Like the entrepreneurs with the next great mining invention, min-ing remediation attracts an equally enthusiastic group. Some are legit-imate, but many are the equivalent of the snake-oil salesmen of old. Since the EPA first came to Leadville, project managers had been lis-tening to men with the next great invention, and they all had their favorite. Bill Rothenmeyer, Leadville's first Superfund manager in the early 1980s, watched a couple of guys burn themselves demonstrating a filter idea that flopped. Liz Evans of the plugging years remembered listening to a man proposing to plug the holes with papier-mâché.

For Mike, it was Envirobond. The men explained that after spray-ing the waste rock pile, an invisible seal would form. Water and snow would run harmlessly off the pile, they promised. If it worked, the residents could keep the Downtown Dumps safely where they were. So on a sunny day in November, Mike watched as a sprayer truck coated the Ponsardine with Envirobond. "Oh man, what have I done," he remembered thinking. The colorful waste rock pile—and the surrounding trees, rocks, and sagebrush—had been whitewashed. The dazzling white cone, shimmering in the sunlight, was an eye-catching scar in the autumn setting and yet another insult to

Leadville. Jim Martin was not pleased. The company assured the townsfolk that Ponsardine would be back to normal by the following spring. Mike put buckets below the pile to capture and test the runoff. Envirobond couldn't solve Mike's dilemma with Apache and its owner, but if successful it could save Ponsardine, the Coronado piles, and a dozen other Downtown Dumps. After the snow fell, the pile blended into the background, and everyone waited to see what would happen in the spring.

17

Kids First

Few people in Leadville knew it, but their town was the national headquarters (along with Palmerton, Pennsylvania) for the Superfund Coalition Against Mismanagement, or SCAM—on paper anyway. SCAM's press releases called itself a coalition of Superfund communities that were banding together in the hopes of bringing about meaningful reform to the Superfund law. Jim Martin was a board member, as were his two fellow commissioners, the mayor of Leadville, and Carl Miller, back before he was a state representative. In reality, SCAM was run by a lobby firm in Denver that was paid behind the scenes by ASARCO.

SCAM formed in October 1992 as an attempt to build political strength in Congress against Superfund under the guise of a grassroots movement. For Martin, who was listed as chairman on the letterhead for a time, all SCAM meant was a trip to Aspen to watch a film about the yard removals taking place in Midvale, Utah, and some classes to learn how to talk to the press. "Not that it did us any good."

In late 1993, SCAM attacked the EPA's soil lead policies and the IEUBK computer model used to predict children's risk to high blood lead levels from lead in the soil. The federal government had determined that soil lead levels between 400 and 1,200 parts per million cause elevated blood lead levels, and the EPA was leaning toward setting a policy that established an "action level"—that bright line above which yards must be removed or capped—at 400 parts per million. The EPA called it a "guidance," more than a suggestion but not quite a mandate. SCAM was demanding a public review process not normally given to guidance setting. "We believe that this proposal is tantamount to a rule or regulation and we will not stand for EPA to hide behind calling it a guidance or directive as a means of circumventing the public comment process," SCAM's then chairman from Granite City, Illinois, a lead smelter town, was quoted in a press release. The EPA's preoccupation with dirt sterilization, SCAM contended, wasted billions of dollars of taxpayers' money, threatened the survival of mining communities, and took the focus away from "real" environmental problems.

SCAM seems to have received little attention from the media, though its press releases were dutifully reported in the *Herald Democrat*. By the summer of 1994, the EPA had issued its guidance on leaded soils. Four hundred to twelve hundred parts per million was a "trigger level" for further investigation, not an action level. If one of its ten regions wanted to institute an action level above 1,200 parts per million, personnel there were required to come to headquarters for a "consultation" to justify allowing a higher level of lead to remain in place. In a press release, SCAM vowed to continue fighting the "devastating lead-in-soil policy. . . . As dozens of communities across this country know all too well, the EPA interprets and applies their lead-in-soil policies as regulations."

If EPA headquarters truly intended for its guidance to have the weight of a regulation, as SCAM contended, then Leadville was fated to a Midvale remedy—wholesale yard removal. Nearly every yard in Leadville contained more than 400 parts per million lead and 7 percent had over 2,000 parts per million, the interim number allowed in the Consent Decree 1994 that outlined the mining companies' cleanup responsibilities. The short summer season could mean years of yard removals during the economically vital tourist season—and would reinforce the message that Leadville was diseased and dangerous.

Determining risk in a one-contaminant town like those near a battery plant or lead smelter is relatively straightforward, but add a complex jumble of lead types in the form of smelter soot, waste rock, tailings, and slag blanketing nearly twenty square miles in a mining town like Leadville, and the toxicologists' task is complicated considerably. As the release of Leadville's health risk assessment neared, Jim Martin and other locals were nervous. An early draft had been the subject of much bitterness when it had estimated that 41 percent of children would be lead poisoned. Mike and Rebecca were new project managers, and no one knew if they would be willing to go against the guidance coming out of Washington, D.C. "Our experience has shown that EPA, for the sake of a totally unrealistic model spewing from headquarters in Washington . . . has been prepared to destroy the mining heritage of this community, the quality of life our citizens enjoy and one of our primary sources of livelihood—tourism," Commissioner Martin said during a Superfund panel discussion held in Leadville. "We make comments and the EPA does as it damn well pleases."

In late 1995, when the report detailing the risks of living in Leadville was finally released, it proved anticlimactic. The toxicologists made no predictions of the percentage of lead-poisoned children, instead sanctioning Bornschein's blood-lead results that had shown an 8.8 percent overall risk and calling it a "reality check" to the IEUBK model. The report did conclude that blood lead levels in children are "higher than acceptable" and that the EPA's national policy that no more than 5 percent of children have a risk of blood lead levels greater than 10 micrograms must be met. But that had been expected.

The most disputed finding in the risk assessment was that lead in the soil was the primary cause of elevated blood leads in the children—not lead-based paint. But the report did not draw a bright line—the soil lead action level—that had everyone so nervous. "Based on the IEUBK model," the report read, "the estimated target soil levels needed to meet these objectives range from as low as 400 parts per million (assuming intake of 50 milligrams per day each of soil and dust) up to 5,500 parts per million (assuming intake of 5 milligrams per day each of soil and dust). Because of the uncertainties in the IEUBK calculations, especially in soil and dust intake rates, it is not possible to identify any one specific target soil level as most appropriate." However impossible, one would be coming.

Estimating ingestion rates plays a critical role in determining risk, and in Leadville the subtext was weighted with controversy. Simply living around lead, even touching it, wasn't harmful. Lead had to be eaten or breathed to be toxic. That's why the slag layered on the roads for a hundred years, ground up by cars, and blown into the air had been perhaps the most widespread lead exposure pathway related to mining in Leadville, but the lead bound up in hardened slag was the least. Now, the concern was young children playing in the dirt and putting their fingers and toys in their mouth. That behavior varied tremendously among children, making estimating ingestion rates the most difficult and controversial part of the equation. Officially, the toxicologists had left a wide margin in the risk assessment. Now, it was the project managers' more challenging task to take that information and navigate a web of science, politics, and economics to come up with a number.

In 1994, the Consent Decree had identified a bright line of 2,000 parts per million, but that had been based as much on politics as on science. In fact, toxicologists didn't see a statistical correlation between elevated blood leads and soil composition until soil levels reached 3,500 parts per million, three times higher than the guidance coming out of Washington. "The difference between 2,000 and 3,000 sounds like a lot, but it's not," explained EPA toxicologist Chris Weis. "A child who's exploratory and prone to lead exposure is going to be at risk far below levels that we could ever hope to clean up to and perhaps even ranging into natural background levels in a mining district like Leadville." Rebecca faced a decision: go with a guidance-satisfying 1,200 parts per million and somehow force Leadville to comply or challenge EPA headquarters by advocating a higher threshold. Her decision would depend largely on the Leadvillites themselves.

Much was riding on the success of Kids First. It was a health program and an environment program rolled into one. The county's health department would conduct the blood-lead testing; ASARCO was to test and remove all lead sources—soil, indoor paint, and leaded pipes. Parents of children with elevated blood leads were encouraged to have their homes and yards tested, but anyone could request it, free of charge. Homes that tested over the trigger levels would be rectified. But the program was entirely voluntary. No child had to have a blood-lead test, and no home, even if its lead level were above a trigger level or a child living there had elevated lead, was forced to accept remediation. To be successful and avoid wholesale yard removal, Leadville citizens had to participate voluntarily. Lake County, with ASARCO money, began reaching out to families with children under seven. Newspaper ads, door-to-door visits, and presentations introduced the community to Kids First and encouraged families to come in for free blood lead screenings.

Rebecca was convinced early on that a 3,500 parts per million action level and the Kids First program was worth fighting for in Leadville. The county health department was doing an excellent job of reaching the community, and, despite some vocal opposition, residents were responding. "If we didn't have a strong Lake County Community Health Program like we did, we might have weighed in with a much more conservative soil action level because you wouldn't have any other way to address the exposure," Rebecca said later. "I had very strong convictions about it. I was very comfortable that we would address the lead exposure, and I thought it was the only remedy that would work for that community so I was willing to really work for it." The EPA estimated that about 150 homes exceeded 3,500 parts per million.

Everybody would win under this plan. The town would be spared the disruption and negative implications of a Midvale remedy; ASARCO estimated that Kids First would save the company $3 million over wholesale yard excavation; and the EPA would have only minimal involvement—a valuable distinction for the independent town. Most importantly, Leadville's children would be more protected. "In cases where you can institute a long-lived, active public health program such as Kids First, it's preferable," toxicologist Weis insisted. "If we had cleaned up to 400 parts per million, the EPA would have basically brushed its hands off and walked away with no further action. And in a place like Leadville, the kids are still going to be at risk because they can go play on a pile on the east side of town or they can go to Bernie Smith's cabin down on the river flats, which are still highly contaminated, and there's no safety net for them whatsoever. Whereas with the Kids First program and Lake County's independent involvement in that, there's at least some safety net for those kids. The existence of an active public health program is almost always better than some engineering remedy that you can't really check up on."

But at the EPA, the engineers far outnumber the health professionals and dismissing an engineering remedy in favor of an educational health program ran directly counter to headquarter's policies on soil leads. A second, updated guidance that would come out in 1998 reinforced the 400 parts per million trigger level and the IEUBK model to determine action levels. A comprehensive blood lead study should not be relied upon solely, according to the document. The guidance also stated that Superfund had little authority to remediate indoor lead-based paint. And finally, the EPA emphasized the superiority of engineering remedies over "institutional controls" that rely on compliance—like Kids First. "You should have a lot of institutional controls right when you get to the site because you need to educate the community," explained Shahid Mahmud, a member of the Lead Sites Workgroup at EPA headquarters that came up with the guidance. "But as time goes on, those efforts should be going down and your engineering controls and your actual remediation should be going up. Institutional controls over time are really questionable. Who pays for it? Who maintains it? Who enforces it? The jury is still out on that. We're encouraging more and more engineering controls so you take care of it once and for all."

At Leadville, Rebecca wanted a remedy based on blood lead levels not soil lead levels, and 3,500 parts per million was by far the highest residential soil action level ever requested in the nation—and even that was to be voluntary. "D.C. was difficult," Rebecca recalled. "They looked at our proposal and had many concerns. They felt we weren't doing enough to protect the citizens. The same modeling that led us to 3,500 parts per million has led other communities around the country to accept 500 parts per million."

The debate swirled around two inexact sciences. Blood lead measurements are a "snapshot" in time. They record the amount of lead circulating in the blood at that moment, not a child's total accumulation. Bornschein's study had been conducted in September, after a summer of playing outside when blood lead levels should have been at their highest, but it was still only measuring a moment in time and may not have accurately reflected a lifetime of risk. The IEUBK model, on the other hand, was only as accurate as the data and assumptions that were fed into it. A great deal of the EPA's time and money had been spent determining the model's default values and, in many cases, the model worked as it was intended. The EPA could point to such Superfund smelter sites as Jasper County in Missouri where the IEUBK had established an action level of 500 parts per million. After more than two thousand yards were replaced, blood lead levels had dropped dramatically. The model was intended to provide a cost-effective method of determining risk and setting action levels. A potentially responsible party, however, was welcomed to spend its own money on site-specific studies to refute the model's results.

The EPA had been in Leadville a long time gathering specific information, and ASARCO had paid for a blood lead study. Chris Weis, the EPA toxicologist, was eager to use the information. "There was a lot of debate and hand-wringing about using blood leads to make judgments on children. I think it would be unethical, if not negligent, to ignore that data in the decision making," he would say later, and he questioned the use of the IEUBK model in complex mining sites like Leadville. "It's very good for conducting exposure assessments and discussions with the public, but I don't think it's a very good tool for setting action levels. It doesn't allow very much room for public health and common sense to operate."

To persuade its headquarters, the Region 8 team needed to understand why the model had been so far off in the first place. They turned to the educational efforts, ongoing since the late 1980s, that had most likely reduced ingestion rates. The infamous "pig studies" that many in town found so insulting had helped Leadville's cause as well by proving that not all lead was equal—some types had to be ingested in greater amounts to show up in the blood than the model's default values had assumed. ASARCO was also willing to pay for a program that investigated and remediated all sources of lead, including lead-based paint, which exceeded the company's legal responsibilities. But perhaps the most compelling argument was Leadville's climate. The highest town in the nation was snowed under nearly nine months of the year. Children simply had less opportunity to play in the yards, waste rock piles, and tailing ponds than their lowland counterparts.

Headquarters and officials from other regional offices were still not prepared to endorse a nonengineering approach. State and federal representatives throughout the West feared that Kids First and 3,500 parts per million would set a precedent. Mining companies, and ASARCO in particular, might use Leadville to undermine remedies being negotiated at other Superfund sites. "There was a concern because we know for a fact that when we've gone in and removed down to at least a foot or two, then you've really eliminated the exposure to the kids," Mahmud explained. "We're more confident with that because you've taken care of the source. This was out of the norm."

It would take more than pig studies and snow to convince headquarters to allow a voluntary public health program run by a mining company and the locals themselves, neither of which were even admitting that a health problem existed. Many townsfolk didn't buy into the idea that the dirt harmed their children, and they didn't care about "action levels." This was just another excuse to exploit ASARCO. Those "Kids Farce" advertisements in the weekly newspapers encouraging parents to have their children tested gave Leadville a bad name.

Jim Martin didn't believe a health problem existed either, but he understood that the alternative—wholesale yard removals—was far worse, and he was willing to fight for Kids First.

A previously unthinkable alliance took shape. Leadville, the EPA's Region 8 office, and ASARCO agreed to fight together for Kids First. The mining company's opinion wouldn't count for much, but local citizens would play a pivotal role. The first step for this new alliance was to convince the state to climb aboard. It took some doing, but after months of discussions, the health department and attorney general's office agreed to endorse Kids First and 3,500 parts per million action level. Colorado's governor, Roy Romer, sent a letter of support to Carol Browner, EPA's top administrator. Even Ken Chlouber participated in this odd alliance, though in his own political style. Attempting to strong-arm headquarters into surrendering, he unsuccessfully lobbied Colorado's U.S. senators to add an amendment to the EPA appropriations bill that would have prohibited any further remediation in Leadville unless the 3,500 parts per million standard was approved.

Leadville's town officials and the Region 8 office agreed on a more temperate method. In early 1998, it was time for Leadville to present its case directly to the decision makers in Washington, D.C., and a trip to EPA headquarters was planned for the spring. Rebecca Thomas and three others from the Region 8 office would go, as would a representative from the state health department. Jim Martin and John Ozzello, director of the Lake County Health Department, also packed their bags. Leadville buzzed with the news that two local officials would soon travel to the nation's capital to appeal directly to the EPA's top brass. In the local newspapers, Jim Martin explained the significance of his upcoming trip. The difference between 2,000 and 3,500 parts per million is "the difference between tearing up every damn yard in town and tearing up a few or none," he explained to the reporter. "Thirty-five hundred will be a record high, but we deserve it. We believe it's a safe level. The whole Region 8 supports it. It's the national people that are giving them fits." When the reporter for the *Leadville Chronicle* asked Mike Holmes what would happen if EPA headquarters didn't approve 3,500 parts per million, Mike laughed and said, "I'm going to duck."

On April 1, a few weeks before Jim's trip, a front-page headline in the *Herald Democrat* announced: "EPA ends Superfund after new study on lead: New program to promote benefits of eating dirt." Based on new study results, the article reported, lead is now believed to be an "essential part of every American's diet." Leadville's lead and acid mine drainage would now be bottled and sold to the nation's health-conscious public. It was, of course, an April Fools' joke, and it showed just how far the relationship between Leadville and the federal government had come. With the emerging "new era of cooperation," as the *Leadville Chronicle* had recently proclaimed, the newspapers reflected that new spirit as well. The occasional editorializing still encroached, but the acrimony was gone. The laid-back and collaborative approach Mike Holmes and Rebecca Thomas brought to Leadville had taken much of the bitterness out of the EPA's presence to the point that the *Herald Democrat* could poke fun at the situation.

Jim Martin looked forward to a trip to Washington, D.C. For the boy raised in remote Canadian mining camps, living in the nation's capital during World War II had been his most exotic childhood home. The trip got off to an inauspicious start when the airline lost Jim's luggage and, after their red-eye flight, the hotel rooms weren't available. But with a day to themselves before the meetings began, Rebecca, Jim, and two Region 8 officials rented bikes and enjoyed a long ride from Old Town to the Washington memorials, riding back in a downpour.

The entire group trouped to the EPA's offices the next day. They were escorted into a windowless conference room crowded with attorneys, technical experts, and members of the Lead Sites Workgroup. An assistant administrator, the highest-ranking official at the meeting and the person who would decide Leadville's fate, was fifteen minutes late. After the meeting got underway, Rebecca presented an overview of Region 8's position, but the meeting belonged to Leadville. It would be up to Jim Martin and John Ozzello to convince this room full of Washington suits that they knew what was best for their mountain community and could be entrusted to run their own residential soils remedy. The contentiousness that had surrounded Leadville just a few years earlier and its vocal dismissal that a health threat might exist were well known to those sitting around the table.

Rebecca sat down and watched as the two Leadvillites made their case. She was impressed. John Ozzello, she recalled, "started by saying, 'I really want you to remember me. I know I'm just a small-town guy from a small town in Colorado a thousand miles away from here. But I want you to remember me, and I want you to remember what I'm going to say.' It was very well done. It helped that he was a Leadville-looking guy with a long, gray ponytail and wore blue jeans to the meeting." Ozzello explained the blood lead program Lake County had initiated and their successes in just the first few years. They were targeting areas where the danger was highest—the east side of town, Stringtown, and the Lake Fork Mobile Home Park. Blood lead levels were already dropping. At Lake Fork, the percentage of children with elevated blood lead levels had dropped in half since 1993, and more than eighty homes had already had or agreed to have their soils tested.

Jim Martin was also convincing, Rebecca recalled. "When he gets really angry, he tends not to say too much, especially if he's not allowed to yell. So he didn't say much in the meeting, but it was very clear to everyone in the room that he felt very strongly about it and would be satisfied with nothing less than what we had proposed." The Leadville men obviously knew the issues, knew their community, and understood what was at stake.

At the end of the meeting, the administrator verbally agreed to Kids First and the 3,500 parts per million action level. It would be considered a pilot program and would include an agreement from ASARCO that the company wouldn't mention it at other sites. Factors, including Leadville's unique weather, played a role, but Jim Martin and John Ozzello had convinced EPA headquarters that the community was willing to accept the long-term commitment. "Working toward the same goal went a long way toward building trust with the community," a delighted Rebecca said later. "It was us against every-

one else, and it was very much a team-building experience. We could-
n't have done it without each other."

After the delegates triumphant return home, the *Herald Democrat*
announced that Leadville residents could "put away your shovels."
Carl Miller was jubilant, proclaiming at a meeting, "It shows how
much can be accomplished when we all work together." It took another year and a half before Leadville's Kids First remedy was officially
sanctioned with the signing of the Record of Decision, the ROD, for
Leadville's residential soils. As of September 6, 1999, Kids First was
known as the Lake County Community Health Program and 3,500
parts per million became the highest action level in the nation. Thirteen years had passed since the state had first raised the alarm about
health hazards in Leadville, and a decade since the EPA's Ken
Wangerud had picked up the gauntlet. Now the EPA would step back
and let ASARCO and the county run the program's day-to-day operations.

The ROD was a momentous occasion, but much work was yet to be
done. The residential areas were divided into two "statistical units."
Each unit would have to meet performance standards before the EPA
would delete the town's residential area from the Superfund site.
Within each unit, no more than 5 percent of children up to six years of
age could have a blood lead level over 10 micrograms, and no more
than 1 percent over 15 micrograms. At least 180 children and 50 percent of newly eligible children had to participate in the blood lead
program each year. To be considered representative statistically, those
children had to live in all of Leadville's neighborhoods—not just in
low-lead zones. After putting all the dots on the map, were there any
gaps? These standards had to be met for three consecutive years
before the remedy was considered complete. To encourage participation, ASARCO's trust fund gave each child a $50 savings bond and each
family a $25 certificate for purchases at the local grocery store.

The community also had to create a local ordinance—not an easy
endeavor in this independent town—to ensure that residents digging
up their yards in the future or any new construction sites have the
soils tested and any contamination disposed of properly. The cash-

strapped county would have to set up a system to monitor and enforce permits and find a place where residents could take contaminated soil and pick up clean dirt. This ordinance was the only aspect of the remedy that wasn't voluntary and it extended across the entire site, not just current yards, and to future residential areas as well. Rebecca, John Faught, Jim Martin, Bob Litle, and state representatives sat back down at the negotiation table to hash out an ordinance. The alliance had laid the groundwork for a harmonious approach, but four years later they would still be sitting there, trying to make it work. (Some would blame the delay on the EPA for dragging out the process, others would blame the state for requiring too many built-in assurances, and others would blame the county when newly elected commissioners would come to the table with new concerns and demands.) In a few years' time, a panel of outside scientists would decide if 3,500 parts per million and Kids First had been the right decision. Were blood levels going down or was 3,500 parts per million just too high and Leadville too uncooperative to participate? Would Leadville have to undergo widespread yard removal after all?

The fate of the Downtown Dumps was also riding on the final soil action level. The higher 3,500 parts per million level saved many of them, but two of the three Coronado waste dumps and twelve others were still on the chopping block. The cheapest solution was to simply haul them away, and ASARCO had the bulldozers gassed up and ready to go.

"We said, 'Surely, we'll be able to get somewhere with ASARCO,'" said a newcomer passionate about mining history. "They're our own. They won't remove the mine dumps over there. But, man, I'm telling you what. Before the summer even got over, they were already up there removing mine dumps. You could hardly believe it." Preserving a mine dump up on the hill, and having one in your backyard were two different things to the dumps' neighbors, however, and most were glad to see them go. By the end of the year, fourteen Downtown Dumps had been hauled to an underground disposal site way up Stray Horse Gulch at another mining complex called Ibex, where the unsinkable Molly Brown's fortune had been made.

18

Doc's Meadows

While residents up in Leadville had been arguing year after year over residential soils and waste rock piles, down in the valley, Doc had been waiting for the cleanup of his land to begin. A few years after receiving an anonymous warning and awakening to find his river running red, a MacNeil/Lehrer NewsHour reporter had visited him. The cameras had captured a "city slicker's" fantasy. On the wide Arkansas Valley before the snowcapped Rocky Mountains on an overcast November day, Doc Smith maneuvered his horse in a sharp turn to stop a calf as he rounded up his cattle. Only Doc's seed cap and leather shoes (Doc usually eschewed the typical rancher's cowboy hat and boots), violated the setting. At that time, Doc was still in his fifties and raising the last of his eleven children. He couldn't imagine a life spent anywhere but on the ranch on which he'd been raised.

But later, leaning against a wooden fencepost, his brown cap tipped back revealing his thinning, gray hair to the camera, the frustration in Doc's voice was evident. If mining runoff hadn't contaminated his meadows, his hay production could triple, his cows would be larger, and his income could double, the reporter explained when the segment aired. "He's been waiting since 1936, when his first colt died, for action." Half a century later, Doc was tired of waiting. When the NewsHour visited the Smith ranch, California Gulch had been a Superfund site for only five years. Up the hill, Leadville's new mayor, Jim Martin, and the townsfolk were fighting the EPA's plan to plug the Yak Tunnel. But down in the valley, the federal government was telling Doc that cutting off the source of the contamination had to come first. Only then would they address the damage already done downstream. Doc would have to wait longer. "No one knows really what to do with it," he told the NewsHour reporter. "And so, if you don't know what to do with a very large problem, you either scoff at it or push it back in the background."

For the ranchers, the first signs of hope came in 1992, when the Yak Treatment Plant came on line. "It was like a miracle," Doc recalled. "In May of that year, when I crossed the Arkansas River to attend to the release ditch, it was the first time that I didn't kick up some yellow boy, some iron hydroxide. Now, there are a few fish clear up to Edith Seppi's."

Doc was the most affected by heavy metal contamination. But his neighbor to the north, an energetic woman who turned seventy that year, lived at the confluence of California Gulch and the Arkansas River, her log cabin home sitting just a few hundred yards upstream of that juncture. Edith wasn't a native. She had grown up on the plains of southeastern Colorado and had come to Leadville as a young woman with her parents during the booming World War II years. Her mother worried that Leadville was "much too rough for a woman" and cautioned Edith to keep her distance from the locals. But Edith enjoyed dating the mining boys, who would tell her about their lives in the mines. "They always said that the dripping of water on the track—drip, drip, drip—within twenty-four hours would eat the track through," she recalled. "It was very, very toxic, I'd guess you'd call it." Two years after arriving in Leadville, Edith married one of them—a Zaitz boy—from an old and respected Leadville family. The young couple was happy in Leadville, but Joe Zaitz had never fully recovered from a bout of rheumatic fever as a child, and his doctors recommended he move down the mountain to see if his health improved. So in 1950, Joe and Edith packed up and moved to

Pueblo, but Joe's health continued to decline, and he died the following year.

Edith, a baby in tow, returned to Leadville. A year later, she married Aldo Seppi from another old mining family. Aldo, a hoistman at ASARCO's Irene mine, had been Joe Zaitz's business partner in a service station they had renovated in town. In 1956, the couple bought twenty-three acres of valley ranch land from the Younger brothers—cousins, Edith said, of those other Younger brothers, the outlaws who used to steal horses from Kansas and bring them to the ranch just south of Leadville. Aldo and Edith moved into a 1943 log cabin house and raised two children where California Gulch met the Arkansas River.

Aldo remained a miner while tending to the horses and cattle on the new ranch, which the couple eventually expanded to about 170 acres, and he became good friends with his downstream neighbor. Together, Aldo and Doc experimented with ways to counteract their livestock's health problems. Both men knew that young animals—foals, calves, and lambs—raised on their pastures got sick and died. Older animals grazing on the meadow's grasses didn't fair well either. Their bones were weak, the sheep's wool was poor quality, and the cows didn't reproduce or grow as well as they should have. Over the years, Doc had learned to make the best of it. He and the Seppis didn't allow young animals on their property, and older animals spent most of the year down valley to beef up on other ranches.

As time went on, Doc came to believe his animals suffered from osteochondrosis dissecans, a debilitating bone disease caused by insufficient copper. By the 1990s, scientific evidence was proving that consuming high levels of cadmium and zinc is one cause of the copper deficiency that leads to osteochondrosis. Doc was convinced his animals suffered from heavy metal poisoning. As his grandfather had first confirmed in the letter from the Agricultural College in 1905, acid mine drainage flowing from the mines had brought heavy metals to his pastures.

Officially, no studies had been done to prove Doc's theory. But unofficially, it seemed obvious to scientists studying the Arkansas

River that the cause of the copper deficiency stemmed from livestock grazing on land contaminated with zinc and cadmium. But even as the EPA and the mining companies began cutting off drainage from the hills, the impact of past contamination to the river and meadows would last thousands of years without intervention.

For eleven miles downstream of the confluence, the land was pocked with barren ground. Mine waste and fluvial tailings from the mills had washed down the gulch and accumulated along the banks, killing huge swaths of the neighboring meadows and riparian habitat that benefited both aquatic and land animals. Erosion was an ongoing problem. Without the willow bushes and grasses to bind the soils and hold them in place, the soil—tailings—eroded back into the river. Nearly three million square yards of two-foot-thick fluvial tailings containing zinc, cadmium, copper, and lead had been deposited along the riverbank, most of it within the first three miles of the confluence of the Arkansas and California Gulch—Doc's land.

The ranchers' problems extended beyond the banks of the Arkansas River. Whenever the river overflowed, tailings from the deposits washed over the meadows. Doc's land, in particular, was also webbed with his grandfather's irrigation ditches that had long ago spread the river's water—"rolling mud" as Henry Smith had described it—across the pastures. The metals bound up in the meadows' soil weren't as concentrated or as deep as the tailings deposited along the banks and nearby meadows, but now that they were there, it would take thousands of years for them, too, to erode away.

Biologists had long understood that acid and heavy metals in the Arkansas River harmed and killed the fish. Above the confluence with California Gulch, there were brown trout; directly below it, there were none. Even after the Yak Treatment Plant went online, a report would show that metals immediately below the confluence "grossly exceeded" the state's water quality standards. As the river progressed south through the valley, more and more brown trout appeared as some metals dropped out and tributaries added clean water, diluting the acidic, contaminated Arkansas River. But the level of metals remained elevated for another hundred miles downstream, and the brown trout within that span were stunted and short-lived.

Mining had disrupted the delicate river basin ecosystem up and down the food chain. The metals that accumulated in the plants and insects were then consumed by fish and birds, beaver, deer, elk, and the rancher's livestock. Doc's grandfather had eventually built a ditch to bring water from another stream to avoid use of the river water running right down the middle of his ranch, but the land was locked into what would become the heart of Superfund's Operable Unit 11. The Seppis were more fortunate. When they bought their ranch, it came with a significant amount of prestigious—1874—water rights in California Gulch (like the miners' claims, water rights are also subject to first come, first served laws). "We owned the land, but the water was always highly contaminated that I didn't dare irrigate with it," Edith would say later.

Like Doc, when the Clean Water Act went into effect in 1972, Edith was excited. She took time away from the Sugar Loafin' Campground business she had started a few years earlier, to attend government meetings about the Arkansas River. "They said nothing could be done for California Gulch. They said it was so contaminated it could never be clean." Then, Edith and Aldo received notice that they would lose their water rights to California Gulch because of a previous owner's oversight. Edith petitioned to switch the rights to the Arkansas River—above the confluence—that flowed right by their home. The diversion was accepted, but it cost them more than half their water rights. "I've always been angry about it, but that's what the courts did to me." But now the Seppis had clean irrigation water.

Just a year after the blowout that had Doc calling the news stations, Aldo Seppi died. Edith, sixty-one years old and now widowed a second time, was left with a 170-acre ranch and a business to run. So she did what any savvy, hardworking ranch woman would do—she bought another forty acres. By the time Edith turned seventy, her ranch spanned more than two hundred acres. At eighty, the spirited woman was still going strong.

"Edith and I are like two old pimples on the backside of a pick-pocket," Doc has said. Around town, Doc was considered the one who had brought the EPA to town—a sentiment voiced with various degrees of respect or disdain. For years, he and Edith attended meetings and cooperated with researchers who knocked on their doors for permission to take samples. Some of the bureaucrats and scientists who came around considered Doc a "gruff old guy"; others, especially the women, thought he was "sweet," even "cuddly." Mike Holmes respected him. Once, on a mild December day, Mike brought a couple of EPA toxicologists to meet Doc and look at his land. "He comes out looking like he just climbed out of bed, or out of a bottle, being his country bumpkin self. These two Ph.D. toxicologists said, 'Why are we wasting our time with this guy?' But he's a vet and very involved in the water quality and metals issues. Doc starts talking about absorption of metals, and one metal's effects on the absorption of nutrients, and this really heavy stuff. He impressed them big time. He knows his stuff."

Even after California Gulch had been a Superfund site for a decade, neither the landowners nor the town recognized the gorilla hiding in the closet. The Comprehensive Environmental Response, Compensation, and Liability Act (CERCLA) empowered the EPA to contain or eliminate the source of environmental contamination, but addressing the damage already done—the distinction that, for the most part, separated the valley from the mining district—fell under another powerful CERCLA provision. The federal, state, and local governments, as "trustees" of the environment, could sue the potentially responsible parties for destruction or loss of natural resources, which can potentially cost companies two or three times more than stopping the contamination. For the Natural Resource Damage (NRD) phase of CERCLA, the EPA steps out and another federal agency, usually the Department of the Interior, takes over. Normally, Interior waits until the EPA is done to begin this second phase of addressing damages, marching into town as the EPA is on its way out.

If the EPA seemed a federal behemoth in the eyes of the small mountain community, townsfolk and ranchers would learn that they now would be dealing with a new, even bigger bureaucracy. At other sites around the country, Interior had come in and filed a lawsuit to use the power of the courts to muscle the mining companies into a settlement. When the Department of the Interior came to Leadville, the legal battle would begin anew. More years of studies, settlement negotiations, and perhaps a court trial would follow. The federal government and the mining companies would spend millions more fighting over who was responsible for damages to the natural resources, and Doc Smith and the other ranchers along the Arkansas River would wait additional years, if not decades, to see any restoration. That's what was happening in Coeur d'Alene, Idaho, in the dispute between ASARCO and Hecla Mining Company and the Department of the Interior over contamination of the Coeur d'Alene river basin. That case was destined for a trial, and it would cost both sides millions.

The NRD gorilla stayed hidden until, in Denver, the EPA, the Justice Department, and the mining companies were close to settling the mining district cleanup in the early 1990s. Justice asked the Interior Department if it wanted in on the action, to settle any Natural Resource Damage claims while the mining companies were at the table and cooperating. The Interior Department was left flatfooted. "We said, 'We don't have a clue. We haven't worked on it, and we don't know what's going on up there,'" recalled Andrew Archuleta, at the time a biologist with Interior's U.S. Fish and Wildlife Service. One look at what would be required to understand the damages and how to fix them, and the agency quickly realized that the project was too massive to figure out within the EPA's settlement time frame. Interior bowed out of the negotiations, but the Justice Department's question prompted the agency to turn its gaze on the Arkansas River.

It wasn't until 1996 that the Department of the Interior was ready to proceed in earnest. It put Fish and Wildlife in charge, but three other divisions were also named trustees: the Bureau of Land Management and the U.S. Forest Service, which both owned property in the area, and the Bureau of Reclamation, which still owned the unfortunate Leadville Mine Drainage Tunnel. The Bureau's Frying Pan-Arkansas transmountain water diversion project that brought water from western Colorado to the populated east side by way of the Arkansas River had also left its mark.

"Oh my God, there's something even worse than Superfund," Mike Holmes remembered Doc Smith and other locals reacting to the news of this next phase in CERCLA. The landowners didn't see Interior and more lawsuits as the answer to their problems, and they decided to circumvent what they perceived as an obstruction to restoration heading their direction. Spearheaded by the local Soil Conservation District, of which Edith and Doc were members, they formed a work group, the "Core Team," to find a way to restore the Arkansas River and its floodplain—cooperatively. The membership roster included Doc Smith, representatives from the Fish and Wildlife Service and the Bureau of Reclamation, the state's health and natural resource departments, ASARCO, Resurrection, and Mike Holmes. Though nearly everyone with a stake in the restoration process was represented, maintaining local control of that effort was a key element.

The Department of the Interior had a decision to make: stick to the normal NRD path and send the mining companies a "Letter of Intent" to sue and let the lawyers take over; or take a cue from the cooperative approach the locals had initiated with the "Core Team" and from the relationships Mike Holmes, Jim Martin, and ASARCO's Bob Litle had established up on the hill that were finally getting work done.

Though little effort to restore the damages had taken place, scientists had been studying the river and its environs for decades. It was so well investigated, in fact, that researchers used to joke that you had to get in line to take samples of the Arkansas River. A cooperative approach could take advantage of the studies already done but, just as with Superfund up on the hill, gathering evidence for court requires a stringent methodology to acquiring data. The government and mining companies would have had to start over, jostling each other in line to take more samples.

A nonlitigious, cooperative approach had never been tried before, and advocates both for and against it within Fish and Wildlife's various offices and headquarters debated the decision. Newmont and ASARCO were willing to cooperate. Newmont just wanted to get Superfund over with; ASARCO had already spent $7 million and years just preparing to litigate in Coeur d'Alene, Idaho. "There needs to be a way to spend the money on the ground, not to spend it in courts and on lawyers," Bob Litle explained later. "Why not spend the money figuring out the problem? It's hard to do anything innovative after the battle lines are drawn and you're entrenched in court." Litle's cooperative attitude was key, but he credited Leadville's influence, Doc Smith and Jim Martin in particular, for pressuring the companies. "Mining companies tend to be immune to pressure," Bob said with a laugh, underscoring the understatement. "But their attitude was 'cut the crap. Let's get the mining companies to spend some money on the ground.'"

With the mining companies offering their collaboration, Fish and Wildlife agreed to work out a Memorandum of Understanding (MOU) to establish the ground rules for this unique approach. The two groups wanted to include the EPA. Though not normally involved in the Natural Resource Damage phase, the agency was tied to the process, partly because of its responsibilities in Stray Horse Gulch that had contributed to the Arkansas River's contamination but also because of Operable Unit 11. The heaviest damage extended for eleven miles below the confluence with California Gulch, the area Fish and Wildlife agreed to investigate restoring, but the first three miles of it were also designated Operable Unit 11, where liability determination had been postponed. If it worked, the MOU process could resolve both problems, another potential innovation.

The bureaucratic interests didn't end there. The state had filed the original NRD lawsuit back in 1983 and designated three state-level agencies—Natural Resources, Public Health and the Environment, and the Attorney General's office—as trustees. If the mining companies were going to cooperate, they wanted to settle with the state as well.

No one disputes that the state got in on the MOU negotiations late and lengthened the process, but why it did so depends on who is telling the story. It was a miscommunication, a deliberate attempt to cut the state out, or a state so fearful of budget cuts and local discontent that it was "scared to death until they knew there were no downsides," as a member of the MOU process characterized the state. Several state employees acknowledged that "What would Chlouber think?" was an open topic of discussion when decisions were being made both during the MOU process and in cleaning up the mining district, but opinions differ about just how much Chlouber actually influenced the state's decisions.

With the state finally involved, everyone made room for three more government agencies at the table—which now included a large group of people representing widely varying interests. The MOU process had never been attempted before, and no template existed. "We started with a two-page MOU, and then the lawyers got it," recalled Archuleta, the project leader at the time. As had occurred with Superfund a few years earlier, disagreements between the lawyers and the technical staff, between the government agencies and the companies, between the feds and the state were raised and settled. After several years spent negotiating the Memorandum of Understanding—the ground rules—Archuleta, the biologist, remembered sitting at the table, getting ready to lead another meeting: "Everybody's lawyer was there, but ours was sick. So I started out by saying, 'Well, we decided that for every week this MOU doesn't get signed, we're going to get rid of one lawyer. We got rid of ours. Who's going next?' Their jaws dropped, and I started laughing."

A few weeks later, on April 15, 1999, the Memorandum of Understanding was signed. Despite the rough patches, the Natural Resource Damage phase was way ahead of the game. The group had identified five scientists who would analyze the studies already conducted on the Arkansas River scattered across numerous federal and state governments, research institutions, and other organizations. Their report was due by the end of 2000. The scientists would then determine the best methods for restoring the river, issuing another report the following year. As with everything about this Superfund site, the timelines were years off, but by 2004 the real test of this cooperative approach would begin—divvying up the responsibility for restoring the Arkansas River and its natural resources.

During the years of MOU negotiations, tensions had mounted within the Core Team. Doc Smith, Jim Martin, and other locals on the team were feeling left out. As with Superfund, the legal liability settlement took place behind closed doors. But the Core Team had highlighted the need for local input, and the MOU parties agreed to a Local Liaison Committee, which included Doc and Jim.

Mike Holmes, always eager to get the work going, helped ease tensions with the landowners. Without waiting for the Memorandum of Understanding, the EPA began stabilizing the river banks and experimenting with ways to decontaminate the tailings, by adding lime and biosolids, or sewage sludge, that neutralize the soil and bind up the metals to allow grass to grow again. The technique has been used in mining sites worldwide, but in Leadville it had to work at ten thousand feet. Early efforts to revegetate the land had been only marginally successful, but researchers say they just need to find the right recipe of chemicals and growing conditions to make it work.

In the West, ranchers are not known for harboring warm feelings toward the federal government any more than the miners are. But seventeen years after the day Doc's river ran red, Mike Holmes had earned Doc's respect, "He hears a remark, takes the barbs off, moves it around, and everyone ends up hugging," Doc said. "Mike hasn't shot anyone and no one has shot Mike; he's that close to being a genius. He's honest and admits his mistakes. You can't find that in the Interior Department."

A few months after the Memorandum of Understanding was signed in 1999, Doc Smith faced another camera. This production was for the EPA public relations machine. It was summertime in the valley, and Doc, in a seed cap and large sunglasses, stood on a small acreage of barren ground before his glorious Rocky Mountain backdrop. "This was termed a moonscape," Doc said to the camera. "This was mill tailings, mine waste, up to three feet thick with those petrified willows that had been dead for over a hundred years. No grass of any kind growing here. The results of the amending with lime and biosolids and the seeding last fall has given us, not an outstanding crop, but we have more green grasses here than in my lifetime, gentlemen." Doc gestured to the little tufts of greenery scattered around him that barely reached the edge of his shoes. "I think this is neat."

To Doc, signs of life growing out of the fluvial tailings represented hope for his meadows and his cattle. But for the landowners, a potential wrinkle existed. Legally, Interior and the state are trustees of the natural resources—the fish, insects, birds, grass, elk, deer, and water—not to livestock or even necessarily to the pastures. Would the trustees conclude Doc's and Edith's meadows provide habitat for wildlife and are, thus, eligible to be cleaned up under the Natural Resource Damage provision of CERCLA? And if they do, would the mining companies go along with a plan that included restoring the meadows and not just the obvious tailings piled up on the riverbanks? Or, when the EPA, Interior, the state, and the mining companies finally all go home, will Doc and Edith's meadows still be covered with a layer of heavy metals? "With limited dollars and everything else to resolve issues, we may not be able to solve every problem at the end of the day," said a state trustee.

Doc, sitting at his heavy wooden dining-room table beside the antique woodstove, his artificial leg stretched out straight in front of him, was resigned. He was now in his mid-seventies, the lines of a hard life working a ranch at ten thousand feet etched in his face and cracked hands. A plaque from the region's Soil Conservation District hung on his wood-paneled living room wall: "Bernard Smith Landowner of the Year 2002 for a lifetime commitment to Lake County and her natural resources." Except for Doc and his wife, Carol, the house was empty now, all of their eleven children grown and long gone. "I'm feeling better because someday somebody is going to have to figure out how to deal with the metals on the land," Doc said. He looked out the window at his old, weathered barn, Mt. Massive rising behind it. "I don't think I'm going to live long enough to see all of this happen."

19

Appalachia of the West

While the world celebrated the approach of a new century, Leadville faced it with dismay. The last boom days–era town still mining in Colorado could no longer claim that distinction. The Black Cloud was finished. It wasn't a surprise. The mine had been hemorrhaging $200,000 a month for several years as ASARCO searched for more ore without success. It had been a good run. The company had sunk the Black Cloud shaft in 1971 expecting about ten good years of zinc and lead. Twenty-eight years later, the mine was finally exhausted. That metal prices were at a twelve-year low was incidental, but it gave ASARCO little incentive to keep looking.

One hundred miners lost their jobs when the Black Cloud shut down in early 1999, sending the last of Leadville's miners tramping. Some headed for the Henderson moly mine eighty miles away. Others took off for mines in Nevada or Arizona. More than a few faced a heart-wrenching decision. Their families had been Leadville miners for generations. Now they had to decide between Leadville and mining. For the first time in 130 years, they couldn't have both.

There were economic consequences as well. Leadville and Lake County lost another $6 million in taxes and wages, but compared to the tidal wave of change the Climax shutdown had started seventeen years earlier, pulling the pumps on the Black Cloud caused little more than a sentimental ripple through town. No one blamed the company; miners have always accepted that they were working themselves out of a job, and ASARCO had kept the mine going longer than most companies would have.

But now that mining was gone, was Leadville no longer a mining town? The Climax shutdown had taken away the town's mining economy, but had the Black Cloud taken away its identity? That contention was far more disputable. "We may not have an active mine, but Leadville's always going to be a mining community," the director of the Chamber of Commerce told the *Washington Post*. Leadville had always known its place in the world. It was the Silver Queen, the Magic City, feeding the industrial machine with raw materials. Many in town didn't want that to change. But change had already come.

Every morning, early, before the sun rose over the mining district, men and women bundled up in coats and gloves lined up on Harrison Avenue in front of the county courthouse for the buses that would take them north over the passes to Copper Mountain or Vail. Others piled into cars, trucks, and sport utility vehicles to make the forty-five-minute journey over winding, snow-covered mountain highways to work in the ski resorts or nearby towns. More than half—perhaps as many as two-thirds—of Lake County workers commuted over the hill for jobs. A few were white-collar professionals; more worked construction jobs; but most cooked, cleaned hotel rooms, or washed dishes.

Standing in the cold darkness, waiting for the bus, the workers murmured to each other in Spanish. The Mexican immigrants were the new, largely ignored faces of Leadville, but their presence has had a profound impact on the town. Names like Martinez, Sanchez, and Jimenez were not new to Leadville. Spanish Americans and Mexicans had migrated north to work in the mines alongside their European neighbors beginning in the early twentieth century. They had joined an extraordinarily diverse community that brought the variety of customs, faiths, and languages that marked the West's mining camps. In Leadville, the Irish brogue had dominated. The Maid of Erin, Robert Emmet, and Wolftone celebrated the Irish presence. The Scots provided the Highland Mary and Highland Chief, among others. The Swiss gave Leadville the Luzerne. The Germans, the Hamburgh. The Irish lived in rough wooden houses on the east side; Finntown was farther up Stray Horse; the Austrians lived on the west side; the Scandinavians took Chicken Hill alongside California Gulch; the Cornish, or the "Cousin Jacks," lived in Jacktown down by the smelters; and "Coon Row" was on west State Street. Intermixed were the French, Canadians, Italians, and many other nationalities. Absent were the Chinese and the Indians. Like many of their fellow westerners, Leadville's early leaders had feared and hated both groups and had outright banned "John Chinaman" from entering the city limits.

Sharp ethnic divisions had survived well into the twentieth century, but eventually McCrackens were marrying Windorskis and Stefanics could attend the Catholic Church once dominated by Donovans and Kerrigans. When Mexican immigrants began flooding into Leadville in the late 1980s, one of Leadville's two Catholic churches had added services in Spanish. Immigrants were recruited by resorts to provide cheap labor after the skyrocketing cost of living drove out the young "ski bums."

By the dawn of the twenty-first century, Hispanics accounted for one-third of Leadville's population, perhaps half of them recent immigrants—much more, some say, if undocumented workers were counted. Many lived in crowded trailer parks surrounding Leadville and traveled over the hill to work long hours for low wages and no benefits. Leadville was required to provide basic social services, such as medical care and schooling for their children. More than half of Leadville's schoolchildren spoke Spanish. Some blamed the resulting strain on Leadville's resources on the Mexicans; others placed it on the rich ski resorts for driving their labor force out of their own counties. Vail's Eagle County had a tax base of $2 billion for its 42,000 residents. Lake County, with a population of 7,800, was now surviving on $80 million. Many had tried, regionally and legislatively, to compel the rich resort counties to compensate the neighbors caring for their workers, but without success.

Occasionally, overt bigotry was expressed toward Leadville's "other" inhabitants in conversations and in editorials, but Leadville's new immigrants suffered more from invisibility. Language barriers, transience, and long hours spent working and commuting that left time for little else isolated the Mexican population. And established Leadville had made little effort to reach out to them. Few resources were available in Spanish, a few trailer park owners allowed their tenants to live in trash and sewage with no government oversight, and neither newspaper had gotten to know them.

Leadville had become a bedroom community, surviving off cheap housing, a modicum of tourism, and its proximity to more popular destinations long before the Black Cloud had closed. Twenty years after Climax, Lake County had dropped from the highest per capita income among Colorado's rural counties to one of the lowest. Nearly half of the county's one thousand schoolchildren qualified for free lunches. Leadville's schools were particularly hard hit. Without tax revenues from Climax paying the bills, snow drifted into classrooms through warped windows, roofs leaked, and children had to share textbooks. Leadville no longer boasted the highest number of graduates continuing on to college as it had during the Climax years. By 2000, barely half of the town's students graduated from high school. A conspicuous number of parents began home schooling or sending their children thirty miles south to Buena Vista. Some families moved away all together. The town's municipal pool, built with Climax money, fell into disrepair in 1998 and stayed that way. Teachers, hospital staff, and other professionals necessary in an isolated community earned substantially less than their counterparts over the hill and they, too, tramped often. The junk cars were still there, dogs still ran loose, and men still staggered out of bars along Harrison Avenue at ten o'clock in the morning. A travel guidebook described Leadville as the "Appalachia of the West." Many townsfolk liked Leadville dirty and

trashy. It kept people away. A hardworking mining town was supposed to look gritty. Even when the town was flush with Climax
money, Harrison Avenue was crumbling.

The pervasive mind-set in Leadville had remained that of feeling
victimized by outside forces. There were many to blame for
Leadville's economic woes. The ski resorts were both the town's sav-
ior and its abuser; Mexican immigrants were moving in, literally
changing the face and character of the town and draining its
resources; and the federal government—perceived as the ultimate Big
Brother outsider—received much of the scorn, blaming the feds being
a long-standing tradition in the independent West. The U.S. Forest
Service and Bureau of Land Management owned two-thirds of Lake
County, something Ken Chlouber reminded citizens of in public
forums recounting federal abuses. It was believed that if the land were
in private or local government hands, it would benefit residents—
though no mention was made of the mostly undeveloped one-third
that was left.

But to many the demise of mining—the root of Leadville's woes
and its most bitter pill—lay squarely with the environmentalists who
ran mining out of the United States and with the Environmental Protection Agency that helped them do it. "I think a lot of people in government want the government to go socialistic and take our freedoms
away from us. They should have never been allowed here to begin
with. There was never a need for it. None of it. They like our climate
so they like to spend their summers up here. Hmm, hmm," a diminutive, elderly woman complained, echoing Ken Chlouber. "It's the
EPA's fault that mining is dead in Leadville. And they're still doin' it!"

For twenty years, many residents—most vocally Ken Chlouber and
Carl Miller—had blamed Leadville's depressed economy on the
Superfund label. Who would want to move into a Superfund site and
open a business or buy a home? But clearly not all of Leadville's woes
could be blamed on the federal government. It was difficult to tease
apart the economic impact of Climax from Superfund. Leadville's
population had climbed steadily in the past twenty years, and EPA
officials liked to point to Aspen, just over the Sawatch Range. Aspen

had spent thirteen years as a Superfund site. The resort wasn't dealing with acid mine drainage as in Leadville, but it had shared a similar bitter fight over metal contamination of residential soils from historic mining waste. Aspen's money and power had eventually kicked the EPA out (an ordinance controlling future disturbances to the land had been instituted instead). That the EPA had submitted to the wealthy community's demands while remaining in Leadville was another grievance voiced by resentful Leadvillites that even some EPA officials acknowledge is accurate. But throughout its stint as a Superfund site, Aspen's popularity among the rich and famous hadn't diminished or put a dent in the resort's skyrocketing housing prices, among the highest in the nation. In any case, any stigma over Superfund that Leadville might have encountered diminished over the years. Many new residents didn't even know their town was a Superfund site.

After the Climax shutdown shattered the status quo and challenged Leadville's identity as a viable town, the fault lines that had formed in the community early on widened over the ensuing years. Some hated what Leadville was becoming, others feared it, but a growing number wanted to embrace the changes and shape Leadville's future before outside forces did it for them. Conflicts— rarely seen in the Climax days—erupted, dividing the town into warring factions. Town and county meetings often turned venomous; recall votes were commonplace. By the turn of the century, nearly twenty years after Climax, many in Leadville still defined the town by what it had lost, though more and more residents had concluded that it was time to "get over it" and move on.

Everyone seemed to agree about what they didn't want. Residents rejected a prison, a machine gun factory, and a Christian camp, a proposed $50 million ranch with a conference center, lodge, and luxury housing for three thousand—bigger than the town itself—on nine hundred acres of wilderness seven miles northwest of Leadville. Townsfolk, unwilling to "sell their soul," as one resident commented, successfully united against the zoning changes that would have been required for such an immense complex, even though it would have meant new jobs and taxes.

Residents also didn't want to become a "tinsel town" along the lines of artificially historic Breckenridge, faux-Europe Vail, or completely over-the-top Aspen. All proposals for the town were measured against that unifying antigoal. But finding a consensus about what the town *did* want was much more challenging. Like so many towns that have lost their economic centerpiece, particularly in the West, Leadville had turned to tourism. It seemed innocuous: Leadville could market itself as a mining town, reaffirming its identity—at least in the brochures. But tourism changes communities in unanticipated ways.

To be successful, Leadville would have to clean itself up. Most tourists aren't attracted to a real mining town, a gritty, blue-collar community with junk cars and loose dogs, shops supplying the locals with everyday needs and toxic scars evident on the land and in the rivers. They want a cleaned-up, pretty version with boutiques and restaurants in renovated historic commercial districts surrounded by cute Victorian houses—the authentic *appearance* made more real by a tour to look down a mine shaft while a local tells tales about the past. But as the town begins to take on this picture-book appearance and learns to cater to the tourists, its authentic *character* inevitably begins to change. Long-time residents, particularly those who don't directly benefit from tourism, grow resentful and uncooperative in the face of what they see as a betrayal of the town.

Leadville's character was manifested in its gritty "Appalachia of the West" reputation—that stubborn independence that says you don't mess with your neighbor or his junk cars, even if a prettier Leadville would attract more tourists and further boost the county coffers for everyone's benefit. That unwillingness to impose rules left Leadville vulnerable. An independent, hands-off attitude allowed for the very changes those same residents feared as outsiders move in with their own ideas of what Leadville should be. That dilemma created yet more conflict as residents struggled with the growing contradictions in their lives.

Leadville

Perhaps nothing symbolizes loss of independence as much as the creation of architectural controls, the rules that enforce how the town wants to look and to protect it from undesirable changes. In Leadville, the city council instituted an architectural review process. The board had no authority, but when residents realized the city government intended to "invade their private property rights," the review process was rescinded. A sign ordinance was also revoked. But residents were clearly conflicted. They didn't want the government telling them what color to paint their houses, but they also didn't want Vail-style condos moving in either. "It would make Leadville look like hell," said a city council member. "I think we need to have a guideline so that we don't have a Vail- or Summit County–looking Leadville." So you do want architectural controls? the mayor had asked, mockingly. Well, no.

The county's building code inspector was similarly frustrated. During inspections of two trailer parks on the outskirts of Leadville, where Mexican immigrants crowded into trailers, he had found inadequate sewage systems, effluent seeping to the surface and toys all around. Trash was piling up. The trailer parks were health hazards, he told the county commissioners, and neither owner was willing to clean up the trailer parks. In another example, he told of a man living up East 5th Street during the summers who used his backyard as an outhouse. When the code inspector confronted the man, he had threatened to shoot him. "People come here with their junk because we don't enforce it like surrounding counties," the inspector told the commissioners. He couldn't do his job until the politicians put some enforcement teeth in the ordinances. But the county attorney countered that residents would riot if the government tried to pick up Leadville's trash.

Some feared any concession to tourists would doom Leadville to a Vail fate; others felt turning Leadville into a popular resort was impossible no matter what the town did. The resorts had skiing and were essentially built from scratch by large infusions of outside money. Leadville had a small, family-owned skiing operation ten miles from town and was unlikely to attract the kind of money it would take to become Vail. The year a handful of Texans arrived in town and bought a few local businesses was still considered the "Texas Invasion." Striking a balance continued to elude Leadville. Without community consensus, development or tourism projects that were floated got nowhere.

It would be easy to portray the divisions in Leadville as a struggle between the old-timers and the newcomers—the "'old' and 'new' Leadville" as the *Herald Democrat*, now run by those squarely in the newcomer category, had characterized it. But in reality there were plenty of old-timers and newcomers in both camps. "Old Leadville" wasn't the sleepy, little bedroom community to the ski resorts that put up with a few tourists in the summer, thankful when the first snowflakes fell so residents could have their parking spaces on Harrison Avenue back. It was a boisterous mining camp, open round the clock for the men on swing shift, with plenty of shopping and good schools. Some saw development as a means of recapturing those better economic times. Others stubbornly held to the belief that Leadville was a mining town. Residents must be patient and wait out this latest bust for mining's return. "Mining wins out over development" the *Leadville Chronicle* announced in the summer of 2002. The planning commission had unanimously refused a zoning change that would have allowed development in the mining district. "We shouldn't build houses on potential mineral reserves in our country, especially with all that is going on around the world currently," said one board member. "You don't develop on your future." Still others—newcomers and old-timers alike—preferred the isolation and quiet of this new Leadville.

Much of the resistance to change stemmed from fear, not just of obvious Vailization, but of the more subtle changes anything new might bring. A sizable number of people had been carpetbaggers, moving to Leadville to buy houses during the rock-bottom prices of the post-Climax years. Many of them were either on fixed incomes from small trust funds or business payouts or preferred the lifestyle of the near jobless. Housing costs and property taxes had risen since those first chaotic years after Climax, but compared to the exorbitant cost of housing in the resort areas, Leadville was still a bargain. Those on fixed or low incomes in Leadville feared that by encouraging new businesses, residents and second homeowners, the cost of living would go up. Leadville's schools, roads, and public services might suffer without economic growth, but Leadville would still be affordable.

The clashes over change that made the town and county meetings so animated came in small bites, and it came in large gulps. In the fall of 2002, Leadville's mayor, Chet Gaede, asked Leadville and Lake County to help develop a business park on the west edge of town. Chet Gaede was a newcomer with ideas—change was on his mind. He had spent twenty years as a fighter pilot in the Marine Corps before enrolling in law school; after graduation Chet and his wife, Sherry, went looking for a small town "with warts." They had watched their previous neighborhoods in Hawaii and Southern California explode with people. But a town with warts would stay small, much like Chet's native Woodstock, New York. Leadville's long winters, high altitude, remoteness, and innate quirkiness ensured a long existence without strip malls and luxury resorts. Chet Gaede was in his mid-40s when he and Sherry moved to Leadville in 1996. He opened a law practice and was mayor two and a half years later.

As mayor, Chet tried to inspire the town into reaching a consensus about its future. He brought in consultants to conduct surveys, hold town workshops, and issue reports about economic development. He thought the town needed more families and upscale tourist shops on Harrison Avenue. That didn't require strip malls, but it did mean more businesses, jobs, affordable housing, and better schools. The joke in Leadville was that you couldn't even buy underwear in town. There were a few mechanic shops, one grocery store, a pharmacy, bookstore, a couple of sporting good shops, and a hardware store, but for other basic necessities residents had to drive over the passes or down valley. The opening of a new, small Family Dollar store on the edge of town was big news in 2003. But when Chet asked the town to help jump-start economic development in Leadville with a business park, the opposition turned out. The plan required the county, which owned the twenty-eight-acre site, to deed the land to an independent council and to pay for water and sewer lines. A couple of tenants were already lined up.

Outspoken councilwoman Carol Hill was perhaps Chet's biggest critic, and the two regularly butted heads during city council meetings and in newspaper op-eds. She first came to Leadville just a year before Climax closed, left a few years later, and returned in 1993 to run the local bookstore. Carol was a libertarian. With her election, Leadville again made the national news. Four libertarians now sat on the seven-member city council, making Leadville the first incorporated town to be controlled by the anti-government party. The distinction was more semantics than a recognizable shift in local politics. One council member had recently changed parties, and another newly elected member registered libertarian just days before the election.

Traditional political parties weren't much of an issue in Leadville politics. In the small town, people tended to vote for personalities, and their elected officials tended to govern the same way, deciding issues based on how it affected their neighbors rather than on any codified vision of the future. Lisa Dowdney, the recently converted council member, explained to the *Herald Democrat* that their job was to "keep Chet in line." If the libertarian bent wasn't new politics in Leadville, it did bring libertarians from around the state to Leadville for their state convention. The libertarian era ended just a year after it began when one member switched parties and another resigned. Carol herself officially became a Democrat a few years later, but she retained her deeply felt libertarian views.

"Growth should pay its own way" seemed to be the town motto. "I'm not sure any tax money is appropriate where there is risk involved," Carol said of Chet's business proposal. The government was venturing into "real estate speculation" and giving away land. In Leadville, another stumbling block to development was the powerful sanitation and water boards, elected bodies independent of town government. Leadville's infrastructure in the new century reflected its transient character of the past two centuries when water and sewer lines had followed the new construction. Back in the Climax days, the town hadn't thought to lay down a foundation for Leadville's future. Now, in the post-Climax world, much of the land couldn't be developed until that infrastructure was in place. The "growth should pay its own way" attitude left potential businesses footing the bill for additional infrastructure costs. Leadville had too many things going against it to throw up more roadblocks. Some on the pro-growth side thought the sanitation and water boards had more control over the town's destiny than the politicians. Chet's business park project died as community opposition mounted.

Later that year, a new development idea was floated. This time more obstacles potentially stood in the way. The EPA, the state, and a potentially responsible party all had to get on board for it to be successful. But the Harrison Slag site became the beneficiary of the EPA's emphasis on brownfield redevelopment that had begun in 1993. After hazardous waste was removed, sites like Harrison—twelve acres of prime real estate littered with leftover slag—were pariahs to developers worried about becoming embroiled in Superfund liability. The Clinton administration initiated reforms to encourage development of these sites, such as assurances to prospective buyers, tax incentives, and grants for redevelopment projects.

Leadville became an early recipient when the EPA funded a study to look at ways to put the Harrison Slag site to use for the town. The consultant came up with a design for a small shopping area that would also finish remediating the site—essentially capping the remaining contaminants with buildings and parking lots. Union Pacific wanted to sell, the EPA was eager to get Operable Unit 3 off the books, and Alco, a discount store, was ready to move in. Leadville had to do its part by purchasing the property from Union Pacific and planning a retail center of which Alco would be a part.

Out came the opposition. There was fear. "It's so speculative right now," Carol said during a city council meeting. The national economy is just too precarious to risk such a venture, agreed her fellow council member, Lisa Dowdney. This was another case of government inserting itself in private affairs and taking away taxpayers' assets, they said. If this project were profitable, then a private enterprise would do it.

About half of the audience applauded. And a new fear arose. Alco's money would compete with local businesses already here, people said, and Carol Hill, the bookstore owner, agreed. "The locals are paying taxes that are now going to help a business put them out of business. That's not fair. You have to draw a line," she explained later. Working together was not a Leadville strong suit. A few years earlier, the Chamber of Commerce had tried to create a brochure advertising Leadville's antique stores, but two of the four owners refused to cooperate because their competition would also benefit. Some residents didn't understand—or perhaps care—that more shopping opportunities would draw people to Leadville and keep residents in town, improving business for everyone.

Over Carol and Lisa's dissention, the city council agreed to at least explore the possibility of developing the Harrison Slag site. "People are saying, 'Do something,'" their fellow libertarian on the council explained. But residents weren't holding their breath. "I've lived here too long to say I'm optimistic. We have a history of shooting things down," one twenty-year resident said. This was "just another spurt that will never get off the ground," said another, an ex-miner, shaking his head. "I don't know why Leadville can't get it together." Jim Morrison, embittered by his experience as county commissioner, considered his new job over the hill a "refreshing change. There, they don't argue about whether to make changes, they argue over the best way to approach it. If you don't control your own destiny, then someone else will." Jim Morrison was firm. Though the Morrisons had been in town since the beginning, retirement was not going to include Leadville. "I've just about had it with this old town."

County politics in the courthouse down the street from City Hall seemed to be faring no better. In 2000, Jim Martin, seventy years old now, had decided to retire from local politics after his term was up at the end of the year. But when he saw the cast of characters running in the election, he was persuaded to run for a third term. Soon after his reelection, he started counting the days until his term was up. The dynamics on the Board of County Commissioners had changed, and he was now the odd man out. He kept a low profile while a fellow commissioner weathered two recall attempts, but he felt his own position had become more stressful. Two years into his term, just before the holidays, Jim woke his wife. Something was wrong. That night he was rushed to Denver in an ambulance with a bleeding ulcer and sky-high blood pressure. Seven hundred and fifty-one days to go, *and* he would have to give up beer.

20

Wedding Cakes and Merlot Ponds

As the first spring in the new century approached, residents awaited the fate of the Ponsardine. Would the downtown dump, whitewashed to clownish brilliance the previous fall, be back to normal? As the snow melted in May, the dump's oranges, yellows and browns gradually reemerged. The lone pine tree at the top of the pile, however, hadn't survived the assault, and as Envirobond washed down 7th Street so, too, did the acid mine drainage the pile was still generating. "The only real long-term effect was they killed one tree and a mouse that had fallen into one of the buckets," Mike Holmes recalled with a laugh. He would still have to do something with Ponsardine. Later, word got back to Mike that the company promoting Envirobond was using Leadville as a preservation success story at environmental conferences. The product apparently did work when the company first churned up the surface to allow it to sink in and bind to the material, but that negated its use as a preservation tool. Mike warned the company that if they kept it up, he'd spread the word that Envirobond had failed in Leadville.

At the other end of Harrison Avenue, the tug of war over the "hydrologic center of the Earth" was still mired in controversy. After vowing that Apache, still the largest source of contamination remaining, would never be capped, Michael the Archangel had disappeared. His partner, Magovich the dentist, was trying to salvage his own plans. The mushroom farm he had envisioned for the now defunct Black Cloud had fallen through when ASARCO broke off negotiations and pulled the pumps, letting the mine flood. And his plans for the Heartbreak Hotel weren't looking too likely either, not with the Archangel in the picture. "Michael Layne has to get out before anything gets done," Magovich told the *Leadville Chronicle.*

As summer neared, Jim Martin, ASARCO's Bob Litle, and Mike Holmes were anxious to finish cleaning up Apache. After Leadville had thawed for the summer, bulldozers surrounded the monstrous pile, ready to attack. Then, Michael Layne reappeared long enough to refuse to grant ASARCO access to the piles. The bulldozers idled, and the standoff continued throughout the summer. As the first snowflakes blanketed Apache, the bulldozers retreated, and another construction year had slipped away. Over the winter, the EPA devised a new plan of attack. It was time to call in the lawyers.

In 2001, as the snow melted, and armed with a federal court order, ASARCO finally sent in the bulldozers. It had taken eighteen years to reach that point, but in just five months, the jagged, debris-littered piles were shoved, shaped, and molded into a smooth, rounded hill and capped with a waterproof liner and clean soil. Then ASARCO ran out of money.

They met once every month or two, normally on the first Thursday of the month, in a chilly, unadorned conference room behind the mining museum. With their sport utility vehicles cooling in the alley after the ninety-minute trip to Leadville, they sat on high-back, tan leather chairs around the oblong table that filled the room. A plain gas stove sent out too little heat, prompting some participants of these Superfund meetings to keep their coats on in the winter. These were casual gatherings despite their importance, blue jeans, sweatshirts or flannel button-down shirts, and work boots the norm, an occasional baseball cap. Every once in a while a suit made a guest appearance, usually on a lawyer. The percentage of mustaches in the room was higher than the national average.

Rebecca was usually the only woman at the table. She dressed more business casual in slacks and a tidy sweater or blouse, a vintage-style barrette holding up her long hair. Other regulars included Mike, Bob Litle, Jim Martin often in a Mister Rogers cardigan, and John Faught, twisting a rubber band around his wrist. A few years into his Leadville tenure, Faught had decided he enjoyed problem solving more than litigating and, citing "quality of life issues," sold his law firm to become a one-man law office, working out of his home. He had been advising the county going on ten years, calmly keeping its interest on everyone's radar and often leading the way through the negotiations.

Jim was the veteran of the group, but right behind him was the state health department's even-tempered Russ Allen, "Sarge" to his co-workers, his rank in the Marines during the Vietnam War, who had been assigned to Leadville in 1990. Other participants occasionally showed as well: Mayor Gaede, the other county commissioners, a variety of ASARCO employees and contractors, and an additional EPA or state bureaucrat. A local reporter, well known to the group, sometimes listened in, but Superfund articles were no longer front-page stories. Newmont's Resurrection was a frustratingly frequent no-show. "Maybe they're not interested," Jim Martin suggested at one meeting, and everyone laughed at the notion.

The meetings were congenial; past grievances came up only as a source of inside jokes. At one meeting, a new county commissioner innocently asked who owned the water coming out of the Yak Tunnel. Silence descended on the room. Finally, Bob Litle smiled and said, "All I know is ASARCO doesn't own that water," and the room erupted in laughter. Another time, Jim Martin admitted he had used slag as roadbed material when he was mayor. In an aside, Mike leaned over to update Mayor Gaede, "We let you off the hook on that one." At another meeting, Jim chastised Mike, "You're starting to sound like a lawyer," as he laughed and put his hand on Mike's shoulder. Consultants who had worked at other Superfund sites thought Leadville was "tame" by comparison; the level of communication and cooperation surpassed anything they had ever witnessed in Superfund before. A decade earlier Leadville, the EPA, and ASARCO had treated each other as adversaries, threats of lawsuits and lynchings clouding their interactions. Though deep differences still divided them and an undercurrent of dissention occasionally swept through the room, the participants now acted more like partners with a common goal—and they were getting much more done.

The new century brought an additional EPA official to the table, Stan Christensen, a tall, mustached Nebraska native. Rebecca Thomas was cutting back. Within a span of five years, she and her husband Stewart had adopted four children, three of them from Belarus, and all of them under five years old. But she kept her hand in Leadville, helping to arrange the Harrison Slag development and the residential soils ordinance still fighting for life. On a trip to Leadville to show the new guy around, Mike and Rebecca warned the laid-back Stan about Jim Martin. He'll explode with anger, but he doesn't mean it personally. ("I drive him nuts," Mike has said. "He screams at me. It's incredible how he loses his temper at me. Afterward, we go have a beer.") As if on cue, Jim Martin, inspecting work on Stray Horse Gulch, spied the Lead Sled bumping up the hill. His face grew red as he turned and marched over. Mike jumped out. "Goddam it, Holmes," Jim began, upset over some facet of the work. "Well, damn it, Jim, I told you. . . ." Mike responded as the two stomped off to work it out. The miner and the bureaucrat were getting along just fine.

The most frequent theme in the Superfund meetings in the new century was money. In 1995, Superfund had been worth $3.8 billion, but eight years after Congress abolished the industry tax that funded it, the Superfund ran dry. During the Clinton administration, Interior Secretary Bruce Babbitt had tried to raise money for abandoned mine cleanups by dragging the nation's hardrock mining laws into the twenty-first century. In 1994, he had pushed to undo the General Mining Law of 1872 that, among other things, allowed mining companies to avoid paying royalties on hardrock metals extracted from public land. Royalties would raise more than $80 million a year, enough to finance environmental cleanups at mining sites throughout the West for decades. "Coal, oil, and gas have been paying royalties on extraction from public land since 1920. Ranchers pay for the use of public land. But hardrock miners have been stonewalling this for 122 years," Babbitt said at a news conference in Denver. But the Republican-led Congress had not only failed to renew the Superfund tax, it had rejected requiring the hardrock mining industry, which grossed perhaps $10 billion a year, to compensate the country for wealth extracted from public lands.

Other attempts by the Clinton administration to regulate hardrock mining operations followed. In 1999, the EPA began requiring hardrock mining companies to report the amount of their toxic emissions each year. That year (and every year since), hardrock mining topped the list as the biggest toxic waste polluter of the nation's soil, water, and air. In 1999, the EPA reported that hardrock mining had released 3.86 billion pounds of pollutants—half of the nation's total. That same year, ASARCO reported that the Black Cloud—a small mining operation—had released 6.5 million pounds of lead, zinc, copper and other toxic pollutants into the environment during 1998, making ASARCO one of the top five polluters in Colorado. One year later, Colorado announced that its toxic releases had declined 16 percent and attributed the drop primarily to the Black Cloud's closure in the spring of that year. The *Herald Democrat* reported the 1998 figure on July 1, 1999: "There is no reason for panic or undue concern in Lake County, a fact which [the Black Cloud manager] wanted to emphasize: 'These numbers are probably the same amounts that have been released over the last ten to fifteen years.'"

In January 2001, hours before President-elect George W. Bush took office, new regulations fought over for years finally became law. Companies would be required to post bonds to ensure adequate reclamation later. The urgency for bonds had been underscored by the Summitville Mine, a cyanide-leaching gold mine in southern Colorado. In 1993, a month after a cyanide spill killed thousands of fish in the Alamosa River, the Canadian mining company that owned Summitville declared bankruptcy and fled back to Canada, leaving taxpayers with a $150 million cleanup bill. Other rules allowed the Bureau of Land Management to veto projects that would irreparably harm public land and to institute standards regulating impacts on natural resources. But before the Bush administration's first year had ended, Gale Norton, an occasional visitor to Leadville as Colorado's attorney general followed by two years as a lawyer and lobbyist for the lead industry and now Bush's secretary of the interior, deleted the environmental safeguards and watered down the bond requirement.

At the same time the Bush administration allowed for the prospect of more Superfund-worthy mining sites like Summitville, it put the financial burden to pay for them on taxpayers. President Bush rejected CERCLA's "polluter pays" principle and opposed reinstating the Superfund tax. After Superfund ran dry in late 2003, taxpayers began picking up the entire tab. Projects, including those like Leadville that had been on the books for twenty years, had to compete for general—taxpayer—money alongside non-Superfund projects. In 2002, that had resulted in a $228 million Superfund shortfall. Additionally, reports revealed that polluters were paying 64 percent less toward hazardous waste cleanup during the Bush administration than under Clinton. Cleanup work at dozens of hazardous waste sites nationwide slowed or stopped, and new listings nearly ceased.

ASARCO's finances were equally troubled. Since the recession of the 1980s that shut down Climax, few hardrock mines survived in the United States. ASARCO still owned copper mines in Arizona, but in those years of low copper prices, its most profitable asset was a copper mine in Peru. Through a hostile takeover bid in 1999, a firm based in Mexico City purchased ASARCO. The hundred-year-old company that had established the Guggenheim dynasty was now a wholly owned subsidiary of Grupo Mexico.

The transaction was a tremendous burden for American taxpayers. The new bosses at Grupo Mexico showed little interest in paying the billion dollars in environmental liability ASARCO owed in about forty sites around the United States, and ASARCO's defiance reasserted itself at a number of Superfund sites. "The retroactive liability EPA is attempting to impose on ASARCO is severe and patently unfair," the company wrote in a 2002 letter to the EPA. (ASARCO's renewed defiance was perhaps encouraged by the demonstrated unwillingness of the Bush administration, unlike its predecessor, to enforce environmental regulations on the hardrock mining companies.) Worse, if Grupo Mexico stripped ASARCO of its assets, the U.S. government would have little leverage against the foreign company to compel them, sticking taxpayers with ASARCO's liability responsibilities as well. ASARCO cleanup projects across the West and Midwest, including in Leadville, stalled. In 2002, when the ASARCO division attempted to sell its Peruvian copper mine, the Justice Department sued to stop them because the sale would render ASARCO insolvent and unable to pay the hundreds of millions it owed the United States.

In Leadville, the gold-mining company Newmont had plenty of reasons to be concerned about ASARCO's dicey financial situation as well. Unlike copper, gold prices were soaring again, and Newmont was flush. If ASARCO ran out of funds, Newmont, as the surviving half of the Res-ASARCO Joint Venture, would be liable for nearly a million dollars in annual maintenance costs for the Yak Treatment Plant, and it would be the only mining company left to clean up Doc's valley.

To settle its dispute with the Justice Department over the Peruvian mine, ASARCO agreed to put $100 million from the sale into a trust fund for environmental cleanups. ASARCO would not have to spend more than that amount unless its copper mines in Arizona began earning a profit. The trust fund couldn't begin to cover what was needed, however. A judge would soon determine that ASARCO's liability at Coeur d'Alene alone was nearly a quarter of damages estimated to total $1.3 billion. The EPA now had to prioritize ASARCO's projects as well. With so little money for cleanup—from Superfund or from one of the nation's largest potentially responsible parties—the nation had to decide which of its hundreds of hazardous mining waste sites—whose rivers and valleys—would be cleaned up.

After EPA headquarters doled ASARCO's money out for 2003, Bob Litle exclaimed, "Hallelujah!" Leadville had done well, considering all of the sites vying for money. A year's worth of operating expenses— $360,000—for ASARCO's half of the Yak Treatment Plant had been funded; Apache would be finished with $100,000; and demolishing the smelters, the low-priority Operable Unit 5, had gotten $300,000, roughly a tenth of what was needed to finish the job. It wasn't much, but for now Litle could keep moving things along and apply for more trust fund money the following year.

Foresight had saved Kids First. Officials estimated that the trust fund set aside in 1994 had about seven years of life left. Even so, Jim Martin worried that the fund and ASARCO would ran out of money before the program's goals were accomplished. But was the program working? Had he been right to trust that his community would cooperate?

The success of Kids First—the ability to meet the performance standards that would keep the EPA away—rested largely with Lake County. In 2003, a group of independent reviewers was commissioned to scrutinize Kids First, and it determined that in fact participation rates exceeded requirements. Most Leadville parents were cooperating, and the county's health program was reaching more than 70 percent of eligible children each year. By the end of 2002, 550 children had had their blood lead levels tested. As predicted, few children living on the west side of town in newer homes and farther from the mining waste had elevated blood lead levels. The levels were considerably higher, however, on the east side of town, in the smelter community of Stringtown, and at the Lake Fork Mobile Home Park down by Edith Seppi's place.

Had the EPA been right to blame the town's soil? And was a 3,500 parts per million soil action level—still by far the highest in the nation—protective? Some folks in Leadville still didn't believe that their mining heritage had poisoned the town. Comparisons still abounded. Leadville is a healthier place to live than the inner cities, than Denver, many insisted, and they pointed to the Mexican immigrants who used lead in folk medicines and pottery, moving to town with high lead levels already circulating in their blood and skewing the results. The citizens were right, in part. A few of the high blood lead levels did come from recent arrivals. The air in Leadville was purer and the water cleaner than in Denver, in most places in the nation, in fact. And overall, blood lead levels weren't as high as in many urban areas where lead-based paint still flaked off walls in neighborhoods too poor to replace it. Levels weren't even as high as other mining sites.

But lead in the soil did play a significant role in the town's blood lead levels. Just look at the results, Rebecca Thomas urged. Since 1996, ASARCO had tested 570 properties for lead in the soil, paint, indoor dust, and water. Nearly a quarter of them had exceeded acceptable levels. It wasn't just the soil. By 2002, nearly sixty homes had been repainted, vacuumed or had their leaded water pipes replaced. But 120 of the yards inspected had exceeded the trigger level of 3,500 parts per million and been removed or capped—the majority of them on the east side and in the Lake Fork Mobile Home Park. Two-thirds of the remedies had been directed at Leadville's yards, and blood lead levels were going down. The numbers were small, but Leadville wasn't a big place, and the east side was even smaller. According to the independent review, these results suggest that the 3,500 parts per million action level is achieving the EPA's blood lead goals.

In 2003, the far western side of town and Lake Fork, one of the two "statistical units," were declared safe—children had a low risk for having blood lead levels over 10 micrograms. About half of Leadville residences could therefore be deleted from Superfund, though any child or property would still be able to participate in the program. Blood lead levels on the east side and Stringtown were going down as well, but children still had nearly a 10 percent risk of elevated blood lead levels, twice the acceptable standard. The program would continue for at least another three years, and most likely for many years to come.

Some in town were still bitter about the ongoing attention to Leadville's yards. "We're trying to attract people into our town at the same time the EPA is telling the world that we're poison," Ken Chlouber said in 2001. "They're still doing it today, checking homes for lead, checking children for high blood leads. It's such an incredible insult and slap in the face to this community." But Kids First had spared the town of wholesale yard removal. More importantly, it benefited the children, whether their high blood lead levels came from playing in their backyards, climbing on a waste dump, paint flaking off the walls, or what they already carried in their bodies from Mexico. Many in town had come to believe Leadville was lucky— enviable—for having such a comprehensive public health and lead abatement program.

For the EPA, Stray Horse Gulch remained the biggest job heading into the new century. It had been three years since the EPA had agreed not to make more Wedding Cakes but to collect the acid mine drainage in holding ponds instead. As soon as the ponds were built, the water draining into them was so mineralized and acidic, with a pH of 1.8, that it turned a deep purple. They became known as the Merlot Ponds. As eye-catching as the Merlot Ponds were to the tourists, they were too small to capture all the runoff, even during Colorado's drought, and were in danger of overflowing. But there underneath the ponds lay the Leadville Mine Drainage Tunnel (LMDT), an express lane to the Bureau of Reclamation's water treatment plant.

To prevent the Merlot Ponds from sending their concentrated contents down Stray Horse Gulch, Mike had channels built to send the contaminated water down the Marian mine shaft, which leads to the LMDT by way of the Robert Emmet. It was an emergency measure that had the potential of becoming a permanent solution to the acid collecting in the Merlot Ponds. But there were numerous bureaucratic and technical obstacles. This solution meant dealing with the Bureau of Reclamation, a federal bureaucracy with a history of avoiding involvement. And an estimated billion gallons of water that should have been draining to the treatment plant was instead backing up in the Robert Emmet shaft that connected near the top of the drainage tunnel. It was a clear sign that something was wrong.

Within twenty years of its completion, the tunnel was already deteriorating badly. Unlike the Yak Tunnel, which ran for four miles through hard rock, the first thousand feet of the LMDT passed through a soft glacial till. It was like tunneling through a sand dune. By the 1970s, wooden timbers had collapsed, blocking the tunnel and causing water to back up and saturate the soft hillside. Sinkholes formed, most conspicuously along Highway 91, the road to Climax that passed over the tunnel near its portal. The hill on the north side of Leadville was in danger of disintegrating and taking out a mobile home park below.

As the Bureau of Reclamation began filling in sinkholes and taking steps to dewater the mountain, the agency reassured citizens that Leadville wasn't in danger. Engineers put in a plug to prevent a blowout and sunk wells to pump water backing up behind it directly to the Arkansas River. Later, a second plug was installed past the sandbox geology and water was piped directly to the newly built water treatment plant. The agency had relieved the pressure that threatened to fluidize the hillside, but the tunnel's wooden timbers above the plugs continued to rot and collapse. Blockages continued to plague the LMDT, and the evidence was creeping up the Robert Emmet shaft.

The EPA considered the situation "ominous." Water in the Emmet seemed to have leveled off. But if water draining into the tunnel wasn't going to the Emmet or to the treatment plant, where was it going? The EPA didn't want to drain the Merlot Ponds into the LMDT only to have the contamination get lost in the fractured geology and then pop out somewhere else, perhaps thousands of miles away.

Leadville's residents considered the situation ominous as well. "A disaster waiting to happen?" ran the *Leadville Chronicle* headline on April 5, 2001. Residents of a modular home village, the article announced, "live with death just outside their back doors." The increasing water pressure, the article continued, threatened to blow out the blockages and Reclamation's plugs, sending billions of gallons of contaminated water exploding out the portal, destroying the treatment plant, releasing thousands of gallons of stored chemicals, and wiping out dozens of homes in a nearby modular home park.

Leadville

"No one told us!" one resident complained to the *Herald Democrat*. "I don't want to wake up one morning and find myself in Pueblo," said another. The inflammatory article started a swell of angry and distressed residents who organized town meetings, hired attorneys, and threatened to sue the Bureau of Reclamation and the park's owners. State politicians promised to look into it. Carl Miller reminded citizens that Reclamation had never been a good neighbor. Ken Chlouber used the occasion for a dig at the EPA: "The EPA has not done well by this town, not done one good thing. And they've been here for twenty years. I'm very hopeful they'll start working with the local community, which would be a pleasant change to how things have been going for years," he said at a meeting.

Reclamation's spokeswoman said the blowout scenario was highly unlikely, a fiction more suited to a "Stephen King novel." But residents kept up the pressure and a month after the uproar began, Reclamation officials came to Leadville and promised to "become a better neighbor." They agreed to build an escape route and install a siren to warn residents of impending disaster. The furor died down, but the blockages remained.

Despite the problems, the tunnel seemed the easiest way to treat Merlot Pond water. By 2003 the EPA had developed a plan, and Mike called a new public meeting in Leadville. After the sun had set on May 1, about twenty people trickled into the mining museum's small auditorium. It was Leadville's twentieth anniversary as a Superfund site, and few residents showed up at the EPA's public meetings. That night, the audience consisted primarily of casually dressed bureaucrats up from Denver who already knew the plan, students from the local community college, a couple of local reporters, and just a handful of residents. Jim Martin was there as always, doggedly overseeing the EPA's work, and the only politician to show. He still wanted the EPA out of town, but he wanted to make sure they finished the job properly first.

Mike, in a dark blue V-neck sweatshirt and a hand in his pocket, stood alone at the front of the room and explained the latest plan. The EPA wanted to continue sending contaminated water collected in the Merlot Ponds down the Leadville Mine Drainage Tunnel. True, the tunnel was in bad shape and would only get worse over time. Dye tests to see where the water was going had added to the confusion—sometimes reaching the treatment plant and sometimes disappearing into the fractured geology. But the EPA planned a third plug in the two-mile-long tunnel about two-thirds of the way upstream of the portal. The water that backed up behind this plug—contaminated water from the mining district—would be pumped to the surface and sent through a buried pipe by gravity to the Bureau's treatment plant. The EPA had determined that water draining into the tunnel below that two-thirds point was clean groundwater and wouldn't require treatment. For $3.5 million, the EPA could avoid building a third treatment plant in the area while also reducing Reclamation's treatment plant costs.

Serious obstacles remained. The Bureau of Reclamation was "cautiously optimistic," but "very concerned" about incurring additional liability and wanted to be reimbursed for alterations to the treatment plant and for treating the EPA's water. The agency was willing to work with the EPA, but nearly a year later, a Reclamation official would hesitate to endorse the project, saying it was too early to tell if the plan would work for them.

Superfund's financial crisis was also threatening the plan. After Mike appealed to the "Priority Panel" for funding, the LMDT tunnel project's "catastrophic blowout potential" still was only ranked in the middle of the EPA's priorities, not high enough for funding. Mike would have to make a more convincing case for money the following year or the LMDT tunnel project would remain on hold.

At the public meeting that night, a local ex-miner who had been sitting front and center for the past twenty years launched into the EPA's ongoing crimes against ASARCO, the taxpayers, and Leadville. "Throughout this whole thing, I've watched nothing but hypocrisy and governmental mess-up," the man said from under a Broncos cap, his heavy jowls accentuating his scowl.

"I can appreciate what you're saying," Mike replied, bobbing his head, his hands buried in his pockets.

"I'm not really mad at you," the man conceded after a brief exchange. "It was those guys down in Denver. You couldn't get anything from them down there. I'm talking about that one that was the Indian that came from Montana. . . . I'm going to bring it up with the senator, if I can get a hold of him, to see if we can get this straightened out here because it sure is a mess."

No one was baited. A decade earlier the miner had had plenty of angry companions; now he seemed alone in his ongoing bitterness. Some others in Leadville felt similarly, but their numbers were dwindling and most no longer participated. Even Senator Chlouber had withdrawn, at least for a time.

Once the LMDT plug and pipeline were laid, the EPA would be just about done, Mike announced at the meeting. Ponsardine was the only other problem left. The downtown dump was slated to go. The only objection came from another ex-miner who lived near the pile on 7th Street. "I'm sorry about my heartfelt views here, but that stuff means a lot to me," Bob Calder said. Mike nodded. "I'll work with you on it, Bob."

And he did, four days later when Mike locked his keys in the Lead Sled. Bob, a tall, slumping, soft-spoken man, was the local locksmith. Mike rolled his eyes: "How's that for effective community relations?" The conversation in Bob's tiny shop just off Harrison quickly turned from keys to the Ponsardine. Bob had an idea to save the colorful dump, and Mike encouraged him to explain it. Bob leaned over the counter, his long, dark bangs hiding his face, and carefully drew a diagram of what he had in mind. Mike leaned in, and the two discussed Bob's plan in earnest.

But more than the Ponsardine, the locksmith was worried about the commotion constructing a pipeline near his home would cause. "I just couldn't take it, man. You know? If you decide to put in the pipeline, it'll mean war," Bob said in a slow, low voice, his head tipped down to look at Mike over the top of his large, gold-rimmed glasses. He almost had a smile on his face. His tone didn't suggest war. "I consider you the most impacted resident, Bob," Mike acknowledged. As he stepped back out onto the sidewalk, Mike believed that, though the pipeline would go in and Ponsardine would face the bulldozers, by keeping Bob informed and minimizing the construction disturbance, he could make the work more palatable and keep from going to war.

"Leadville is a mess. It's not an EPA success story. It's not," insisted Vicki Peters, a lawyer in Colorado's attorney general's office. She and others in the state see the EPA not so much cooperative as "too conciliatory" when dealing with Leadville and the mining companies. "It's like with a horse," Peters said. "If you keep dancing around, pretty soon you're the one backing up. You need to give them a choice, but you need to make the right choice look good. The EPA makes the wrong choice look good."

The state of Colorado has a significant stake in what happens in Leadville. Jim Martin may not believe it, but one day Leadville will no longer be a Superfund site. The state will then be responsible for maintaining the EPA's remedies in Stray Horse Gulch. So before it lets the EPA go, the state is tightly overseeing its federal inheritance. Though both governments tackle similar legal mandates, the interpretation of them—how clean is clean enough in particular—is raising conflicts, particularly as the EPA's departure draws nearer. Fairly or not, it's the state that is now perceived as the obstacle to getting the EPA out of town.

"I am not at all proud of the Environmental Protection Agency because I have felt that they have been so ready to basically slam the door and run while the state has been trying with the highest level of professional dignity and devotion to protect the environment and public health in Leadville," said Felicity Hannay, Peters's colleague in the state's attorney general's office.

The EPA's critics cite a litany of ways that the feds have left Leadville and the Arkansas River Valley vulnerable. When the EPA leaves, Leadville will have a large amount of "waste left in place," in part due to the compromises that have been made along the way—the Merlot Ponds, Oro City, waste rock piles left untouched, and Kids First. Political pressure from Senator Chlouber had prompted two state agencies to urge the EPA to reconsider its plans for Stray Horse Gulch. Switching to Merlot Ponds did save more of Leadville's historic mining district from turning into wedding cakes. But this compromise will require continuous monitoring, will most likely suffer contamination spills in wet springs, and will cost the Colorado government and its taxpayers millions more, perhaps in perpetuity. Was the compromise worth saving Leadville's historic mining district?

The state's biggest complaints seem to concentrate on residential soils and Operable Unit 12, or site-wide water quality, the how-clean-is-clean-enough question. Vicki Peters and others believe the EPA has pandered to the town and left children at risk. Once Kids First's statistical standards are met, ASARCO will go away, potentially—even probably—leaving behind homes that were never tested. "They need to go in and just clean it up. Get it over with," Peters said. "Suck it up and do the right thing. If the lead isn't there, then the kids aren't at risk."

Stan Christensen, the newest EPA project manager to wade in, countered, "You can't run roughshod over the town. We are a risk-reduction program. It's not possible to get risk down to zero. That's not the goal. We try to get the most risk reduction for the money." Even in places like Midvale, Utah, or Jasper County, Missouri, where hundreds, even thousands, of yards were removed, some property owners refused and the EPA legally couldn't force compliance. In an intractable town like Leadville, the project managers believe, a cooperative approach like Kids First has achieved more than a strong-arm tactic could have.

Leadville is one of the most complex cleanup sites in the nation, literally built atop mining's waste spanning sixteen and a half square miles. Cleanup has necessitated a narrow path through competing interests. As Mike Holmes has said, "We only wish our job was good science and engineering. We have residents, folks on vacation, and bike paths going through here." But did Mike and Rebecca sacrifice health and environmental protection for community relations, as state representatives have charged?

The debate is heating up as the EPA, mining companies, Leadville, and the state begin to grapple with Operable Unit 12. With most of the work on the hill completed, has enough acid mine drainage been cut off to protect the valley downstream? Below the surface at the friendly Superfund meetings, deep differences of opinion swirl, and everyone seems reluctant to stir them up.

Down in the valley, Doc and Edith are still waiting. The Natural Resource Damage reports documenting injury to the valley and how to fix it both came out two and a half years behind schedule, the final report making an appearance in February 2004, but compared to the alternative—mired in a Denver courtroom—no one complained too loudly. The next step in this unique cooperative approach to Natural Resource Damage will likely be the most challenging: the state's health department, natural resource department, and attorney general's office, the EPA, U.S. Fish and Wildlife Service, U.S. Forest Service, Bureau of Reclamation, Bureau of Land Management, ASARCO, Newmont, Leadville, and the landowners all have to agree on responsibility—dividing up the work that will finally restore the valley. Ten years earlier, similar negotiations to divvy up the mining district had taken eight years and been nearly insurmountable. The Memorandum of Understanding timeline for the valley allows for an ambitious two years of settlement negotiations. Will this cooperative experiment be successful or is everyone destined for a courtroom? Representatives are "cautiously optimistic."

What happens in the valley is inextricably tied to Superfund's Operable Unit 12. It will take another four to eight years for remedies to stabilize before the EPA can determine how well they are working. But what will the resulting water quality be measured against? The target has not yet been decided.

CERCLA mandates that cleanup goals at each site be based on requirements already established by other environmental laws, such as water quality standards under the Clean Water Act. The EPA must apply laws and standards it deems "relevant and appropriate" to a particular site, and that determination is a matter of judgment. The

Arkansas River falls under Colorado's water quality standards, but the 1994 Consent Decree had not stipulated the cleanup goals, and ten years later there is little hope of meeting Colorado's standards and little agreement about whether those standards should apply. Sending the bulldozers back into the mining district is a politically and financially unpalatable choice. More likely, Colorado's strict water quality standards, based largely on the river's chemistry—how many metals are present—will be relaxed, and a different index of the river's health, one based on biology—how the fish, insects, and plants are doing— will be adopted. But just where to draw that line is a contentious decision.

The law of diminishing returns is in play here. If 85 percent of the cleanup has been done, at a cost of an estimated $100 million, is cleaning up the last 15 percent, at what some EPA officials predict would require another $100 million, worth it, particularly with so many other abandoned mining sites remaining throughout the West? And California Gulch isn't the only source of the Arkansas River's contamination. Other mines, other gulches, other tributaries that feed into the river above and below California Gulch also affect it, as do the ranches, farms, and the Bureau of Reclamation's dams and diversions. "It's never going to get to pristine when you have those other things going on," a federal employee involved in the debate said. "That's not even the goal." But the question—how clean is clean enough— remains.

Nationally, how safe is safe is also being debated. Though the acceptable lead threshold set by the Centers for Disease Control and Prevention remains at 10 micrograms, scientific evidence is showing that there seems to be no level at which lead is harmless. Some scientists and policy makers are pushing to lower the acceptable threshold level to 5 micrograms. As with earlier reductions, it's a proposition with serious implications for the nation. What would a cut in half of the acceptable lead levels mean for communities like Leadville still struggling to achieve current levels? That question may no longer be an issue, at least for now: in 2002, the Bush administration began replacing members of the CDC's lead advisory committee who support a lower lead threshold with doctors and professors who have strong ties to the lead industry.

Even after Leadville is no longer a Superfund site, it will continue to struggle with the consequences of its mining heritage. It is predicted that an additional ten thousand people, attracted by jobs in the ski resorts, will move into Lake County in the next twenty-five years, more than doubling its current population. As they do, they'll inevitably spread to unremediated areas with high levels of lead and arsenic in and around Leadville, raising new public health concerns. When the EPA first rolled into Leadville, cappuccinos and hummus sandwiches weren't on the menus. As transplanted urbanites move in, they bring not only their urban lifestyle, but their urban perceptions of risk as well. Will Leadville someday contend that the EPA "cut too many corners" and demand greater protection from Leadville's mining past?

In geologic time, the dramatic changes mining perpetrated on the Earth for society's benefit are young. Repairing the consequences is younger yet, and no one knows what will happen to these sites over time. Blockages in both the Leadville Mine Drainage Tunnel and the Yak Tunnel are already occurring.

"There are going to be battles coming down in the future," Jim Martin predicted. "We've spent billions of dollars on these remedies and if they're not working, should we just shrug our shoulders and say that's okay?" Nearly twenty years after driving home up the valley when the spectacular blowout of 1985 forced Jim to consider the environmental consequences of mining, he can count thousands of hours spent sitting in meetings, battling for what he felt was right for the town and for the environment. "I think the EPA has done us good," he has concluded. "I know damn well it's done the river good."

Epilogue

In the opening years of the twenty-first century, signs of change in Leadville are everywhere. It can be heard not just in the Spanish spoken in town but in the public debates taking place in local government meetings as Leadville's newcomers demand better schools, more businesses, and a cleaner environment. "The mentality is changing," said one longtime resident. "It isn't even subtle. A lot of people are seeing the writing on the wall." Many of these newcomers bring with them a new energy, a willingness to work together, and the know how to get things done.

The changes can be seen on Harrison Avenue. Outside money is slowly sprucing up Leadville's main street. After a corner of the Tabor Grand, the pigeon coop once eyed for a parking lot, collapsed in a rainstorm the day after its new owner purchased it in 1991, he worked with the federal Department of Urban Housing and Development to create low-income apartments. Some, including the newspaper editor of the time, thought it was beneath the town's dignity, but several million dollars later the Tabor Grand Hotel is the pride of Harrison Avenue, housing a block of shops, including a real estate office, beauty salon, and one of Leadville's two coffee shops selling lattes and cappuccinos. Some buildings remain boarded up and decaying, but the Quincy Block, the turreted Bank Building, the gothic Old Church, and others are in various stages of renovation. A few steps off Harrison on 6th Street, the decaying Italianate-style house once owned by the Guggenheims was also recently restored as a private residence. Live bands play in Leadville's other coffee shop that doubles as a low-key bar. The Silver Dollar with its blended Irish and Wild West themes is still there, as is the Golden Burro, a perpetual "For Sale" sign in its window. Leadville has bed-and-breakfasts, a few upscale gift shops, and many more "rubber tomahawk shops" reminiscent of the 1950s. In the summers, wooden planters of columbines and pansies line Harrison Avenue. Brooklyn Heights, a subdivision featuring "New Victorian Homes," is going up south of town.

In 2003, when Mayor Chet Gaede decided not to run for reelection, the town faced an important decision. The two frontrunners to replace him were Lisa Dowdney, the former libertarian of the "keep Chet in line" philosophy, and Bud Elliott, a motel owner on the town's tourism task force. Lisa had come to Leadville in the 1970s and had the distinction of being one of few women who had ever worked underground at Climax. Now, she was unemployed. Bud had once worked as a nurse on the psych ward in Kansas City. He came to Leadville in 1993 with a young son after his wife died. As a city council member, Bud was the court jester. He looked benevolent, round, and soft as he tipped back comfortably in his chair at the end of the table watching the edgy mayor, unyielding Carol, and the others go at it. His bemused smile suggested that he thought this was better entertainment than reality TV. Every once in a while, Bud righted his chair and zipped in a one-liner. During one argument over spending money to fix the roads, for example, Bud asked the dissenting libertarian if cars ruined by the resulting potholes would be considered a "taking" by the city, poking fun at the libertarian party's aversion to governmental seizing of property. Another time, a county commissioner asked for volunteers to help water a grove of newly planted pine trees. "It'll be a lovely day," he said. "A chance to walk your dogs." "How many dogs are you going to need?" Bud quipped.

Bud campaigned on code enforcement, Lisa on a less-threatening government. The town was divided. But as the two made their cases to the public, other signs of change were taking place: a man was found guilty—by a jury of his peers—for violating the trash ordinance; a dog pound opened and began rounding up Leadville's numerous stray pit-bull mixes; a committee to fix the pool was gaining momentum; and when a "Diversity Committee" held a Cinco de Mayo celebration, more than four hundred people attended. It wasn't diversity—only a few non-Mexicans were there—but restaurant owner Frederico Montez, a Mexican who had arrived in 2001, was amazed at the turnout. "I didn't know there were so many Mexicans here," he said. It was the first time mariachis ever played in Leadville, he added with a smile.

That fall, the voters chose Bud Elliott for mayor by a margin of just forty-six votes—a squeaker, but another sign that newcomers were starting to tip the balance. Within days Bud had twenty junk cars towed, and Leadville didn't riot. The town also passed two school bonds, the first in thirty years. In 2004, voters would face another choice between two opposing visions for Leadville. Chet and Carol both announced their intentions to run for county commissioner when Jim Martin's run spanning sixteen years in local government ended.

Leadville's relationship to Superfund is changing as well. Mention the Wedding Cakes and most residents shrug. The fence along the Starr Ditch is no longer considered the Berlin Wall. The sign had come down long ago. After Mike Holmes sent in a crew to dredge out the sediments and restructure the ditch, he announced that the chain link fence could come down. The response: "We don't want our kids playing in that." So the fence stayed. (When Ken Wangerud was told of the residents' change of heart, he was stunned. "You're kidding me." Ken paused, then added, "Well, you see? That's why you stand up and you take a lot of shit.")

Leadville

Ken Chlouber and Carl Miller hadn't been heard from since the battle over Oro City ended in 1999. Then, in August 2003, the legislators met with the county commissioners (minus Jim Martin) to encourage them to get tough with the EPA. Both legislators' terms expire in 2004. Carl plans to retire from politics and return home to Leadville to help his community prosper. "Leadville is still struggling," Carl said. "The character of our town is our most valuable asset, but you can't close your eyes to change. I don't support the close-the-door-behind-me attitude." After eighteen years in state politics, Chlouber is term limited, but his aspirations have turned to Washington, D.C., and a run for a seat in the U.S. House of Representatives.

In an editorial in the *Herald Democrat*, Mayor Gaede urged peace with the EPA. "It seems to me that we get more by working with the other organizations that have interests in our community than we do by calling them names and insulting them," he wrote, and he cited the EPA's contributions in Leadville—most notably its efforts to help preserve the mining district, the Harrison Slag redevelopment grants, and the Mineral Belt Trail. "Each of these projects came about because the EPA was approached as a partner in the community instead of the enemy."

The Mineral Belt Trail, in particular, is a showcase of teamwork and a source of community pride. Completion of the paved loop around Leadville had taken seven years, $2 million, and tremendous cooperation from groups previously not used to working together. Two years after the Mineral Belt Trail was formally dedicated in July 2000, it was recognized as one of the best bike trails in the nation when Secretary of the Interior Gale Norton designated it a National Recreational Trail.

Within a twelve-mile circumference, the Mineral Belt Trail gives bike riders and cross-country skiers a view of 150 years of mining. The trail travels through pine trees and aspens in pretty Evans Gulch alongside a trickling stream and willow bushes where the wetlands purify the acid mine drainage coming from mines on the hill. Climbing up and turning south, the trail passes Baby Doe's matchbox cabin and headframe, cars with license plates from Arizona and Nevada in the dirt parking lot. A short distance farther south, past Denver City's headframe and shaft where poor John Jones had been hoisted to heaven all those years ago, the view opens onto Stray Horse Gulch, where tourists stop along the road to investigate the Wedding Cakes and Merlot Ponds surrounded by split rail fences, the Robert Emmet, water still backing up in its shaft, the waste rock piles of the colorful R.A.M. and Pyrenees, the Greenback cribwall, and the remaining newly restored timber buildings of Finntown.

Weaving through the heart of Stray Horse Gulch and over a bridge spanning 5th Street, the Mineral Belt continues south on a serene passage through an aspen grove to California Gulch. There, the trail descends, cutting between Oro City farther uphill and Resurrection's basins and channels and passing Guggenheim's Minnie headframe as it climbs back out of the gulch. It then winds its way through a forest of lodgepole pines before heading back into town for a view of slag piles and ASARCO's old Arkansas Valley Smelter.

The trail has many fans, but Howard Tritz, the enthusiastic history buff, wages an ongoing battle with vandals who have stolen or destroyed more than half the signs describing Leadville's history. So Howard tested a steel post. Someone busted a chain trying to pull it out, but the post persevered, and Howard and his partners have begun searching for more money to finance the expensive steel signs.

Most of the money is coming from the EPA. Howard bitterly notes that the Guggenheim Foundation refuses to help finance the trail. The only Guggenheim money to come back to Leadville was a $25,000 donation to the mining museum, a snub not overlooked in the town that started the Guggenheim dynasty. The May Department Store Company, a fortune built by David May after he, too, got his start in Leadville, also refuses to contribute. Howard thinks it's time Leadville pulls out the "tombstone," the monument to the May Empire it erected to itself on Harrison Avenue in 1952.

Historic preservationists in Denver have long voiced frustration over Leadville's refusal to reach out to them. "They're not being thoughtful enough to the needs of the current tourists," Monta Lee Dakin, Colorado Preservation Inc.'s former director, has said. "Maybe it's too much for the town of Leadville to handle, and so maybe they need to seek outside help. My plea to the citizens of Leadville is to think beyond their borders and to understand the significance of the site and to get the proper know-how to turn that into a site that visitors can go to and where the site is protected."

There is much for tourists in Leadville, including a driving tour through the mining district, a train ride, the mining museum, tours of Baby Doe's cabin and the Tabor Opera House among others, and a chamber of commerce that doubles as a visitor's center. But preservationists are right. Tourists have to work at it. Many restaurants close early, events aren't well advertised, and Leadville is far off the beaten path.

The tourists who do come reflect the character of the town they're visiting: adventurers passing through, young families that can't afford Vail luxury, and the down-to-earth sort who prefer Leadville's hometown friendliness to glitzy resorts. Incredible stories of locals going out of their way to help a tourist abound, and a noticeable number of Leadville's visitors reward that generosity with loyalty, returning year after year. Some have been coming for decades. But there aren't many of them.

Attracting the number of tourists needed to sustain a town inevitably pushes locals aside. But Leadville has become primarily a bedroom community for service workers in Vail and Copper Mountain. It doesn't need throngs of tourists to survive, and finding a balance that enhances Leadville for both tourists and residents may yet be achieved. But first, the town must repair the fractures that have divided it since Climax closed. The growing emphasis on partnerships between government organizations and town officials to accomplish difficult projects offers a model to healing old wounds.

With the success of the Mineral Belt Trail in the mining district, Mike Conlin, the trail's chief orchestrator, has taken on another ambitious project down in the valley that also requires the cooperation of numerous federal and state agencies, a variety of organizations, and a few Front Range municipalities. Conlin credits relationships forged during the Mineral Belt years for helping to create new relationships that are conserving the Hayden Meadows south of Doc's land as open space and preserving the historic Hayden Ranch. His strongest ally in this new venture is the EPA. "It's a quantum leap from the adversarial role that was in place in the early 1990s," Conlin said. "When we first started all of this, no one would have thought to ask the EPA for help. But now they are the go-to guys for technical support and for cash. Through this process, we now have a much stronger working relationship."

Another important partner raised eyebrows initially—Colorado Preservation Inc. (CPI), the organization Conlin had considered a "hammer," an outsider brought in by Chlouber and Miller to disrupt the work in Oro City in 1998. But Mark Rodman, CPI's new executive director, is eager to showcase CPI's involvement in what he considers an "amazing partnership": the work to preserve the Hayden Meadows and Ranch. "There were skeptics at first because of Oro City. They weren't sure they wanted to get involved with *that* organization again," admitted Rodman. "How we got involved in this is totally different from how we got involved in Oro City. It was a good eye-opener for us. It also gives us the opportunity to show others around the state what CPI can do. This is an example of how an organization can be effective as a partner."

After more than twenty years as a Superfund site, Leadville is a vivid example of the enormous challenges facing the nation as it cleans up the mess 150 years of mining the Earth's minerals has left behind. To date, approximately $100 million has been spent on Leadville's mining district—a small amount compared to some mining sites (Milltown Dam downstream of Butte, Montana, for example, has entailed $700 million with another estimated $100 million of work remaining). Cleaning up the land and streams continues in or near dozens of mining and smelters towns throughout the West, such as Picher,

Oklahoma; Eureka, Utah; and Lead, South Dakota. Fast-tracking such a complex problem still affecting thousands of streams and acres of land across the West is not possible, and billions more will be needed to finish the job. The task is made even more daunting now that Congress and the Bush administration have allowed CERCLA's Superfund to run dry and have increasingly let industry off the hook.

In the 1980s, the federal and state governments came to California Gulch to clean up an environmental disaster that had denuded the land and continued to kill fish and wildlife for miles downstream. But Leadville is not just a mining district: it's a town with a deeply rooted mining culture already threatened by modern times. The government was determined to force residents to comply, and the Leadvillites responded out of their own fear and hatred of government outsiders. Along the way, other competing interests collided with both: politics, industrial defiance, historic preservation, debates over dangerous precedents versus innovative ideas, and questions of how safe is safe and how clean is clean. To be successful, the EPA and Leadville had to stop fighting and instead start working together.

The result is a visual illustration of the narrow path that can be woven through all of those competing interests. It can be seen in nature's own wetlands in Evans Gulch, the Kids First ads in the newspapers, the Sandhill remedies of the tailing piles, the Yak Treatment Plant, waste rock piles sitting next to Merlot Ponds and Wedding Cakes, and the tufts of grass at Doc's feet. In the end, everyone has had a hand in creating what Leadville has become.

Leadville is a success in ways that those involved in the early volatile years could not have imagined, thanks in large part to the men—and Rebecca Thomas—willing to put aside the stereotypes that separated them and find common ground. In 1997, Mike Holmes won the EPA's first national community relations award in recognition of the transformation he instigated in the EPA's relationship with Leadville. The unpretentious Mike was so adamant about not going to the award ceremony in Washington, D.C., that he talked his buddies in the Emergency Response program into sending him to the floods in Grand Forks, North Dakota, instead.

More than a few historic preservationists lament the EPA's "unnec-essary destruction" done to Leadville's historic mining district and consider the Wedding Cakes in particular a "travesty." But if the relics of the past are preserved as a reminder of our nation's journey, why not the Wedding Cakes? Leadville's story began when the first gold panner squatted next to a little stream in a pristine mountain valley and cried, "By God, I've got California in this here pan!" But it didn't end when Climax or the Black Cloud shut down. The story of mining includes society's growing awareness of the destruction the industry inevitably imparts on the earth and the nation's attempt to repair the damage.

Romanticized visions of the historic past flourish in the West. But in Leadville, the Wedding Cakes and Merlot Ponds give tourists the opportunity to ask the same hard questions that Jim and Doc, Mike and Rebecca, ASARCO, the state, and the other players in this drama have grappled with for twenty years. These visual reminders that Leadville's mining story didn't stop with the miners make the town more "authentic," not less so. Instead of mourning Leadville's loss as a memory laminated in time, the town could be celebrated as a complex and unique demonstration of the arc of time.

Mining has, for the most part, taken place away from public view and, with our compliance, without public scrutiny. For the first hun-dred years, the blasting and dumping occurred in isolated places deep in the Rockies or remote desert landscapes. Now the costs are even farther from view and our consciences, having been moved overseas to places like Angola, Indonesia, and Bolivia. Hidden in the Rockies, mining rarely confronted our treasured ideals of the West's beauty and the earth's bounty. The belief that we can take from that bounty for our own uses without consequences has remained largely intact. But the scars are ugly, far-reaching, and persistent. For thousands of years, mining has been a necessary component of building thriving civilizations, providing the raw materials for Roman aqueducts, weapons, cars, and computers.

In America, economic progress has almost always prevailed over health and environmental considerations. The hunger for material goods feeds society's voracious appetite for more metals. Mining companies are happy to fulfill that desire and historically have done so largely without oversight. For the most part, we, individually, consume without regard to the raw materials or where they come from. As a nation, we must develop the collective will to face our past and clean it up.

ACKNOWLEDGMENTS

This book could not have been written without the assistance of many people. My heartfelt thanks, first, to the citizens of Leadville who welcomed me and shared their stories. Leadville's friendliness and generosity made my stay a happy time. I would especially like to thank Bernard and Carol Smith, Jim and Corinne Martin, and Mike Holmes for the many hours they spent helping me untangle the events of the past twenty years, sometimes while driving me around the mining district, particularly during the early days of my journey.

My deepest thanks to the many people who appear in this book for giving so generously of their time and for their patience. Many others whose names do not appear also gave generously of their time, sharing their experiences, helping me with research, or welcoming me in Leadville. In particular, I would like to thank Jerry Andrew, William Atkinson Jr., Tom Cherrier, Laura Coppock, James Fell Jr., Kathleen Fitzsimmons, Larry Frank, Tom Holford, Karmen King, Christine Londos, Ellen Mangione, Nancy Manly, Jody Martinez, Sam McGeorge, Brad Littlepage, Amy Morrison, Peter Moller, Ken Olsen, Bryce Romig, Donald Seppi, Bill Scherer, Duane Smith, Steve Voynick, the librarians at the Lake County Public Library, and the ladies behind the counter at the Cloud City Coffeehouse in the Tabor Grand building where I spent many hours working and relaxing.

I would also like to thank the Colorado Historical Society, which started me on this journey many years ago. In particular, my thanks go to Patrick Fraker, Aaron and Karen Mandel, David Wetzel, and Carol Whitley for their support, assistance, and friendship.

I am grateful for the invaluable financial support I received early in this project from a *Preservation* magazine fellowship.

I owe a great debt to Jonathan Cobb, my editor at Island Press, who believed in the value of telling this story and in my ability to tell it, and whose diligence and skillful editing helped make this a much better book.

Most importantly, I would like to thank my parents, Robert and Carol Klucas, who have supported me in so many different ways over the years. This book could not have been written without their love and encouragement.

A NOTE ON SOURCES

This book tells the story of the past twenty years in Leadville. I relied on numerous interviews with the people who appear in this book, and with many others who do not, to describe scenes and to understand the motivations and actions of the events and decisions that occurred. I lived in Leadville for a year to learn about the town and Superfund firsthand and to get to know the people critical to the story. I spoke extensively with Jim Martin and Doc Smith and many others while living in Leadville and on previous visits. In the summer of 1991, I had a half-hour interview with state senator Ken Chlouber, when I first began researching what ultimately became a book topic, though I didn't realize it at the time. Except where noted as a quote from that interview, information attributed to Senator Chlouber was drawn from newspaper accounts or government documents identified in the text.

In addition, I utilized the EPA's Region 8 Record Center to research thousands of official documents, from brief memos to lengthy reports. A number of published sources were also invaluable, particularly the *Leadville Herald Democrat* and, after 1998, the *Leadville Chronicle*.

I made extensive use of other newspaper accounts about Leadville, political policies of the past three decades, and the environment from the *Denver Post, Rocky Mountain News, Washington Post, New York Times, High Country News, Engineering and Mining Journal, Business Week,* and *USA Today.*

Many books and articles have been written on the history of Leadville and mining. I relied primarily on the following:

Blair, Edward. *Leadville: Colorado's Magic City.* Boulder, Colo.: Pruett Publishing Company, 1980.

Davis, John H. *The Guggenheims: An American Epic.* New York: William Morrow and Company, 1978.

Fell, James E., Jr. "The Carbonate Camp: A brief history and selected bibliography of Leadville," *Colorado History.* Denver: Colorado Historical Society, 1997.

———. *Ores to Metals: The Rocky Mountain Smelting Industry.* Lincoln, Neb.: University of Nebraska Press, 1979.

Griswold, Don L., and Jean Harvey Griswold. *History of Leadville and Lake County, Colorado: From Mountain Solitude to Metropolis.* Denver: Colorado Historical Society in cooperation with the University Press of Colorado, 1996.

Marcosson, Isaac F. *Metal Magic; The Story of the American Smelting and Refining Company.* New York: Farrar, Straus, and Company, 1949.

Philpott, William. *The Lessons of Leadville, Or, Why the Western Federation of Miners Turned Left.* Denver: Colorado Historical Society, 1995.

Ramsey, Robert H. *Men and Mines of Newmont: A Fifty-year History.* New York: Octagon Books, 1973.

Von Bamford, Lawrence, and Kenneth R. Tremblay Jr. *Leadville Architecture: A Legacy of Silver, 1860–1899.* Loveland, Colo.: Architecture Research Press, 2000.

Voynick, Stephen M. "Another bit of America gone." *Christian Science Monitor,* August 31, 1983.

———. *Climax: The History of Colorado's Climax Molybdenum Mine.* Missoula, Mont.: Mountain Press Publishing Company, 1996.

———. *Leadville: A Miner's Epic.* Missoula, Mont.: Mountain Press Publishing Company, 1984.

Voynick, Stephen M., with Ray Ring and Hal Clifford. "In search of the Glory Days." *High Country News,* December 23, 2002.

In addition to numerous newspaper articles, I relied on the following books and articles for information regarding mining's impact on the environment and the impact of U.S. political policies on the environment, Superfund, and mining:

Applegate, John S., Jan G. Laitos, and Celia Campbell-Mohn. *The Regulation of Toxic Substances and Hazardous Wastes.* New York: Foundation Press, 2000.

Davis, Devra Lee. *When Smoke Ran Like Water: Tales of Environmental Deception and the Battle Against Pollution.* New York: Basic Books, 2002.

Fields, Scott. "The Earth's open wounds: Abandoned and orphaned mines." *Environmental Health Perspectives,* March 2003.

Kline, Benjamin. *First Along the River: A Brief History of the U.S. Environmental Movement.* San Francisco: Acada Books, 1997.

Landy, Marc K., Marc J. Roberts, and Stephen R. Thomas. *The Environmental Protection Agency: Asking the Wrong Questions.* New York: Oxford University Press, 1990.

Lash, Jonathan, Katherine Gillman, and David Sheridan. *A Season of Spoils: The Reagan Administration's Attack on the Environment.* New York: Pantheon Books, 1984.

For background information on the effects of lead and on the nation's policies regarding lead, I drew upon the following books:

Florini, Karen L., George D. Krumbhaar Jr., and Ellen K. Silbergeld. *Legacy of Lead: America's Continuing Epidemic of Childhood Lead Poisoning.* Washington, D.C.: Environmental Defense Fund, 1990.

Markowitz, Gerald, and David Rosner. *Deceit and Denial: The Deadly Politics of Industrial Pollution.* Berkeley and Los Angeles: University of California Press, 2002.

Millstone, Erik. *Lead and Public Health: The Dangers for Children.* Washington, D.C.: Taylor and Francis, 1997.

National Resource Council. *Measuring Lead Exposure in Infants, Children, and Other Sensitive Populations.* Washington, D.C.: National Academy Press, 1993.

Warren, Christian. *Brush with Death: A Social History of Lead Poisoning.* Baltimore: Johns Hopkins University Press, 2000.

Wilson, Des. *The Lead Scandal: The Fight to Save Children from Damage by Lead in Petrol.* London: Heinemann Educational Books, 1983.

Of the many books written about the West, I particularly recommend the following:

Conaway, James. *The Kingdom in the Country*. Boston: Houghton Mifflin Company, 1987.

Limerick, Patricia Nelson. *The Legacy of Conquest: The Unbroken Past of the American West*. New York: W.W. Norton and Company, 1987.

——. *Something in the Soil: Legacies and Reckonings in the New West*. New York: W.W. Norton and Company, 2000.

Reisner, Marc. *Cadillac Desert: The American West and Its Disappearing Water*. New York: Penguin Books, 1986.

Rothman, Hal K. *Devil's Bargains: Tourism in the Twentieth-Century American West*. Lawrence: University Press of Kansas, 1998.

Udall, Stewart L. *The Forgotten Founders: Rethinking the History of the Old West*. Washington D.C.: Island Press, Shearwater Books, 2002.

Worster, Donald. *Under Western Skies: Nature and History in the American West*. New York: Oxford University Press, 1992.

INDEX